Unpacking the Loaded Teacher Matrix

Studies in the Postmodern Theory of Education

Joe L. Kincheloe and Shirley R. Steinberg
General Editors

Vol. 311

PETER LANG
New York • Washington, D.C./Baltimore • Bern
Frankfurt am Main • Berlin • Brussels • Vienna • Oxford

sj Miller and Linda Norris

Unpacking the Loaded Teacher Matrix

Negotiating Space and Time Between University and Secondary English Classrooms

PETER LANG
New York • Washington, D.C./Baltimore • Bern
Frankfurt am Main • Berlin • Brussels • Vienna • Oxford

Library of Congress Cataloging-in-Publication Data

Miller, sj.
Unpacking the loaded teacher matrix: negotiating space and time between university and secondary English classrooms / sj Miller, Linda Norris.
p. cm. — (Counterpoints: studies in the postmodern theory of education; v. 311)
Includes bibliographical references and index.
1. Language arts (Secondary) 2. English language–Study and teaching (Secondary)
I. Norris, Linda. II. Title.
LB1631.N67 428.0071'2—dc22 2006023769
ISBN 978-0-8204-8676-5
ISSN 1058-1634

Bibliographic information published by **Die Deutsche Bibliothek**.
Die Deutsche Bibliothek lists this publication in the "Deutsche Nationalbibliografie"; detailed bibliographic data is available on the Internet at http://dnb.ddb.de/.

Cover design by Kimberly Fleeger

The paper in this book meets the guidelines for permanence and durability of the Committee on Production Guidelines for Book Longevity of the Council of Library Resources.

29 Broadway, 18th floor, New York, NY 10006
www.peterlang.com

Printed in the United States of America

This book is dedicated to all of the individuals who traverse the loaded matrix, past, present and future.

This book is also dedicated to Emily Keyes, whose life was recently prematurely taken at Platte Canyon High School in Bailey, Colorado. While we write this book for her and for so many others who have died untimely deaths, both pre and post-Columbine, we are reminded of the timeliness of unpacking loaded issues during this and any spacetime.

Be the change you want to see in the world.

Gandhi

TABLE OF CONTENTS

Ernest Morrell

What are the unexpected issues that crop up in a teacher education program or with teacher educators within a program that is committed to social justice?

Teacher educators are a population under siege. As a professional and scholarly community, we are constantly challenged to demonstrate that we are doing something valuable when preparing teachers. Ideas and ideologies that run counter to the mainstream are called out as such, while prevailing ideas about how teachers are currently taught rarely face much examination at all, as if they occur within an objective and value-neutral context. "Liberal," "progressive," and "social justice," are terms that are treated with the utmost contempt, as if we were attempting to indoctrinate the next crop of teachers with sinister ideas about fairness, equity, and care for those who are most marginalized. I wonder aloud as I write this, what do teaching and teacher education look like when they are not geared toward social justice? I shudder to think. And who wants to teach and live in a world where social justice is considered as a political term and not a human right?

Yet and still here we are in another moment in time when teacher education is the subject of increased scrutiny, and important allies of the progressive agenda wax and wane in their explicit support. When words and ideas like multiculturalism and equality are placed on the chopping blocks of our important guiding documents and our professional conversations as we turn instead toward talk of standards, and skills, and excellence, and achievement, as if the concepts were mutually exclusive of one another. When the calls are for value-free teacher education (and what is a teacher without values anyway?) abound. And outsiders call for objective and rigorous research that proves that we are actually playing any role at all in producing effective teachers, which, as it is implied in the challenge, we are not.

If there is a bright side to all of this, then it resides with the contexts that lead to the creation of studies and books such as this one. More and more progressive teacher educators are being asked to make public their practice. In times when we are called upon to justify our attention to culturally or socially-situated instruction, we are able to articulate the principles of education (and teacher education) that we stand for. We are also able to initiate discussions with friends and colleagues around the world about the challenges we face in trying to be the teacher educators we know that we should. While dialogue isn't necessarily transformational, transformational dialogue usually is. What our authors invite us into is the space of their transformational dialogue. As they set out to articulate the principles and practice of a social justice-oriented framework for teacher education, they reveal the insights, challenges, and triumphs associated with this work. They also invite us into their conversations as participants; as we read, we too become enlightened, and we are forced to consider our own work, only not as isolated or alone as we might have been before we picked up this text.

Unpacking the Loaded Teacher Matrix is an important text that pushes our grounded theories of critical teacher education through a thorough analysis of practice. In their words, Miller and Norris seek to unpack the loaded teacher matrix:

> by understanding critical issues impacting classroom management, recognizing the timeliness of critical media literacy skills, examining the underlying problems and successes with preparing preservice teachers to use technology in the schools, unpacking how social justice and sociocultural issues are addressed by instructors and how preservice teachers understand and interpret them in the context of their classrooms, and applying standards to lessons with empirical, hands-on data (p.xx)... We look at how preservice teachers can respond to administrators, veteran teachers, cooperating teachers, students, and parents about school safety, censorship, and examine consequences of not addressing harassment. We also offer suggestions to preservice teachers to help them understand their rights to self-expression on each of these issues. (p.xx)

The beauty of this book is that it is at once intensely theoretical and incredibly pragmatic. Through weaving together the narratives of three pre-service teachers, Miller and Norris provide us with a richly described and contextualized case of critical teacher development that holds applications for the scores of future teachers who will read this book, as it also helps teacher educators to contemplate and reframe their practice.

Marshall McLuhan once commented that nothing is inevitable as long as there is a willingness to contemplate what is happening. As I contemplate the challenges that teachers and teacher educators face, I refer to this quote often. Teachers can and do shape the world of the future in their impact on young women and men daily in our classrooms. So too, do our teacher educators. If we want to see a world that is a little more fair, a little more free, with a little more equity, a little more justice, then we must also turn to our teacher educators to consider together the practices and experiences that best prepare tomorrow's teachers with the courage, confidence, characteristics, and capabilities to do this kind of work. The authors remind us of the importance of holding fast to our principles as advocates for fairness, equity, and social change as we help preservice teachers to construct their identities, their philosophies, and their classroom practices, even during times where holding such values may be politically incorrect or as some might say, political suicide for teacher education. To quote from their words:

> As researchers who possess ideas that are consonant with liberal values and who make a stand against prejudice and violence, we suggest that to not be conscientious about preservice teacher identity construction is to reinforce values that perpetuate a status quo society and to not advance into what we hope can be a more open, safe, and free world. Teachers are the vehicle that can further a liberatory pedagogy (Freire, 1970) yet are simultaneously vulnerable to becoming a manufactured identity that placates neo-conservative and Right Wing values.

As we consider our charge and the and the multiple possibilities of the future of teacher education and K-12 classrooms, we must remind ourselves that nothing is inevitable; leaders change, old ideas yield to new ones, and the resilience of the human spirit rears itself in the hands of the change agents time and time again. Current and future teachers consume and apply this text to your practice; let it play a vital role in your being and becoming critical educators. Be happy to be a part of the movement that is teaching for social justice. The authors are unafraid to admit that they are scholars, educators, and advocates with deep commitments to human justice. Nor are they afraid to admit that the road to becoming an empowered and empowering educator is an arduous one with many challenges and many considerations. Most appropriately, though, they are unafraid to show their optimism in a process that they feel can lead us to that Promised Land. It is this process, this optimism, and this conversation that they share with us, their colleagues and friends. For teacher educators, Miller and Norris offer empirically supported processes for their social justice philosophy in teacher education. Enjoy the conversation and maybe contribute a verse. We'll need it. For if we are to be/come the change we want to see in the world, teacher educators must have the courage to teach and embody the spirit of this book.

University of California, Los Angeles
December 9, 2006

ACKNOWLEDGMENTS

There are many people who made this book possible and to whom we are deeply indebted. First and foremost we are grateful to our past, current, and future students who continue to dedicate numerous hours to teaching the English Language Arts. We are grateful to the cooperating teachers who opened doors to their classrooms. We are indebted to Ernest Morrell for the foreword and for his research and scholarship that continues to forge new pathways for all of us to follow and which planted seeds early on that helped conceptualize our book. We are grateful to Janet Alsup, Rick Beach, and Peter McLaren for their endorsements of our book and for inspiring and expanding our thinking. We are grateful to our colleagues Jeremy Price, Judi Franzak, and Nancy Hayward for their thoughtful feedback and insights about terminology, content, and social justice issues. We are thankful to Amanda Godley for her astute questions and ideas about the conclusion of the text. To Margaret Hagood and Kevin Leander, we are thankful for their brilliant minds, their encouragement, scholarship, and proleptic vision of spacetime theory. We are thankful to our editors Shirley Steinberg, Joe Kincheloe, Chris Myers and Sophie Appel, our production supervisor for her prompt assistance. To Linda's family: Kelly Jean Norris for providing insights from an inchoate, inner city, teaching perspective; Kimberly Fleeger whose aesthetic vision as a graphic designer captured the essence of the loaded matrix on our cover; and to Bob Norris, for his total support as a sounding board and for his keen perspectives that are outside of English pedagogy. We would be remiss if we did not acknowledge all of the mentors, teachers, and colleagues who are also lifelong friends who inspired us by trailblazing before us and by now walking the road with us so that together we broaden the scope of English education. Lastly, we are thankful to each other for the unconditional support and friendship that inspired each of us to write this book. See you in the hallway!

sj Miller and Linda Norris
Indiana University of Pennsylvania

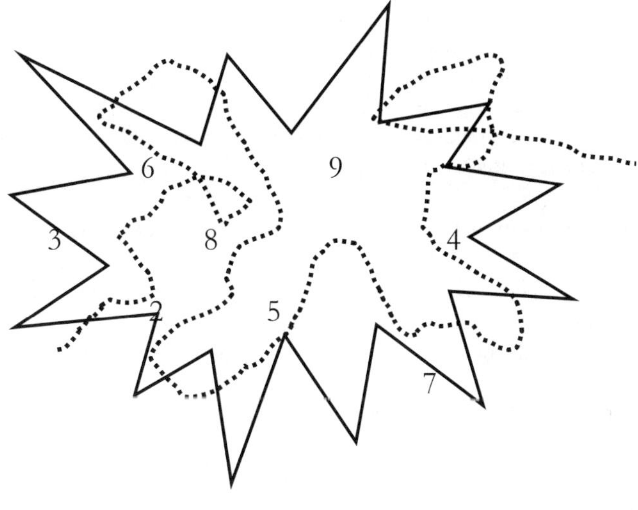

1

Introduction

This book's genesis originated from informal face-to-face conversations between two new colleagues from seemingly dissonant backgrounds in the same English education program. After we began to send emails back and forth about the idea of collaborating on a book about preservice teachers and some of the issues they encounter when preservice teaching, the book and our not-so-dissonant backgrounds took on a life of their own. We were not quite sure how or where to begin, but through our email exchanges, it became more apparent about the likeness and interests in our thinking that excited us about the eventual direction that our book would take. On August 8, 2005, I wrote to Linda, "BTW, I am eager to talk to you about a book prospectus. Let's set up a time to brainstorm, shall we? In which class do you begin to review state standards with the secondary English education students?" Then Linda wrote back, "Yes, I'd like to do a book and we can brainstorm ideas whenever you'd like. What do you think is needed in our field right now? What areas are you most interested in? I would like to do something on preparation for and supervision of student teaching. Let me know if that is something you want to pursue." To this I responded a couple of days later,

> What I have been mulling around is, to prepare a manual, as you suggested which considers the 1, 2, 3s of supervision with a troubleshooting component. More specifically, how can we most effectively prepare supervisors, teachers, administrators, students, and the school communities that absorb preservice teachers for the preservice teacher experience? Some areas might include discussions on: standards social justice issues pedagogy-current and antiquated policies that impact the school, media literacy, and university experiences. What do you think? Tag!

Then before our email exchange evolved into a different phase, she wrote,

> Yes, I like where the book is going already. I feel confident I could do the sections on standards, pedagogy, and media literacy (I already have a ton on that); how would you feel about starting the others, particularly the social and political? I really like the idea of a manual format. You might check out the one I suggested in the 441 syllabus for one way to approach it. I think ours could be more powerful than this, however.

And that was all it took. We then began to build from these ideas and work together on our format, purpose, and audience.

We show this exchange because it is at the heart and soul of our work. We believe firmly in the art of collaboration in all of our professional interactions. We are two university teacher educators who are deeply committed to social justice and who ascribe to liberatory and transformative pedagogies, yet who have had different teaching experiences. Linda, whose focus has been in guiding teachers to become autonomous and self-reflective in their practice, taught secondary English in suburban and rural Western Pennsylvania schools for fifteen years and has supervised preservice teachers for the past fourteen years throughout Pennsylvania including Philadelphia and Pittsburgh. sj, whose focus has been to help preservice teachers think critically about social justice issues and how these impact their emerging teacher identities, has taught secondary English and social studies in urban and rural areas in northern New Mexico and has supervised preservice teachers for the last four years.

These chapters are the fruits of a shared effort. Knowing that we each had strengths to contribute to the text, we decided at times to write individually and at other times collaboratively. We always, however, sent drafts back and forth to each other for feedback, editing, and revision. Together, the melding of our experiences demonstrates and actualizes the transition from preservice to inservice teaching.

Rationale and Purpose: Social Justice and the Loaded Teacher Matrix

We have both seen many texts about what preservice teachers need to know to be prepared for the classroom experience (Alsup, 2006; Alsup & Bush, 2003;

Burden, 2003; Burke, 2003; King-Shaver & Hunter, 2003; McCann et al., 2005, Strickland & Strickland, 2002). However, we have not seen many discussions regarding the more delicate issues that creep up when least expected during teacher training and preparation. In the executive summary from the American Educational Research Association (AERA), a call was put forth for research in both former and in more recent areas within teacher education. Relating to the call for this book, we respond to two of the gaps. First, we seek to fill in research on the "contexts and participants in teacher education" (Cochran-Smith & Zeichner, 2005) and more specifically with research on the "instructional strategies and texts" that our program is using, and second, we research "unexplored topics related to teacher preparation" as it relates to how preservice teachers' "beliefs, attitudes, skills and practices" impact their students' learning opportunities and attitudes.[1] At the core of this text we seek to fulfill a timely need to link teacher education to a social justice agenda as we challenge dominant ideologies through the pedagogies and practices we ascribe to in our teacher education program. Cochran-Smith (2004) suggests that for teacher education to move toward a social justice agenda it must be conceptualized as both "a learning problem and a political problem" (p. 2). For us, this meant that we forefront social justice at the genesis and exodus of our work and "walk the road" with our students' narratives toward equity and transformative pedagogies in our work with our preservice teachers.

We choose to forefront social justice as the common link for our chapters in our efforts to unpack the loaded issues facing preservice teachers. As social justice educators we are committed to multiplicitous levels of social change. We see this change as intimately connected with our own belief systems and how we impart that to our preservice teachers. We align our pedagogy with Howard (2006), who wrote:

> Transformationist pedagogy means teaching and leading in such a way that more of our students, across more of their differences, achieve at a higher level, more of the time, without giving up who they are. In the transformationist classroom the price of success is not assimilation ("acting White"), but rather a process of deep engagement with authentic identity and one's own intellectual efficacy. The reward in such classrooms is that everyone gets smarter together, including the teacher, while at the same time maintaining, strengthening, and honoring our differences, (p. 132)

and Freire (1970), who says that liberatory teaching can help people act on and transform the world around them.

Social justice cannot be reified to one definition because it is subjective to the individual and the contextual knowledge that the person embodies given a specific space and time. We have come to embody social justice as a lifestyle that marries body, mind, and soul or the beliefs married to the actions that leads to an intrapersonal level of awareness. It can mean a lifestyle that is committed to the belief that all people are entitled to the same core basic tenets as stated in the Constitution of the United States: life, liberty, and the pursuit of happiness. As such, each person is entitled to the same opportunities regardless of background or acquired privilege. It means standing up for injustice and discrimination in all forms with regard to: race, ethnicity, gender, gender expression, age, appearance, ability, national origin, religion, weight, height, sexual orientation, social class, environment, ecology, culture, spiritual and animal. For us social justice is not something we *just* do or enact in the classroom to meet NCATE's (National Council for Accreditation of Teacher Education) or NCTE's (National Council of Teachers of English) standards rather it is quite the opposite; for social justice is in our lifestyles and exists on many levels and takes on many shapes and forms. This means that we are conscious about what we eat, where we shop, how we spend our money, what causes we give to, how we become allies for others, what we read, and how we, *not if we*, stand up in situations that require a voice or an advocate. For us standing up no longer becomes a choice; rather it is core to our commitment to social justice and social change. By embodying such a lifestyle, social justice travels through our teaching and impacts our curricular choices, texts, pedagogies, and our professional relationships. We feel that living a life that aligns body, mind, and soul strengthens our core selves and builds emotional and spiritual integrity. Most important to us is that we have to be able to understand and appreciate all of our students, especially those who we perceive are different from how we perceive ourselves, so that we can instruct and facilitate fairly and equitably.

We wanted to create something new and different for the field of English education and so we carefully examined our preservice teachers' words, actions, and thinking as they moved through our program to report more acutely those potentially explosive issues that "no one wants to talk about" or teacher educators may turn their back on because of their controversial nature. Because we want to broaden our understanding of what is empirically constructing preservice teacher identity construction, this study took a unique turn, "a spatial turn" (Soja, as in Leander and Sheehy, 2004, p. xiii), that directs us toward the importance of looking at teacher identity construction in imaginative, spatial, and innovative ways as it transacts with social justice.

This collaborative project emerged out of our similar desire to help preservice teachers "walk the road" (Cochran-Smith, 2004) and navigate through their teaching experiences. We each noticed through our own work experiences that there were gaps in addressing what might be perceived as potentially incendiary or touchy discourse in our methods classes and disconnects between our university instruction and field experiences in actual schools. To us, this meant unpacking the *loaded matrix* of classroom and school environments by understanding critical issues impacting classroom management, recognizing the timeliness of critical media literacy skills, examining the underlying problems and successes with preparing preservice teachers to use technology in the schools, unpacking how social justice and sociocultural issues are addressed by instructors and how preservice teachers understand and interpret them in the context of their classrooms, and applying standards to lessons with empirical, hands-on data.

Our means of unpacking this matrix is to tell three preservice teachers' stories and how their identities emerge through a "heteroglossic" (Bakhtin, 1986) mix of fiction and nonfiction. Heteroglossic privileges us to play with voices in a way that disrupts the typicality of voice sharing and allows us to invent and reinvent the voices of the text as issues are addressed. The stories that we share through our co-authorship create a hybridity of narrative. These narratives then position us, as Bhabha would say, in a space where new meaning is formed wherein "something new and unrecognizable, a new area of negotiation of meaning and representation" (as in Soja, 1996, p. 14), emerges.

Our goals for this book are, first, to provide methods instructors with resources and information about potentially controversial issues in schools and how to instruct their secondary preservice English teachers on those issues; second, we hope that English educators might incorporate some of these topics into their own English teacher education programs; and, finally, we offer empirical assistance and troubleshooting support to English educators about how to communicate effectively *with* their preservice teachers about these topics. This book can serve a dual audience of both the instructor and the student in the preservice methods course. It may also serve and apply as a cross-disciplinary teacher preparation text, although our stories are taken from the work we are doing in secondary English teacher training. Preservice teachers' identities are sandwiched between a larger rhizomatic (Kamberlis, 2004) matrix, which is a network of relationships, co-constructing their identities through veteran teachers, classroom students, their families, social groups, cooperating teachers, clinical supervisors, university instructors, policy, and the like (Miller, 2007). Understanding and recognizing the role of this matrix merits more attention, so that not only can we as teacher educators become more aware of the delicate nuances involved in co-constructing preservice teacher identities, but so too can we help to shift power dynamics that sustain a subservient status and perpetuate divisive hierarchies between student and teacher in classrooms. Our framework is conceptualized by articulating what the loaded teacher matrix is (figure 1.1) in light of the experiences that we have observed our preservice teachers encounter.

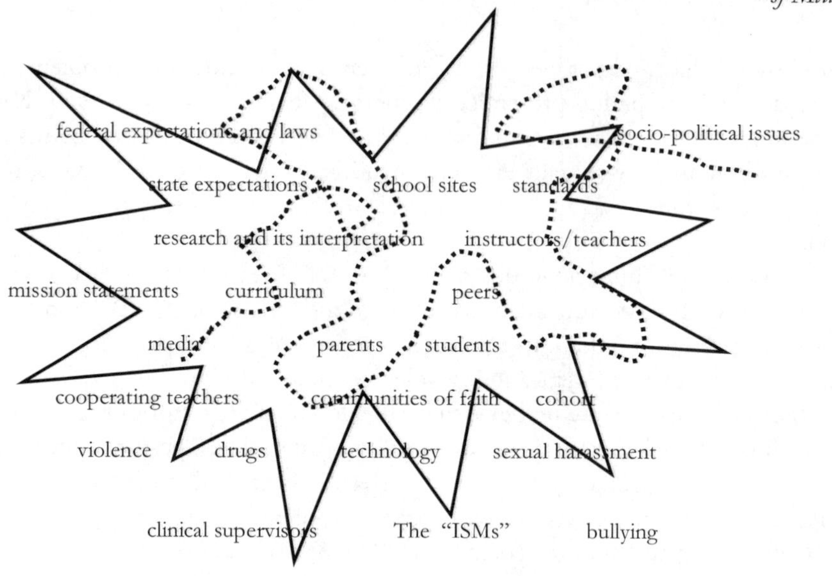

Figure 1.1 Our rhizomatic loaded matrix co-constructing the identity of the preservice teacher. At any one moment in any given space, a number of determinants are impacting the teacher (Miller, 2007).

Lefebvre (1974), in *The Production of Space* (and later in translation in 1991), was instrumental in creating a "spatial turn" (Soja, as in Leander and Sheehy, 2004, p. xiii) that convinced scholars of the importance of looking at history in terms of imaginative, spatial, and innovative ways. Building upon prior concepts of Foucault, Lefebvre developed a critical awareness of spatiality or space as something that was produced in relation to the social relations that inhabit it. Our matrix is thus situated in theories on thirdspace (Soja, 1996) and described through spatiality and hybridity theories (Bhabha, 1994; Leander & Sheehy, 2004; Lefebvre, 1991; Miller, 2005; Nespor, 1997). Thirdspace is best understood by making meaning of firstspace and secondspace. Firstspace is real or actual space such as "concrete materiality of spatial forms, on things that can be empirically mapped" (Soja, 1996, p. 10), and secondspace is imagined space or "thoughtful re-presentations of human spatiality in mental and cognitive forms" (p. 10). Thirdspace is then the amalgam of both the "real-and-imagined" journeys or the "thirding" of spatial awareness and imagination (p. 11). Our loaded matrix as situated within thirdspace is imaginary, yet its personification is quite real as it both frames and forefronts our preservice students' teaching experiences. This matrix will ultimately shift in time and space and can serve as an artifact for proleptic discourse because it will mark the experiences of teachers during a space and time. We examine in detail the shift that occurs from a preservice teacher's instruction in a university space to a secondary school space and how we can best prepare new teachers for these differences. This text will also serve as a springboard for units of study to guide new English Language Arts (ELA) teachers and their instructors to be better equipped for diverse student populations, traditional and nontraditional schools in different settings, and the realities of the first three years of teaching—the most critical time for new teachers to remain in the profession.

Overview of Chapters

Each chapter has a similar choreography. Through the three stories we tell, each fictitious name and their experiences represent students and the cooperating teachers that we have worked with and what they have encountered in our classrooms and in the field. We highlight the preservice teachers enrolled in our program from a weekly methods course during the spring semester of 2006 who wrote about and discussed issues and questions that arose from their teaching placements with us. Through Ethan, who teaches in an urban setting, Beth in a rural setting, and Acazia in a suburban setting, we intentionally play with the notions of space and time as fluid, troubleshoot as we travel with them, and reflect on what we learn from both their and our experiences in methods coursework and in their teaching placements. Since these three individuals represent our experiences as university educators, former classroom teachers, and clinical supervisors, we are also able to laminate other stories of preservice teachers that may be fictitious but, we thought, best speaks of the issue at hand. We share Ethan's, Beth's, and Acazia's field experiences as they relate to the topic of each chapter and highlight one portrait per chapter framed by three focus questions or issues: one which is based on a current issue in English education, one which emerges from the preservice teacher's experience in the classroom space, and one that grows out of the university methods course in which the preservice teacher was enrolled. We also offer units of study to train preservice teachers framed by pedagogical stances to teach them and then share the often dissonant experiences between the school and the preservice teacher from within the matrix.

While some of the writing for the book was done collaboratively, including part of the introduction and the conclusion, some chapters were individually written. Together we wrote chapters 6 and 9. sj wrote chapters 1, 2, 3, and 7, and Linda wrote chapters 4, 5, and 8. In "Introduction," we present the background for the conceptual framework as the loaded matrix and introduce it within a larger social justice agenda. For chapter 2, "The Loaded Matrix: Theoretical and Practical Framework," we ground the theory of our research in our theoretical framework and describe the loaded matrix as frame that illuminates the loaded issues discussed throughout the text. We also discuss the importance of disrupting the commodification of teachers as objects as we work within a social justice agenda. Finally, we describe the practical design of our English education program and provide the overview of the voices of ourselves and the preservice teachers who will help our readers "walk the road" of the text. In chapter 3, "The Loaded Matrix in Classroom and School Environments," we present an overview of some incendiary issues in classrooms and schools. We look at how preservice teachers can respond to administrators, veteran teachers, cooperating teachers, students, and parents about school safety, censorship, and examine consequences of not addressing harassment. We also offer suggestions to preservice teachers to help them understand their rights to self-expression on each of these issues. In chapter 4, "Do We Need Rules in the Loaded Matrix?" we present critical issues that impact classroom management including violence, drugs, promiscuity, and bullying (cyber and in-space). We discuss "transactional" (Strickland and Strickland), "proactive" (Burden) pedagogies that minimize behavioral inappropriateness and tensions among preservice teachers and all the constituents in the schools, not just their own students. In chapter 5, "How Film and Critical Media Studies (Re)shape the Loaded Matrix: Critical Visual Literacy," we describe new ways for preservice teachers to tap into image, language, and sound messages, and promote visual literacy as a key component for learning in today's schools. In chapter 6, "Can Technology (Re)load the Loaded Matrix?" we examine the underlying problems and successes with preparing preservice teachers to use technology in the schools, including topics such as addressing issues about equity, teaching credible Internet searches, creating student web pages, and addressing inequitable budgets for equipment and services. Chapter 7, "Social Justice and Sociocultural Issues as Part of the Loaded Matrix," we unpack how social justice and sociocultural issues are addressed by instructors and how preservice teachers understand and interpret them in the context of their classrooms. Such issues include but are not limited to dynamics of power, students with special needs, ESL (English as a Second Language) learners, the "isms," and the intersections of race, class, and gender. Chapter 8, "Applying the Standards to the Loaded Matrix," walks readers through a hands-on approach that instructs them how to apply standards to the topics previously discussed in the text. We offer working documents, including electronic portfolios, as part of this section and an overview of the standards affecting the English language arts. Prior to our conclusion, in chapter 9, "Unloading the Loaded Matrix: (Re)charging Our Minds," we remember topics previously addressed and offer considerations for English teacher educators and preservice teachers. We also draw our book to a close as we think forward about how preservice teachers and English educators can continue to collaborate on loaded topics as we move deeper into what is on the horizon in this new century.

Since preservice teacher identity is constructed relationally to atomistic components, it becomes all the more crucial that the ways we co-construct their identities aligns with the values and precepts that will help govern a society of democratic ideals. As researchers who possess ideas that are consonant with liberal values and who make a stand against prejudice and violence, we suggest that to not be conscientious about preservice teacher identity construction is to reinforce values that perpetuate a status quo society and to not advance into what we hope can be a more open, safe, and free world. Teachers are the vehicle that can further a liberatory pedagogy (Freire, 1970) yet are simultaneously vulnerable to becoming a manufactured identity that placates neoconservative and right-wing values. While on one hand preservice teachers risk reification, they are also humans with minds and bodies that deserve the opportunity to make decisions for themselves. Preservice teachers are thus caught in a tug-of-war that is situated between two worlds: that of the inchoate educator who is making meaning of what a teacher is and does, and that of still being educated (Britzman, 1991). This is where we converge.

Notes

* We have deliberately inserted different combinations of pronouns in order to challenge the ways we write about gender.

1 Though AERA makes a call for how teacher candidates impact students' achievement and growth, that is beyond the scope of this work.

References

Alsup, J. (2006). *Teacher identity discourses.* Urbana, IL: NCTE.

Alsup, J., & Bush, J. (2003). *But will it work for REAL students?* Urbana: NCTE.

Bakhtin, M. M. (1986). *Speech genres and other late essays.* Austin: Texas University Press.

Bhabha, H. A. (1994). *The location of culture.* New York: Routledge.

Britzman, D. (1991). *Practice makes practice.* Albany: State University of New York.

Burden, P. R. (2003). *Classroom management: Creating a successful learning community.* Hoboken: Wiley/Jossey Bass.

Burke, J. (2003). *The English teacher's companion* (2nd ed.). Portsmouth: Boynton/Cook.

Cochran-Smith, M. (2004). *Walking the road: Race, diversity and social justice in teacher education.* New York: Teachers College Press.

Cochran-Smith, M., & Zeichner, K .M. (Eds.). (2005). *Studying teacher education: The report of the AERA panel on research and teacher education.* Mahwah: Lawrence Erlbaum Associates.

Freire, P. (1970). *Pedagogy of the oppressed.* New York: Continuum Publishing.

Howard, G. (2006). *We can't teach what we don't know.* New York: Teachers College Press.

Kamberlis, G. (2004). The rhizome and the pack: Liminal literacy formations. *Spatializing literacy research and practice* (pp. 161–197). New York: Peter Lang.

King-Shaver, B., & Hunter, A. (2003). *Differentiated instruction in the English classroom.* Portsmouth: Heinemann.

Leander, K., & Sheehy, M. (Eds.). (2004). *Spatializing literacy research and practice.* New York: Peter Lang.

Lefebvre, H. (1991). *The production of space.* Oxford: Blackwell.

McCann, T., Johnannessen, L. R., & Ricca, B. P. (2005). *Supporting beginning English teachers*. Urbana: NCTE.

Miller, S. (2005). *Geographically "meaned" preservice secondary language arts student teacher identities*. Ann Arbor, MI: Umi Dissertation Publishing, www.lib.umi.com/dissertations/fullcit/3177097.

Miller, s. (forthcoming, 2007). (Re)/Re-envisioning preservice teacher identity: Matrixing methodology. In J. Flood, S. B. Heath, and D. Lapp (Eds), *Handbook of research on teaching literacy through the visual and communicative arts* (Vol. II). Mahwah: Lawrence Erlbaum Associates.

Nespor, J. (1997). *Tangled up in school: Politics, space, bodies and signs in the educational process*. Mahwah: Lawrence Erlbaum Associates.

Soja, E. W. (1996). *Thirdspace: Journeys to Los Angeles and other real-and-imagined places*. Malden: Blackwell.

Spring, J. (2005). *Political agenda for education: From the religious right to the green party* (3rd ed.). Mahwah: Lawrence Erlbaum Associates.

Strickland, K., & Strickland, J. (2002). *Engaged in learning: Teaching English* (pp. 6–12). Portsmouth: Heinemann.

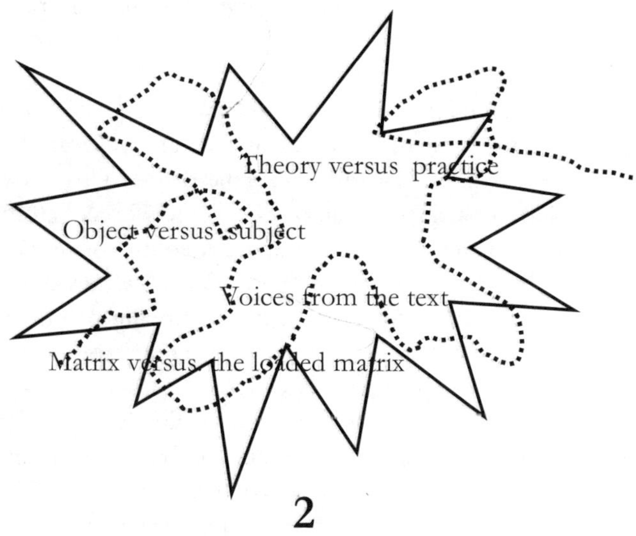

2

The Loaded Matrix: Theoretical and Practical Framework

This chapter presents the conceptual framework for the loaded matrix and illustrates how preservice teachers' subjectivities are vulnerable to competing sociopolitical agendas that attempt to split the mind from the body. This chapter also describes the practical design of our English education program and the overview of the voices of the preservice teachers who "walk the road" (Cochran-Smith, 2004) with us in the text.

The Matrix

Preservice teachers and teachers alike are embedded within a vastly complex web of social, political, and cultural relationships, each of which influences either individually, collectively, or at their crossroads, the identity of the individual at any given point in time (Miller, 2005, 2007). Because English teaching is not an isolated profession nor immune to changes in policy at the international, national, state, and local levels, teachers' identities[1] are vulnerable to shifts along with the profession. As a result of the shifting nature of our field and the multiple contexts in which teachers engage, teachers identities will be reconstituted during the spacetime in which the identity is being constructed. Because of this complexity and the imminent whimsicality of change, it is difficult to understand how concurrent competing forces are impacting the preservice teacher. Therefore, in order to more readily conceptualize how preservice teachers' identities are impacted, we reference a matrix as a theoretical concept that is both an invisible and visible space, which embodies all of the forces co-constructing the identity of the teacher (Miller, 2005).

The matrix is a simulation for the real, or the hyperreal, that Baudrillard (2001) suggests is a space that is divested of the "antireal" and because of that must vanish into simulation. For our study, the matrix is both a hyperreal and an imaginary creation contrived to illuminate the networked, atomistic relationships together that impact preservice teacher identity construction. Although imaginary and real, it provides a way to frame and show how in spacetime intricate relationships are networked so that the fluid nature of the matrix is applicable and has efficacy in other research contexts and spacetimes (Miller, 2007). Depending on the time in which preservice teachers teach, although they will be embodied by a different network of relationships, the concept of the matrix can be lifted to suit other contexts. By foregrounding the matrix as an environment for activity, we invite our preservice student teachers and their instructors to also participate in discussions about their teaching experiences so that they can be co-collaborators who seek to understand their own identity co-constructions. Moreover, by inviting preservice teachers into such thinking and new spaces, we can give them a starter set of tools to help them realize that they are not objects to be constructed but are subjects within a system, with viable ideas and vulnerable identities.

We articulate against the dualism of the mind/body split that divides the preservice teacher into compartments and can render them helpless against combating sociopolitical agendas. The empowerment that can arise from the teacher as a whole being, not as object, can lead teachers to be conscientious about their power in constructing their own as well as students' identities in the classroom. The importance of such empowerment shifts the binary dynamics and power structures within hegemony and helps individuals become nonbinary agents capable of acting on and transforming the worlds in which they live. On this Bhabha (1994) admonishes us not to simulate the discourse of dominant culture because it reinforces status quo constructs. Nonbinary thinking can liberate and open doors to new possibilities that over time may lead to subvert traditional paradigms once used to keep people silenced and marginalized (Freire, 1970). When we teach preservice teachers to co-opt their own identities, we can liberate them from binary and dominant perceptions that may have once had their time and place in education, but which are now antiquated. Rose (1993) advocates for transcending binary constructs and believes that a politics of "difference and identity built on the opening of new spaces" relocates us to a place where counterhegemonic principles can lead to a liberal democracy (Soja, 1996, p. 111). Such a politics lifts us out of binary identifiers and relocates us to a space where ideas can "co-exist concurrently and in contradiction" (Rose, 1993 quoting deLauretis, as in Soja, p. 112). Teacher education has the power to greatly challenge and subvert dominant paradigms through each of the constituents impacted.

The matrix then is a networked space where relationships intersect, are concentric, do not intersect, can be parallel, nonparallel, perpendicular, obtuse, fragmented, and even marginalized (Miller, 2005, 2007). Such relationships are concomitant and cannot be looked at atomistically, because it is their intersection in a spacetime that creates their matrix. The dotted line inside and outside of the matrix is an example of the interconnectedness of all issues and is randomly embedded. The terms that fall in, on, around, or outside of the line, are incidental. Often when a relationship within the matrix sours or shifts, other concurrent relationships impact the stabilization of the preservice teacher and (re)stabilizes her/his positionality within the teaching profession during a spacetime. The networked matrix that is co-constructing a preservice teacher's identity is massive and it will continue to expand in time and shift in new contexts. Since a preservice teacher's identity is ultimately vulnerable to the larger spacetime in which that identity is coming to be and is affected by those who wield discursive, interpretive, and textual power, it is important to identify the nonbinary networked matrix that is constructing the inchoate teacher so that we can, if necessary, shift the conditions in our preservice methods classes so as to suit the needs of our sociopolitical agendas during a given spacetime.

Competing Subjectivities within the Matrix

The matrix co-constructing a preservice teacher's identity or subjectivity is not neat, clean, nor even linear; rather it is full of intersections and intercontextual links. By intercontextual we reference the notion that contexts are "produced, negotiated and hybridized within the flow of dialogue" (Gee, 1992; Leander, 2001, p. 637). Within the matrix, then, preservice identities are entwined with the discourses and the social spaces in which they engage (Gee, 1992). Gee says that our discourses are more than our uses of language; they are the combinations of the "saying-writing-doing-being-believing-valuing" (p. 127) and ways of participating in a variety of social contexts. He further suggests that "each of us is a member of many discourses and each discourse represents one of our ever-multiple identities" (p. ix).

Social spaces are places that have been formed by intercontextual discourses and bring together multiple identities, discourses, and identities and which have great significance upon an individual's identity co-construction (Brooke, 1991; Gee, 1996). Social spaces are formed for all kinds of reasons but are often constructed out of necessity and are impacted by political (power) and social ideologies (Foucault 1980, 1986; Lefebvre 1991). Foucault (1986) and Bourdieu (1980) suggest that the effects of power construct identities, and that the embodiment of identities is vulnerable as a result of power. Social spaces become central to understanding an identity in terms of "race, ethnicity, social class or gender … those identifications shape engagements in spatial tactics of power and in everyday social, cultural and literate practices" (McCarthey & Moje, 2002, pp. 234–235). Because social spaces are defined in relationship to society, such as a school, café, or bar, identities are highlighted by those social spaces and by the way their identities have been defined in relationship to society. Selves therefore are illuminated by their identities within specific social spaces and yet can be excluded when their identities are not defined by their relationship to that space. Identity can therefore be destabilized when a social space excludes a particular identity. As individuals change and merge with other social spaces, their identities can become hybrids layered with a multitude of subjectivities. Preservice teacher identity formation is therefore sociospatial (Leander, 2002) and teacher identities are discoursed.[2]

The landscape of the matrix is cyclical, because something that is potentially passé, such as a bill or an ideology, is likely to be recycled back and disguised into a new shape or form as soon as there is a new consensus. Varying political ideologies and hidden agendas of private constituents and government decisions greatly constrain teachers and instructors in teacher education programs (Apple, 2002). Thus, the identity of the teacher becomes a tug-of-war on the mind and body in which the individual is being co-constructed by factors well beyond the individual's control. On this Fiske articulates (1989):

> Though the body may appear to be where we are most individual, it is also the material form of the body politic, the class body, the racial body, and the body of gender. The struggle for control over the *meanings* (italicized for emphasis) and pleasures (and therefore the behaviors) of the body is crucial because the body is where the social is most convincingly represented as the individual and where politics can best disguise itself as human nature. (as in Nespor, 1997, p. 119)

It is important to keep in mind that within the preservice teacher's identity there co-exists a complex sociopolitical web laden with hidden agendas and that their minds and bodies are fodder ripe for competing political agendas. Teacher educators can thusly disrupt or further agendas depending on where they fall politically by either challenging the mind/body dualism or by advocating for the rupture. On this Nespor (1997) says, "bodies as well as physical structures define the divide: Inside the body becomes the space of control and intellect, and the exterior of the body, its extensions and emissions, become uncontrolled spaces, celebrated by kids and suppressed by adults" (p. 121). The identity of the preservice teacher is vulnerable to being co-constructed by power far beyond the individual's control. Preservice teacher identity though is a delicate subjectivity that should be carefully crafted and not objectified. If a teacher is looked at as an object to be sculpted or "made" (Haraway, 1991, p. 208), Bourdieu (1977) tells us that "in taking up a point of view on the action, withdrawing from it in order to observe it from above and from a distance, constitutes practical activity as an object of observation and analysis, a representation" (p. 2). If teachers are treated from this perspective, they become reified for consumption of larger agendas, and who they are and what they represent to those of us who want reform in the educational system is diminished. Ultimately, how preservice teachers' identities are co-constructed and the conditions under which their identities are being co-constructed reflects how professors and even the teachers themselves have negotiated between competing forces and their own belief systems within the larger matrix.

Challenging the Mind/Body Split: Teachers Not for Commodification

The Ancient Greeks saw the mind and body as dual entities that had no interaction or relationship. This absolute split between mind and body was later identified by many philosophers, but Descartes has been revered as the father of the philosophical discussion of the mind/body theory of interactionism called Cartesian dualism. Descartes saw the mind and body as two distinct entities. Challenging this dualism was Spinoza in the seventeenth century, who believed that the body and mind were intimately related because they are extensions of each other and therefore are one and the same. He redefined the relationship between the two entities and dissolved their conceptual gap. Spinoza's theory of neutral monism grounds our work here with preservice teachers whom we see as entirely whole beings. Our book offers ways of working with preservice teachers that unites the mind to the body and challenges the disembodiment that teachers are malleable objects for resale and recycling.

The challenge of uniting the mind with the body can be read throughout the chapters and observed through the examples we share. We are of the mindset that we cannot separate our teachers' minds from their bodies because what they do in the classroom embodies both the physical and the mental aspect of their beings. To separate the two is to devalue the self and to lay dormant a piece of the self that is a necessity in teaching. To separate the two is to make preservice teachers into sacrificial lambs who perpetuate sociopolitical ideologies. Vygotsky (1978) suggests that formations of the self and self-awareness are a "critical aspect of consciousness of the mind." On this, McCarthey and Moje (2002) suggest that "because it seems that selfhood and identity are linked, and because mind and consciousness (as socially constructed) have something to do with learning and using literacy, we can argue that identity and literacy are linked in important ways" (p. 228). We want our teachers to move, laugh, dramatize, perform, smile, point, sigh, joke, gesticulate, write, and move around the room as necessary, and we want them thinking through each of these transitions. We want our teachers to be aware of their feelings, thoughts, and emotions as they respond in kind and thoughtful ways to students. We value praxis, the reflection, and action (Freire, 1970) that comes from revising pedagogical applications in the classroom and that act of reinventing or shifting what may not be effective is a conscious and deliberate act that requires a fully embodied self. By embodied we mean that the individual is aware about how the mind and body work together through expression of discourse. To ignore the mind's relationship to the body in preservice methods is to further political ideologies that serve to perpetuate divisive hierarchies and feed patriarchy in our democracy.

Preservice Teachers as Object versus Subject

Preservice teachers are agents of sociopolitical change and therefore potential weapons for dangerous ideologues. It is important that we present preservice teachers with the tools to help them recognize how their pedagogical choices impact the classroom environment and encourage them to make choices that align with their belief systems and multiple subjectivities. In reconsidering our approaches to a nonbinary understanding of preservice teacher identity construction, we can continue to compare our "spatial turn" to the work of Bruno Latour, who attempts to bring technology and science into social science in order to understand them as "accomplishments of human social practice" (Brandt & Clinton, 2002, p. 344). Latour (1996) suggests that "any time an interaction has temporal and spatial extension, it is because one has shared it with nonhumans" (p. 240). He sees interaction as a place for meaning making. According to Latour, interactions occur within frames, and within frames certain objects stabilize the actors. While something may happen within the frame locally, it can be relocated or redistributed globally. For instance, while teachers may teach in a classroom, and hence, the classroom acts as a frame, what students learn or make meaning of may be taken out of the local and be transported or distributed globally. Within the frame, things like paper, pens, computers, and so on may stabilize the environment, but the students or the actors who use those objects may distribute the learning to places that are far reaching. So while "actants" (Latour, 1996) may experience literacy at one time, literacy can be relocated in other spaces. If we think about preservice teacher identity as something that is being co-constructed and therefore can shift, we can reconsider that "the what" and "the how" of teacher education that can have an even greater impact globally in the classroom. Considering that technology will likely continue as a fundamental means by which knowledge is disseminated in our world, thinking of preservice teachers along the same lines relocates the extension of what we are doing in teacher education to further locations.

Along the same lines of Latour (1996), Brandt and Clinton (2002) in their study "Limits of the Local: Expanding Perspectives on Literacy as a Social Practice" further expand our understanding of preservice teacher identity co-construction. They suggest that teachers are agents or actors in the field of literacy and that literacy is not deterministic. They purport that literacy is not a situated social practice; rather it has the ability to "travel, integrate, and endure" (p. 337). They suggest that literacy is not just a thing to be done but is a mediator or participant who can connect actors locally and globally. By awarding literacy with a pseudo-reified status, we open up to the possibility that it shifts in contexts as it participates and can be shifted by the actors in contexts as they participate in literacy. In considering that teachers are literacy agents, what we teach them in teacher education, they distribute across different times and spaces.

When placing preservice teachers into Brandt and Clinton's concept of "literacy as a [pseudo] thing" we can view them as agents of literacy who cannot only act locally in schools but impact the globalization of literacy through the students they teach. Thus teachers are surrogates for technology because they participate in the vast distribution of knowledge that can be disseminated to infinite places around the world. Brandt and Clinton ask, "Can we not approach literacy as a technology—and even as an agent?" (p. 343). Keeping this in mind, English educators can be viewed as agents of technology. If we approach preservice teacher education with the understanding that preservice teachers are agents for literacy dissemination, we open up to the possibility of becoming more conscious that those same preservice teachers not be treated as objects to be acted on, but rather as actors capable of infinite ways of distributing literacy across space and time. Another way to view this is to consider that preservice teachers, once they become in-service teachers, and even after they pass on from this world, the literacy practices that they have mediated will live on after them and their legacy will transcend the transient nature of time. This is not to be taken lightly, for English educators have the potential to help transport literacy practices globally through the preservice teachers that they are teaching and impact literacy practices across time and space.

English educators can continue to transcend the local by reconceptualizing how they create the conditions in which preservice teachers' identities are being co-constructed. We must reconsider for what purposes we are constructing our teachers if we intend to have far-reaching implications for our work in teacher education programs. Building on Brandt and Clinton's concept that literacy is both a thing/subject and the actor in a context, preservice teachers can also be viewed as ontological subjects, capable of negotiating meaning, not as an object for manipulation, but those whom we can impact as technological agents of disseminating literacy practices across time and space. If we de-localize our conception that teachers impact students only during the times and spaces in which they are teaching, we can expand our conversation around the kinds of interactions and conversations we have in our teacher education programs and create spaces to reconsider the conditions in which our preservice teachers are coming to be. This notion will be addressed in successive chapters through the experiences of the preservice teachers.

When preservice teachers begin to see how they have been co-constructed in their role as teachers, this may lead to liberation or dissension from conforming to thought and other institutional expectations that run counter to social reproduction theories imbibed by institutions. As preservice teachers understand their own identity co-constructions, they may seek to emerge and transform their own teacher identities that bump up against social norms and educational values (Miller, 2007). This is why learning how to support counter beliefs that may be nonbinary or nontraditional is a fundamental addition to teacher education: "Dangerous knowledge begins with a critical re-examination of identity representation" (Carey, 1998 as in McDermott, 2002, p. 1). It is only dangerous to teach teachers to be self-reflective if English educators are not equipped to handle the issues that emerge. We should intentionally teach to our preservice teachers consciousness about how they can obstruct, deconstruct, reconstruct, and then construct their teaching identities and maintain a fully embodied self. In so doing, we empower them to be self-reflective and transformative.

Danielewicz (2001) says that teacher education programs should foster teacher identity development to the highest degree possible. In helping preservice teachers recognize their own identity co-constructions, they become more informed about their own subjectivities that can empower them to challenge being co-opted by hegemonic-based discourse and thinking. Recognizing that their own teacher identities are situated within a complex networked matrix of spacetime relationships can help them negotiate their identity co-constructions and help them relocate to spaces that stabilize and affirm their teacher identities. They then can be technological "actants" who participate in co-constructing the identities of their own students across time and space and can teach their students how to co-opt their own identities so that they are not caught up in hegemonic thinking and power structures. Slattery (1995b) affirms this when he suggests that "postmodern schooling must reconnect students and teachers, space and time, meaning and context, knowing and the known, humanities and sciences, and especially past, present, and future" (p. 628) and that "a proleptic understanding of the integration of time, place, and self is one of the most essential elements of curriculum development for the postmodern era" (Slattery, 1992, 1995a, p. 631).

We would be remiss, as Maxine Greene (2000) tells us in "The Ambiguities of Freedom," if we did not seek to free the minds of those we taught or if we did not honor the words of one of the greatest thinkers of democracy and education, John Dewey, who spoke about the "qualities of selfhood" and reminded us of the crucial linkages between the self and interest. We as teacher educators must be relentless in our quest to create conditions that enable our student teachers to be reflective in all aspects of their own identity constructions and create meaningful and self-reflective opportunities for their minds and bodies to be imaginative, inventive, and to take risks that will ultimately lead to "opening up alternative possibilities" for their own students (Greene, 2000, p. 12). We must free our students from hegemonic paradigms that have reinforced their own subjectivities and give them the tools to be "deconstructive" in their own teacher identity co-constructions and be proactive in their own teacher identity co-constructions, and so in turn, they can be conscientious about the conditions they are creating that are constructing their students' identities. On this Greene articulates, "most of us realize that, if we consciously keep our own questions open and take intentional action against what stands in the way of learners' becoming, of our becoming, the spaces for freedom do enlarge" (p. 13). We must broaden our understanding of teacher identity co-construction even further so that the landscape of teacher identity has room to grow and expand authentic educators. To help preservice teachers and their educators to be cognizant about how they are co-constructing the identities of the students in their classrooms is to ultimately shift the power dynamics in society. Popkewitz and Pereyra (1993) say that by using the theoretical work of Foucault on power and knowledge. "substantial change in teacher education occurs as a result of changing patterns, regulation, and power. They contend that changes occur as a result of tensions and conflicts" (Imig & Switzer, 1996, p. 216).

Conceptualizing the Loaded Matrix

Our matrix is not exhaustive; rather it offers a conceptual framework that suffices to explain what impacts teachers' subjectivities. In order to construct our matrix for you, we must provide some necessary contexts that will serve as a path to help the reader more readily understand from where we are drawing our insights. We each believe that aside from some of the less common and less popular "mainstream" topics that have been addressed in preservice research such as attire, sexual relations with students, religion, and politics, there are other loaded, incendiary issues that merit our attention in preservice methods. Such issues we believe have yet to be addressed because they are indeed loaded, because of their potentially explosive nature. For us, these issues include: understanding critical issues impacting classroom management, recognizing the timeliness of critical media literacy skills, examining the underlying problems and successes with preparing preservice teachers to use technology in the schools, unpacking how social justice and sociocultural issues are addressed by instructors and how preservice teachers understand and interpret them in the context of their classrooms, and applying standards to lessons with empirical, hands-on data.

Our matrix thus is not just a matrix then, but a matrix that is loaded, or cocked, with issues that have the potential to both explode and backfire in schools if not carefully addressed with preservice teachers. We feel it is a social responsibility and a moral obligation to help prepare preservice teachers with the necessary discourse tools in methods classes that will both protect as well as arm them to have a sense of some of the invisible issues that underlie and may undermine the classrooms in which they teach. Because these issues are time sensitive and even potentially life threatening, they require the full attention of the preservice teachers' minds and bodies. The issues facing our preservice teachers today do differ from the issues that they faced in 1910, 1950, 1990, and what they will face in 2040. We can count on the fluid nature of change and the inevitability of shifts in the economy and politics. Such shifts make our schools and the identities of those who teach vulnerable to how to negotiate between one's belief systems and society at large. It is this dissonance that we want to unpack and identify because its efficacy can be applied toward future understandings in the context of preservice teaching and inevitable shifts in the sociopolitical world.

At the core of this work on the loaded matrix is furthering and rededicating ourselves to an agenda for social justice in teacher education. We see preservice teachers as the agents upon whom the penultimate of change rests, and by instilling in them tools that can help them "walk the road" as a teacher education community, we provide a service that can help to protect us from psychasthenia (Olalquiaga, 1992, as in Soja, 1996), a state in which we are unable to demarcate our own personal boundaries and become engulfed by and camouflage ourselves in the scholastic milieu. With this book, we hope to provide a type of heterotopia for you and your students in methods classes, which can be a "real" place where there is a "sort of mixed, joint experience" or a "counter-site" occupied and created by those who contest the dominant sites (Foucault, 1986, p. 24), so that preservice teachers can refer to the skills that they have learned to embody as a tool of resistance against larger and more dangerous sociopolitical agendas. Gee (1992) reminds us that an embodied experience helps to affirm particular identities; when we live something, we can become something. As our field comes to (re)conceptualize[3] preservice student teacher identity co-construction within a networked matrix of relationships, we can help preservice teachers recognize their agency in the process, thereby informing them about their own subjectivities that can empower them to challenge being co-opted by hegemonic-based discourse and thinking.

The loaded matrix that we see contains all of the elements that border preservice teachers' identities and is bound by the specific space and time, or spacetime (Nespor, 1997, p. xi), that a preservice teacher is teaching. By spacetime we reference the spatial (space), a place that "brings them [specified factors constructing identity] all together and substitutes itself for each factor separating and enveloping it" (Soja, 1996, p. 45). Space also references the physical layout of the factors (social groups, communities that apprentice a teacher, institutions, media, classrooms, schools, policy, and research) and other places in which an identity comes to mean. By temporal (time), we reference the literal time in which the identity is being formed. The spacetime relationship is based on the premise that time and space are fluid and are therefore constantly changing. Most theorists have written the actual word spacetime by using a hyphen (-) so it appears as "space-time": we, however, eliminate the hyphen to show that the terms are co-relational (Miller, 2007). The boundedness of identity by the relationality of spacetime suggests that preservice teacher identity then is fluid and constantly shifting along with the shifts or changes in the matrix. Consequently, preservice teacher identities are subject to stabilization and destabilization during any spacetime. Stabilization means that a preservice teacher identity is steadied by some factor of the landscape that is co-constructing it, such as a space or a person, while destabilization means that a preservice teacher identity is invalidated or unsteadied by some element that is co-constructing the teacher, for example, like by a person or changes in policies in a particular space (Leander, 2002). Preservice teacher identities are likewise subject to (re)stabilization when they are (re)validated.

For our work, identity is something then that is co-constructed through competing forces and that one's position in a space is "offered, accepted, rejected, and otherwise continuously negotiated" (Leander & Sheehy, 2004, p. 116) as individuals engage in social spaces. Within these spaces identities are "produced, negotiated and hybridized within the flow of dialogue" (Leander, 2001, p. 637). Ritchie and Wilson (2000) suggest that

> As we have watched teachers develop over several years, we've come to see, as Judith Butler (1990) suggests, that if we conceive of teacher subjectivity as an "effect that is produced or generated" (p. ix) by multiple institutions, discourses, and practices, new possibilities also open up for agency. The understanding that human identity isn't "natural" or something fixed or essential, but that it is always an effect or construction of complex and competing forces, allows much more play and possibility for intervention. (p. 13)

Such an understanding of identity through a spacetime lens paves the way to making meaning of preservice teacher identity in spacetime. Postmodernism underscores that identities and ideas are not black and white but rather provides a kaleidoscopic lens that allows us to view concepts from a space or matrix outside of the preservice teacher.

Preservice teacher identity construction as a whole has been insufficiently researched, yet in so many ways the pinnacle of social change rests on how preservice teachers are taught and are teaching in their placements. Britzman (1991) says that preservice teachers are sandwiched in between several relationships. To a large degree, although the preservice teacher identity is vulnerable to being co-constructed by competing agendas, the preservice teacher identity is predetermined because of institutional and social expectations. As such, we must push the boundaries of binary constructions and understandings of preservice teacher identity by disrupting the cycle of teacher as object, encouraging the voice of teacher as subject with unified mind and body, and then (re)locating its placement within a larger matrix that transcends the boundaries of teacher education that gives rise to its hybrid identity formation and subjectivities that can have far reaching sociopolitical implications. Through the stories we share, we address such concerns and offer suggestions for how other English educators and their students can fight against their own commodification and utilitarianism as they find ways to be whole and integrate their multiple subjectivities into their preservice teaching.

History of IUP English Education

The individuals who came to the Indiana University of Pennsylvania (IUP) English education program have unique and distinct stories. In order to understand their relationship within each of their own matrices, we share the context in which their stories fortified. The IUP has a long history of teacher education dating back to 1875 when it was a Normal School with 225 students, and as far as we know, the institution has granted English teacher certification from that time onward. A Normal School prepared individuals to teach in schools. It became a State Teachers College in 1927 and by 1959 was the fifth largest institution of higher education in Pennsylvania. In 1965, the IUP achieved university status.

We are now the largest of the fourteen State System universities with the largest English department. We currently have eighty-nine English education undergraduates enrolled with an application program that admits on average eighteen students each semester.

The IUP English education program offers a competitive and application-based, four-year undergraduate program of 120 credits leading to a Bachelor of Science in Education and also a two-year master's in the teaching of English (MA/TE). For the MA/TE degree, students teach six hours in addition to the core coursework and must complete either thirty-six credit hours without initial certification or forty-two semester credit hours with certification. The programs are each accredited by the Pennsylvania Department of Education, NCTE, and NCATE. Graduates of our programs are prepared to teach in middle, junior high, and senior high schools. The programs certify teachers in secondary English in Pennsylvania and forty-five other states, provide practical experience in methods courses, and include content preparation in a variety of literature, language, and composition courses and philosophical background in current theories of teaching, two 35-hour per semester clinical observations, and a semester of student teaching with a cooperating teacher. As part of the clinical experience, students may opt to take a two-week intensive urban experience in Philadelphia as a substitute for one of their clinicals. Our students are highly encouraged to develop themselves as part of the professional teaching community by participating in the NCTE-IUP student affiliate chapter. Throughout the program students must complete a three-step process for teacher certification and an electronic portfolio review required by our Council for Opportunity in Education.

The Voices of the Text

As an exercise to spark discussion about teacher identity in methods, we ask our students to think briefly about how their past has affected their teacher coconstruction. In so doing, it was also important for us to reflect on the same task as their role models.

Linda

Linda is a fifty plus, white, Irish-Italian from an urban middle-class Catholic background. She grew up in a steel mill town in a three-story house with her parents, paternal grandparents, and six other younger siblings. As the oldest, she had the desire to teach at an early age and often took the role of a teacher while she "played school" with her siblings. Her grandfather completed only up to sixth grade but could speak bits of seven different languages from having to communicate with so many other Ellis Island immigrant steel workers; he was disabled in a mill-related accident and became her stay-at-home caregiver along with her mother until she was nine. Linda became attached to different generations, other cultures, and developed a facility for languages since often she heard various nonnative voices on the street, and Italian was spoken daily at home. Her grandmother skipped two grades in school, graduated at fifteen, married at sixteen and fed the unemployed at home through a makeshift soup kitchen during the Great Depression. She and Linda's father were the breadwinners. Her grandmother sold "foundations" at a large retail store in the inner city for over thirty years and often took Linda on the forty-five minute bus ride with her to work. Linda admired and respected the energy and excitement of the metropolis. They often went to the "picture show" after work; there she fell in love with everything about the movies. Little did she realize that this was the beginning of her passion for media literacy and that she would eventually be instructing preservice teachers in film pedagogy in the secondary English classroom.

Linda's mom was born from Irish immigrants so poor that some days her only food was a cup of tea and one slice of dry toast. Her family grew their own vegetables in their front yard and slaughtered their own chickens when they could get them. A subservient and compliant stay-home mom, she completed high school, sowed tobacco in Connecticut during World War II, and didn't learn to drive until she was sixty years old. Linda's dad, the total opposite, was a privileged only child, well-to-do, first-generation college student who was a district soils engineer for the state department of transportation in a white-collar job. A dominant husband and Air Force drill-captain father, he provided the paycheck each week, never changed a diaper, and drove her mother to get groceries every Saturday. Linda's father, with her grandmother's financial help to pursue the American dream, moved the family without the grandparents from the black-white segregated mill-town neighborhood to a white suburban neighborhood where Linda spent all of her adolescent and early adult years. Because she had two sets of mixed parental influences from two different generations and classes, and because she had six siblings within a twelve-year range, in her formative years, Linda could communicate relatively comfortably with people of all ages and began, albeit subconsciously, to understand and appreciate class, ethnic, gender, and political differentiations at home and at school. On her parents' insistence, Linda attended twelve years of parochial school, but at eighteen, she shifted away from private education and chose a large, land-grant rural undergraduate education, subsequently swinging back to teaching secondary English and French for over fifteen years in private suburban academies, followed by graduate school for a master's and PhD at a large public city university.

Upon receiving her undergraduate degrees, Linda married two years later and moved to a white, rural, conservative neighborhood where her husband grew up on a family-owned and operated tree nursery and where they reared their two daughters. Linda's current educational views are most aligned with the Green party, but her political and public identity is perceived differently by her discourse communities. In her current hometown she is considered a far-left liberal, but in her university environment, she is considered conservative, although she has heard rumors by her students that she was once a hippie. She has been married for the past thirty years to her husband, and her daughters are now two adult college graduates, one a single high school physics teacher in Philadelphia, and the other a married graphic designer in Pittsburgh. She didn't break ties with the Catholic church but chooses to worship at a Protestant church where her husband and daughters attended regularly. Her eclectic life experiences have allowed her to move within very different social, educational, religious, and political milieus and observe a myriad of communication dynamics. Linda always respected her parents but frequently rebelled against her father's control, chose an equal as a life partner, and sought out strong females as role models, trying to become a stronger female role model herself for her own daughters, but with the nurturing instincts her mother had instilled, and teacher of gender equality. These roots have taken hold and often manifest themselves in her preservice methods classes through texts and assignments including topics not limited to gender bias, bullying, NCLB, media literacy, and creating a positive classroom climate as well as her student teaching supervisory role in such disparate environments as a multilingual Philadelphia public high school and a rural, 99 percent white, seven–twelve junior-senior high school.

Linda's teacher identity is co-constructed through her involvement in campus, regional, and national educational organizations and committees and strong ties to family and friends. She enjoys international and continental travel and her quest for "home," watching and critiquing fiction and documentary films, the food network and preserving family recipes, mining the latest English education materials, and caring for her Golden Retriever.

sj

sj is a thirty plus, first born, white, Jewish, transgendered (biological female who identifies as male) academic, who grew up in a semistrict, working-class, racist home in urban Metairie, Louisiana, which neighbors New Orleans. Her maternal grandparents were immigrants from eastern Europe who escaped during the Russian pogroms. Her grandfather did not go beyond fifth grade in school and later owned a janitorial supply store that supplied goods to New Orleans Public Schools and her grandmother did not go beyond tenth grade and later became his secretary. Her father was a doctor with conservative politics and her mother once an English and math teacher and somewhat liberal was initially a stay-at-home mom. At the age of eight, her parents divorced. Over the next several years, she switched between parents until finally settling in Santa Fe, NM, with her mother and ex-military stepfather. After their divorce, her family fell from class and she and her sister worked to support the family and earn money for the household. She was forced to live in the living room during her senior year of high school because of their economic situation. Excelling in both school and athletics, she earned a division one academic and athletic scholarship to attend a top-ten school in an urban city. While in attendance at college, s/he unlearned much of the brainwashing about people that s/he had been taught to believe and even embody while growing up that motivated her/his in a path of unpacking oppression in all forms through teaching. sj's graduate experiences were in two large cities, one in the West and the other in the Southwest, in urban settings, which furthered her/his thinking around social issues and the manifestation of oppression in all forms. As a registered Green party member, her/his work embraces leftist values and fighting for social change and social justice through his/her teaching and the preservice teachers s/he trains. Now teaching at IUP, which is a rural university situated in Western Pennsylvania, he is learning about the kinds of issues that preservice teachers face in rural schools while straddling and embodying a cadre of multiple subjectivities. sj currently lives in Pittsburgh, which is an urban location, and commutes between very different worlds that feed each other. Some of his influences include: popular culture (films, Reality TV, cyberculture, SLAM poetry[4]), café culture, youth culture, athletics, academic organizations, spacetime and hybridity theory, identity studies, travel, and his cat. Such subjectivities feed him and co-construct his teaching identities.

Ethan

Ethan is a twenty-one year old white, heterosexual male from a middle-class family. He hails from a rural Christian conservative neighborhood with industry and schools that support their unions. His father owns an auto body shop, and his mother is the manager of a women's fitness center. He is the oldest of three children and a first generation college student, who was awarded an IUP men's basketball scholarship as most valued player during his senior year in high school. Upon graduation, Ethan would like to go back to his own community to teach English and to coach basketball at his alma mater. Ethan's grades have fluctuated, but he has managed to keep a 3.25 Grade Point Average (GPA). His favorite courses are in film study and his favorite pastimes are hanging with his buddies at the local sports bar and renting the latest DVDs. He is very visible on campus because of his sports' activities and his role as the vice president of the IUP preservice English teachers' affiliate. The student body likes and respects him; he has a big, booming voice and is not afraid to speak up in class. Ethan holds right-wing views on most educational issues, and he believes in teaching by the book through a building-blocks methodology. Ethan requested to student teach in an urban setting so that he could experience a school environment different from his own secondary school.

Ethan was placed at Longview Science Academy, a large, poor, inner-city magnet school with over 1,200 students in grades 9–12. He teaches three junior English courses, of which one is honors. Over 60 percent of the school population are students of color, primarily African-American, and over half are in the free lunch program. Longview has both general and honors courses and encourages students to participate in science-related activities such as the robotics club, botany club, and the Junior Academy of Science. Ethan eagerly agreed to help with coaching boys' basketball at Longview at his students' request, as some of his junior and senior students were on the varsity team and have had a losing record for the past three years.

Beth

Beth is a twenty-two-year-old, Asian American female, from an upper middle-class family. She was raised in a medium-sized suburban city on the cusp of the Midwest. Her father is a doctor and her mother is a history professor. They are practicing Buddhists and high achieving in their professional lives. Her family is centrist in their political beliefs and tend to vote based on who they think the stronger candidate is as he/she aligns with their family's values. During Beth's senior year in high school she came out as bisexual and her family willingly embraced her.

Beth is a talented student and has achieved high marks in the English education program at IUP. Currently she has a 3.8 GPA and is a popular student amongst her peers and her professors because of her warm and bubbly nature. She has a known penchant for the piano and singing and is often asked to play at social events. She has also taken an active role in the NCTE-IUP student chapter and has attended the last two NCTE conferences. Beth teaches at Hillcrest Junior/Senior High, a seven–twelve grade school, which is located in a rural farming community that neighbors IUP. The community is ultraconservative, and there is a large emphasis on the local sports especially men's basketball, and football. Hillcrest offers regular, honors, and AP courses as well as vocational courses in farming, service production, and mining. The school make-up is homogenous with approximately 300 students, 95 percent who are white and 5 percent who are of color. The school offers mainstream education and includes aids in courses to assist students with special needs.

As a preservice teacher through her lesson plans and discourse, she pays homage to venerable institutional values, standards, and norms while also taking risks. One of her strengths is that her extroverted nature has helped her become likable amongst her own students that has helped her build up a cadre of students who asked her to help them with the school musical and coach them in drama. Although slated to teach ninth and tenth grade English classes, both honors and nonhonors, her talents have additionally awarded her a drama class.

Acazia

Acazia is a twenty-one-year-old mulatto (an amalgam of African-American and white) female who grew up poor and in a single-parent female-headed household. She never knew her father, and her mother worked long hours in retail. Acazia was raised in a poorer section of a major Midwestern city and developed an affinity while in high school for Hip-Hop music, SLAM poetry, popular culture, street slang, and drugs. Her English teacher in high school noticed that she was in trouble and that helped to redirect her life. Now, a self-proclaimed agnostic, she came to the IUP program wanting to give back to her teacher that helped her make it to college because she felt she was someone who beat the odds and could help students who came from difficult backgrounds.

Acazia is a hard-working student with a solid 3.5 GPA. She came to IUP with the desire to give her life more focus and structure so she would not end up in retail like her mother. Although she is still working a second job and is a commuter, in her studies she is diligent, attentive, and dedicated to bettering herself through school.

Acazia was placed at Doverville Middle School, a 6–8 grade school, located in suburbia outside of a major city in Midwestern Pennsylvania near several large shopping malls. The values of the surrounding community are mid-to-right of conservative. Doverville has 600 students, with approximately 80 percent white and of that 20 percent are Jewish, and 20 percent are students of color. Sports are equally important to fashion, hairstyles, and popularity. The school is mainstreamed and offers both honors and nonhonors courses. She has been assigned to teach three seventh grade honors and nonhonors English classes on a middle school family team.

Because she has a strong sense of who she is and what is progressive and hip within youth culture, she has the ability to design lesson plans that are highly innovative, engaging and creative. She also quickly established herself as a popular student teacher amongst her students and their peers and she was asked to start a SLAM poetry club and often spent lunch recesses talking with students about their poetry.

Conclusion

Each of these stories differently articulate the matrix of relationship that is co-constructing each person either in this current spacetime or in past spacetimes. Each of these stories further describe in some way how one's interests impact who they are in the classroom. Each of our teacher identities is a pastiche of how we have come to balance the tensions between our ethics of the past, present, and future with that of institutional agendas and how we have been shaped and/or marginalized by social groups (families, friends, discourse communities, church groups), institutions and their policies (schools, governments), and the media (images in popular culture, film, TV, video), and other factors too immense to name. Because discourses and social spaces are vulnerable to changes that occur in political and institutional spaces, teacher identities are impacted by these changes: often stabilizing and destabilizing them. Articulating what is in the matrix of the preservice teacher is essential in furthering our understanding about how they are co-constructed, so it may inform our own practices and the conditions in our methods courses in which future teachers are co-constructed. As preservice teachers co-opt their own identities, we can encourage them in their growth as teachers and help them fight against the mind/body split. This is why we articulate how critical it is that we open ourselves up to dialogue about both the matrix and loaded matrix in our classrooms. On this, hooks (1994) reminds us that by teaching "in a manner that respects and cares for the souls of our students is essential if we are to provide the necessary conditions where learning can most deeply and intimately begin" (p. 13).

Glossary of Terms

Cooperating teacher	the teacher assigned by the institution to supervise the preservice teacher during her/his tenure student teaching.

Discourses	more than our uses of language, they are the combinations of the "saying-writing-doing-being-believing-valuing" (Gee, 1992, p. 127), and ways of participating in a variety of social contexts.
Embodiment	is the act whereby we develop our "discoursed-identities" (Gee, 1992) that are socially constructed and emerge out of our experiences.
Loaded Matrix	is a matrix that is loaded, or cocked, with issues that have the potential to both explode and backfire in schools if not carefully addressed with preservice teachers.
Matrix/rhizome	a matrix is synonymous with the term rhizome, which is a networked space where relationships intersect, are concentric, do not intersect, can be parallel, nonparallel, perpendicular, obtuse, fragmented, and even marginalized. As a theoretical concept, it is both an invisible and visible space, which embodies all of the forces co-constructing the identity of the teacher. Such spaces cut across borders of space, time, and technology and can be lifted into different contexts.
Praxis	reflection on teaching and pedagogy that leads to action or change.
Preservice identity	the illumination of the individual as a preservice teacher by the expectations placed upon them by their teacher preparatory program and by the school spaces in which they preservice teach.
Preservice teacher	university student who is becoming and being educated as a secondary English teacher.
Psychasthenia	a state in which individuals are unable to demarcate personal boundaries and become engulfed by and camouflage themselves into the scholastic milieu (Olalquiaga, 1992, as in Soja, 1996).
Rhizome/matrix	a rhizome is synonymous with the term matrix, which is a networked space where relationships intersect, are concentric, do not intersect, can be parallel, nonparallel, perpendicular, obtuse, fragmented, and even marginalized. As a theoretical concept, it is both an invisible and visible space, which embodies all of the forces co-constructing the identity of the teacher. Such spaces cut across borders of space, time, and technology and can be lifted into different contexts.
Social spaces	places that have been formed by intercontextual discourses that bring together multiple identities and discourses, and that have great significance upon an individual's identity. Social spaces are formed for all kinds

of reasons but are often constructed out of necessity and are impacted by political (power) and social ideologies.

Notes

1 The term, identity, will be interchangeable with the term, subjectivity.
2 The term, discoursed-identity, is something that I coined with permission from Gee on 12/14/05 via email correspondence.
3 The use of the ( ) parentheses delimits its current place in our educational vernacular. When it becomes part of the nomenclature, the parentheses will not be necessary.
4 SLAM is a hybrid of spoken word and performance poetry that draws from Hip-Hop culture.

References

Apple, M. (2002). *Official knowledge.* New York: Routledge.

Baudrillard, J. (2001). *Impossible exchange* (C. Turner, Trans.). London: Verso.

Bhabha, H. A. (1994). *The location of culture.* New York: Routledge.

Bourdieu, P. (1977). *Outline of a theory of practice.* Cambridge: Cambridge University Press.

———. (1980). *The logic of practice.* Stanford: Stanford University Press.

Brandt, D., & Clinton, K. (2002). Limits of the local: Expanding perspectives on literacy as a social practice. *Journal of Literacy Research, 34*(3), 337–356.

Britzman, D. (1991). *Practice makes practice.* Albany: State University of New York Press.

Brooke, R. (1991). *Writing and sense of self.* Illinois: NCTE.

Butler, J. (1990). *Gender trouble: Feminism and the subversion of identity.* New York: Routledge.

Carey, R. (1998). *Critical art pedagogy: Foundations for a postmodern art education.* New York: Garland.

Cochran-Smith, M. (2004). *Walking the road: Race, diversity and social justice in teacher education.* New York: Teachers College Press.

Danielewicz, J. (2001). *Teaching selves: Identity, pedagogy and teacher education.* Albany: State University of New York Press.

Dyson, A. H., Bennett, A., Brooks, W., Garcia, J., Howard-McBride, C., Malekzadeh, J., Pancho, C., Rogers, L., Rosenkrantz, L., Scarboro, E., Stringfield, K., Walker, J., & Yee, E. (1995). What difference does difference make? Teacher reflections on diversity, literacy and the urban primary school. *English Education, 27*, 77–139.

felman, j.l. (2002). *Never a dull moment.* New York: Routledge.

Fiske, J. (1989). *Understanding popular culture.* Boston: Unwin Human.

Foucault, M. (1980). *Power-knowledge: Selected interviews and other writings, 1972–1977.* New York: Pantheon Books.

———. (1986). Of other spaces (J. Miskowiec, Trans.). *Diacritics, 16(1)*, 22–27.

Freire, P. (1970). *Pedagogy of the oppressed.* New York: Continuum Publishing.

Gee, J. (1992). *Social linguistics and literacies: Ideology in discourses* (2nd ed.). New York: Falmer Press.

———. (1996). *Social linguistics and literacies: Ideology in discourses* (2nd ed.). New York: Falmer Press.

Greene, M. (2000). The ambiguities of freedom. *English Education, 33*(1), 8–14.

Haraway, D. (1991). The politics of postmodern bodies: Constitutions of self in immune system discourse. In D. Haraway (Ed.), *Simians, cyborgs, and women: The reinvention of nature* (pp. 203–230). New York: Routledge.

hooks, b. (1994). *Teaching to transgress.* New York: Routledge.

Imig, D. G., & Switzer, T. J. (1996). Changing teacher education programs. In J. Sikula, T.J. Buttery, & E.G. Guyton (Eds.), *Handbook of research on teacher education* (2nd ed., pp. 213–226). New York: Simon & Schuster Macmillan.

Latour, B. (1996). On interobjectivity (G. Bowker, Trans.). *Mind, culture, and activity: An international journal,* 3, 228–245.

Leander, K. (2001). This is our freedom bus going home right now: Producing and hybridizing space-time contexts in pedagogical discourse. *Journal of Literary Research, 33*(4), 637–679.

———. (2002). Locating Latanya: The situated production of identity artifacts in classroom ineraction. *Research in the Teaching of English, 37,* 198–250.

Leander, K., & Sheehy, M (Eds.). (2004). *Spatializing literacy research and practice.* New York: Peter Lang.

Lefebvre, H. (1991). *The production of space.* Oxford: Blackwell.

McCarthey, S., & Moje, E. (2002). Identity matters. *Reading Research Quarterly, 37*(2), 228–238.

McDermott, M. (2002). Collaging preservice teacher identity. *Teacher Education Quarterly, 29*(4), 53–68.

Miller, S. (2005). *Geographically "meaned" preservice secondary language arts student teacher identities.* Ann Arbor, Umi Dissertation Publishing, www.lib.umi.com/dissertations/fullcit/3177097.

Miller, s. (forthcoming, 2007). (Re)/Re-envisioning preservice teacher identity: Matrixing methodology. In J. Flood, S. B. Heath, & D. Lapp (Eds.), *Handbook of research on teaching literacy through the visual and communicative arts* (Vol. II). Mahwah: Lawrence Erlbaum Associates.

Nespor, J. (1997). *Tangled up in school: Politics, space, bodies and signs in the educational process.* Mahwah: Lawrence Erlbaum Associates.

Popkewitz, T. B., & Pereyra, M. A. (1993). An eight-country study of reform practices in teacher education: An outline of the problematic. In T. Popkewitz (Ed.), *Changing patterns of power: Social regulation and teacher education reform* (pp. 1–52). Albany: State University of New York Press.

Ritchie, J. S., & Wilson, D. E. (2000). *Teacher narrative as critical inquiry.* New York: Teachers College Press.

Rose, G. (1993). *Feminism and geography: The limits of geographical knowledge.* Cambridge: Polity Press.

Slattery, P. (1992). Toward an eschatological curriculum theory. *JCT: An Interdisciplinary Journal of Curriculum Studies, 93*(3), 7–21.

———. (1995a). *Curriculum development in the postmodern era.* New York: Garland.

———. (1995b). A postmodern vision of time and learning: A response to the national education commission report prisoners of time. *Harvard Educational Review, 65*(4, Winter), 612–633.

Soja, E. W. (1996). *Thirdspace: Journeys to Los Angeles and other real-and-imagined places.* Malden: Blackwell.

Vygotsky, L. S. (1978). *Mind in society* (M. Cole, V. John-Steiner, S. Scribner, & U. E. Souberman, Trans. and Ed.). Cambridge: Harvard University Press.

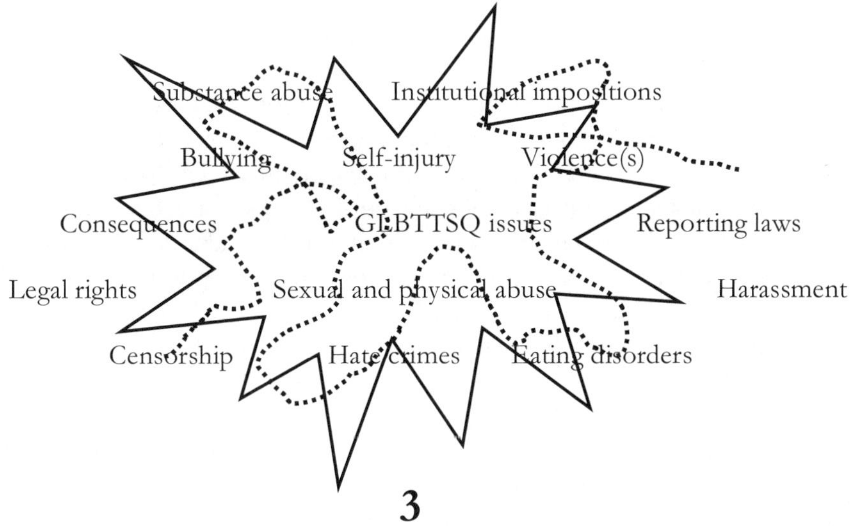

3

The Loaded Matrix in Classroom and School Environments

This chapter presents an overview of violence and school safety, censorship, and the consequence of not addressing harassment in public classrooms and schools.[1] We see censorship in similar ways to violence because it is a way of limiting free speech and perpetuating silence on issues that may lead to social action.[2] We also review various laws and how they affect the speech and actions of preservice teachers. This chapter will reveal how preservice teachers can respond on these loaded issues to administrators, veteran teachers, cooperating teachers, students, and parents. We offer suggestions to preservice teachers in order to help them understand their rights to self-expression and protection on each of these issues. It is important to keep in mind that some of the issues presented in each of our chapters will resurface in the matrix during a different spacetime in successive chapters.

Loaded Matrix Chapter Context

This chapter's genesis emerged out of a situation in Beth's preservice classroom when she was approached by two students at separate times who each disclosed that they were being sexually and physically abused at home. She asked them about their current feelings of safety and if they had told any other adults. They said they were terrified and no other adults had been informed. She then told the school counselor about the students who responded that she would investigate the disclosures further. As her supervisor, Beth called me and explained what had transpired earlier that day in school. I told her she had taken the right steps and tried to give her assurances about the students about whom she was terribly worried. Although I helped assuage her emotions, inside I was cringing. I felt I had not provided her adequate answers and because I was uninformed about Pennsylvania state statutes on reporting rights, I feared that I had not taken ample steps to protect the students or my student teacher. Concerned, I called Linda and she told me I had given Beth the right advice. Still, I felt dissatisfied in my answers to her as her supervisor. I took it upon myself to look at the laws on reporting by state and school district. After discussing this more with Linda, we agreed that faculty, teachers, and preservice teachers each needed to be informed about the laws on reporting abuse and neglect. We also decided that we need to explore what preservice teachers can and cannot say without redress. This meant unpacking and understanding laws protecting preservice teachers. The following questions emerged as a set that guide and are addressed throughout this chapter's discussion.

Focus questions for chapter 3:

1. **How can preservice teachers' emerging understanding of pedagogy enhance their ability to address censorship, violence and school safety, and discrimination in all forms in classrooms and schools?**
2. **How do preservice teachers negotiate between their own beliefs and values and those imposed upon them by schools, individual districts, and the Constitution?**
3. **How do preservice teachers apply and articulate university-based learning with regard to their rights when the pedagogy they would choose to practice runs counter to or is absent or invisible from their cooperating teacher's classroom?**

Emerging Pedagogy

When preservice teachers begin their work in methods classes, many of them latch onto pedagogies that align with their personal beliefs and values. As an inchoate teacher, the preservice teacher may not be fully conscious about why s/he embraces a particular pedagogy. Teacher educators often spend the semester helping preservice teachers to unpack those reasons and then encourage students to articulate their pedagogies into a teaching philosophy or pedagogy. Many of us tell our students that pedagogies are likely to change and shift over time and in different contexts and that it is important to be open and adaptive to the spacetime of teaching (Darling-Hammond, 2005; Miller, 2005a). How then can we best prepare students and then affirm their pedagogies if they bump up against pedagogies in their student teaching placements that counter both what they are being taught in the university and their own? How can preservice teachers' emerging understanding of pedagogy enhance their ability to address loaded issues?

Issue #1: Violence and School Safety

Violence and school safety is of great concern to us. We feel it is our social and moral responsibility to not only inform our preservice teacher students to the greatest extent possible about the different types of both invisible and visible violence that they may encounter in the schools, but also how they can help themselves and their students find safety if necessary.

Violence is a multifaceted beast that manifests itself in different shapes and forms in various spacetimes. I define violence by turning to a former group of my high school seniors with whom I conducted research. According to them, violence is "an unsolicited attack that causes trauma to its victims," "some form of battery against another," "lack of restraint against another," and "it inevitably seeps into our lives through keyholes, windows, radios, newspapers, magazines, novels, young adult literature, TV, movies, and our dreams" (Miller, 2005b, p. 87). As such, violence in schools manifests in many ways but can be taxonomied as: against other humans (sexual harassment, bullying, and cyber bullying), emotional (mental or psychological problems), spiritual (conflicts about belief systems), social (substance abuse), society against self (such as appearance, body, eating disorders, self-injury), and institutional (such as with standardized tests and "expressions of dominant societal ideologies and function as a mechanism of social control" [Herr, 663, as in Franzak & Noll, 2006]) (Miller 2005a/b). The danger herein is if preservice teachers are not made aware of the particular manifestations of violence, they may inadvertently be complacent in perpetuating acts of violence on their own students and thereby continue the cycle of oppression (myths lead to socialization that leads to internalization, which leads to behavior[3]). If the cycle is not interrupted, someone may end up internally oppressing the self, hurting others, committing a hate crime, or worse case scenario: dead. In this section, we detail some of these different manifestations of school violence and their current regulations as well as describe other forms of violence that may be less visible. Schools tend to label forms of violence under the umbrella term "harassment."

We cannot discuss violence in schools without also discussing student safety. Because we want students to feel safe in schools, we must prepare our preservice teachers to consider their well-beings. Morrow (2004) describes three kinds of safety for school students in terms of school excellence: physical, emotional, and intellectual. By physical he means the actual environment, the first space of the school such as in the classroom, the hallways, the bathroom, the cafeteria or the nurses' office. By emotional he means the mental and psychological well-being of the student, which tends to be less obvious to observe. And by intellectual, to provide a space for students where they are free to take risks and challenges in an environment that supports inquiry, free of put-downs. Unless all three of these safety issues are met, it is difficult for a student to achieve excellence in school. By addressing violence with our preservice teachers, we hope to instill in them a sense of understanding about what students need in order to feel safe and successful in school. Each of the issues of violence addressed in the next section also addresses some element of how to help students feel safe and reach homeostasis again.

Against Other Humans: Sexual Harassment

Title VII of the Civil Rights Act of 1964, as amended in 1972 and 1991, prohibits discrimination on the basis of sex in all terms, conditions, or privileges of employment. Title IX of the Educational Amendments of 1972 prohibits sex-based discrimination in any educational program or activity that receives federal funding. Although these measures are in place, it does not necessarily guarantee that sexual harassment will not occur in the schools and schools must still have precautions in place when a sexual harassment happens for anyone.

Sexual harassment is defined by each and every school district with some variation. Most school employees are "expected" to attend sexual harassment trainings and be informed of their working rights. If preservice teachers are not made aware of their rights, they should take it upon themselves to be informed of the sexual harassment and reporting policy of the district and the school site. The Pittsburgh Public Schools offers an example of sexual harassment as:

> Sexual harassment is unwanted and unwelcome behavior of a sexual nature which interferes with an individual's work or academic performance or of creating an intimidating, hostile, or offensive working or educational environment or of adversely affecting the employee's or student's performance, advancement, assigned duties or any other condition of educational programs, employment or career development. (Pittsburgh)

Sexual harassment can be classified into two categories: *quid pro quo* and *hostile environment harassment* although both can occur simultaneously. In *quid pro quo* situations, a person in authority connects some aspect of a student's education to the student's response to sexual overtures such as with a grade. *Hostile environment harassment* does not necessarily involve sexual blackmail (although it may), and its perpetrators may be college employees, students, or other people on a campus. This kind of harassment is either unwelcome verbal or physical conduct that is sufficiently severe, pervasive, or persistent to create an abusive or hostile environment from the perspective of the affected student and a reasonable person in that student's shoes. This can include sexual assault, offensive language, and other forms of unwanted sexually lewd contact. If a teacher sexually harasses a student, the district can be sued for monetary damages and the teacher is likely to be fired. Along similar lines, it is likely that if a preservice teacher sexually harasses a student, the attending university's education department can be sued for monetary damages and the preservice teacher will be removed unequivocally from the teaching placement.

There are three standards of liability to schools for sexual harassment (Gorian, 2002). Under the federal courts, the "no fault" liability would hold a school district liable for every incident wherein a teacher molested a pupil. "Constructive knowledge" liability (which falls under Title VII) is for employer-employee sexual harassment, regardless of gender, and if the school district knew but failed to take action, it is liable. Last is the "actual knowledge" standard that says a school district cannot be held liable unless it knew of the abuse and did nothing to stop it. In all three instances, if a preservice teacher is involved in a sexual harassment incident, it is likely that the binding university department would advise the student teacher, offer services, and depending on the circumstances possibly relocate the student to a different teaching placement pending investigation. We now cover in more detail some of the loaded issues around sexual harassment that may emerge for preservice students.

Teacher-Student Sexual Harassment

We are opening the discussion about erotics and not erotica in the classroom. Such discussion is perceived as taboo territory and often tends to be ignored or avoided in teacher education altogether. This unspoken territory may be avoided for exactly that reason: that it is all too intense and erotic to discuss and those who open the Pandora's Box may not feel equipped for what spills forth either from their students or from themselves. However, we do our preservice teachers a disservice and may even be complicit if a boundary is crossed if we do not prepare them for the erotics involved in teaching. We must be able to discuss the erotics in heterosexual, homosexual, bisexual, and transgender terms. If we are unable to do so, we are complicit in our student teachers' misdeeds.

felman (2002) describes the unspoken and intense connection between student to teacher as "when intellectual and emotional passion spark in tandem, igniting the perpetually dormant Eros[4] of the classroom...," "a deep intellectual penetration that, when experienced, becomes physical because it has so viscerally entered the body and not just the brain alone" (p. 109). felman (2002) suggests that the combination of mind/body becomes the erotic charge. She writes:

> Through watching me while simultaneously participating, the class understands that the body must be present too, active and engaged in the learning process. The body moves the mind as the mind moves the body. The feminist body, embodied as man or woman, when present or alive, electrifies the pedagogical space. And causes a current

> of radical intellectual sparking to surge through the entire academy, disrupting previously passively rendered, albeit highly elevated, intellectual spaces. Thus the feminist body performing femininities threatens the very heartbeat of the traditional patriarchal academy. (p. 101)

A preservice teacher can be taught to understand and recognize that the charge a student may feel toward the teacher does not have to be sexualized though. felman's work is important to teacher educators so that we might better prepare ourselves to discuss the erotic discharge that can happen in a classroom and which might be misread or misused if preservice teachers are not aware of the erotics they might inadvertently protrude. She is not suggesting that teachers become de-sexualized mannequins, but by opening up discussions and understanding what a teacher embodies in the classroom, we can help our preservice teachers recognize that they are conduits of erotics. Often when that which is perceived as "taboo" loses its eroticism, it ceases to be loaded. It is important we name some of the potential charges that preservice teachers bring with them into the classroom in order to thwart a possible explosion. How can we broach this already charged topic? Here are some examples for reflection in multiple genres that can be approached through writings, diagrams, art, dramatizations, role-plays, and class discussions:

- Ask student teachers to describe a time when they found themselves aroused by or crushed out on a teacher. What did that feel like? How did they respond to the teacher? How did the teacher respond to them? How did the infatuation subside?
- Ask student teachers what they think the warning signs are of a student's attraction to him/her and vice versa.
- Discuss proper attire while teaching.
- Ask students to reflect on these questions: Were you ever a favorite student? If so, what did that feel like? Is it wise to have favorite students? Why or why not? What are the complications involved?
- Discuss a plan if a boundary is crossed by a student or by the teacher.
- What is appropriate touching with students? What would appropriate hugging look like?
- Ask student teachers to consider what to do if she/he manifests a crush/infatuation on a student.

Johnson (2004), through her bold research, addresses how as a young, new educator she wore trendy clothes to make herself more appealing and, hence, effective with her students. In fact, she recognized her own need to manipulate them into learning. She also admits that nowhere in her teacher education preparation had she been told that she might develop romantic feelings toward students. In her study she worked with her own student teachers around questions pertaining to boundaries, appearance, favorite students, student crushes, role of Eros in the classroom, and working with sexual content in literature. Based on findings that emerged in her study and in my own talks with student teachers, we have compiled a top ten list of ways to avoid putting yourself in a possibly compromising position with a student:

1. If you are alone with a student in the classroom, always have the door open;
2. Never tell a student that s/he is your favorite;
3. Always hug a student by turning sideways so it is shoulder to shoulder, not face on;
4. Never discuss your intimate relationships with your students;
5. If teaching sexually explicit material, be sure to consider the age of the students, have discussions about how to approach the material with your cooperating teacher, clinical supervisor, and administrator (if necessary). Be sure you have done sufficient research first;
6. Do not ask students about their intimate relationships;
7. Be thoughtful about your attire and, when making choices, consider what it was like to be an adolescent. If a student gives you a compliment on your dress or appearance, simply say "Thank you," and let it die there;
8. Never have students over to your home or let them be in your car;
9. Do not engage in intimate contact on the Internet with any of your students or students in the school; and,
10. Do not post sexually explicit materials or photos of yourself on a blog, or reveal much about your personal life on an Internet site such as those often frequented by students like myspace.com, facebook.com, or friendster.com.

Johnson (2004) concludes her work by telling us that there needs to be more dialogue and research conducted on teacher embodiment.[5] She encourages us with:

> Teacher educators could play a role in creating space within a larger framework of teacher education discourse such that bodily knowledge is considered along with pedagogical and content knowledge as a necessary component of teacher training and professional development. (p. 24)

With the increased media attention on teachers who cross the line with students such as: the recent Tampa Bay middle school reading teacher, Debbie LaFave, who had sex with a fourteen-year-old male student (charges were later dropped); or high school English teacher, Sandra Geisel (served jail time), mother of four, who had sex with a sixteen-year-old male student; and, the notorious Mary Kay Letourneau (served jail time),[6] who had two children with her student and later married him, we might wonder had those teachers had discussions earlier in their careers about the charge between teacher and student, perhaps they would have never crossed into the taboo.

Peer Sexual Harassment

Peer sexual harassment is an issue in schools and one that is often much more prevalent than some might suspect. In fact, schools can be the training grounds for future domestic violence if not interrupted early on. In 1993, The American Association of University Women conducted a survey of 1,632 middle and high school students and found that 85 percent of girls and 76 percent of boys reported experiencing some kind of sexual harassment.

Research suggests that sexual harassment in schools stems from ignorance about appropriate sexual behavior and language use about gender that has been socialized and then internalized (Fineran, 2002; Miller, 2005b). With this in mind what can preservice teachers do to assist students to cope with some of the pressures of adolescence and try to interrupt the cycle? What tools do we need to arm them with in our teacher education courses that can help to prevent or dissipate potential sexual harassment? We must provide them with the knowledge, discourse, pedagogy, and reporting issues that involve their students.

First, in taking a preventative stance, we must update and educate ourselves about gendered-discourse and from there be deliberate about our use of discourse, curricular choices, pedagogical stances, and actions. As we work with our students, it is important to model gender inclusivity and gender-varied language. This means that we present a thorough picture of humanity through our use of language. As we do so, we arm our students with language that is sensitive and applicable to their classrooms. The following are examples of tools to use with our preservice teachers:

1. When we speak we must be sure that we explain that all genders should have equal opportunity and that none is privileged over others, although laws are not yet completely equitable or inclusive for all transgender people. By saying all genders, we mean male, female, transgender, and intersexed. *Transgender* is an umbrella term for people or behaviors that diverge from the gender commonly, but not always, assigned at birth. It is the space in which one's gender identity or gender presentation does not match the assigned birth gender. A transgender person may be a transvestite (one who cross dresses), a transsexual (one who may live outside of the biological gender or who has sexual reassignment surgery), or someone who does not live within the construct of binary notions of gender but self-defines who s/he is outside of dominant society. Transgender is fluid and embraces all kinds of gender variant identities. Transgender is the third gender. *Intersexed* (commonly known as a hermaphrodite) is someone with genitalia, not necessarily born that way, that does not fit into either male or female genitalia but is inbetween the two.

The way we also speak about gender and gender expression should be nonbinary because while there are commonly regarded definitions, beliefs, and meanings for gender, there is also a continuum that allows for people to fall outside of what we commonly perceive as binary. As we stay open to a nonbinary understanding of gender, we challenge ourselves to reflect on the changes that occur in our language use every day.

2. Be sure the pedagogy you employ is inclusive, nonbinary, and multidimensional. Examples of such pedagogy include: equity pedagogy, critical pedagogy, critical hip-hop pedagogy, liberatory pedagogy, engaging pedagogy, feminist pedagogy, queer pedagogy, and transformative pedagogy.

3. Carefully consider the texts you use and how language is written or discussed. Ask questions of your students about texts such as: how is language used? Who is speaking? Who is the intended audience? What is the purpose of the writing? Who is excluded? How is gender portrayed in the text? Describe any variations of gender. Is the text current or dated? Are the voices of the disenfranchised present? What resources were used in writing the book? What is the ethnicity of the author? What is the gender of the author? What are the politics of the press and who published the text?

4. Discuss options with your preservice teachers to cultivate, develop, and foster safe spaces at school. An example of this is starting a gay/straight/alliance (GSA)(see *GLSEN.org* for how to start a program at a school site).

5. Help them consider their curricular choices by providing them with reading lists that support gender and gender identity in nonbinary ways.

6. Remind them to use gender-inclusive language in all their communications with students, parents, school administrators, and peers. Talk about the broader issues of gender bias, sex-role stereotyping, and discrimination and work to promote gender equity.

7. Encourage preservice teachers to create a class library (when possible) that has a diverse range of texts that embrace differences of culture, class, ethnicity, gender, ability, weight, religion, national origin, sexual orientation, size, and gender expression.

8. Empower preservice teachers with a starter set of questions that promote critical inquiry as in number 3.

9. Review types of peer sexual harassment. According to Fineran (2002), examples of peer sexual harassment include:

- sexual comments, jokes, gestures, or looks,

- sexual messages or graffiti on bathroom walls or locker rooms,
- sexual rumors,
- shown sexual pictures, photographs, illustrations, messages or notes,
- called gay or lesbian with derogatory terms like "fag" or "lezzie,"
- spied on while showering or dressing at school,
- being flashed or mooned,
- touched, grabbed, or pinched in a sexual way,
- having clothing pulled in a sexual way or clothing pulled down or off,
- brushed up against in a sexual way,
- blocked or cornered in a sexual way,
- forced to kiss or forcing other unwelcoming sexual behavior other than kissing, and
- having names listed in slam books with derogatory sexual comments.

Next, we can prepare our preservice teachers to talk to students about these situations and encourage them to consider how they might respond. This can be done through role-plays, discussions, writings, journals, art, or multigenre writing.

10. Encourage preservice teachers to post sexual harassment policies in and posters (when possible) around the classroom that honor and celebrate all people.

11. Finally, we all must walk our talk and honor the fact that when we commit to teaching social justice it continues even when we leave our classrooms at the end of the day. Who and how we are outside of school builds emotional and spiritual integrity, and the more we work on our inner lives and learn from others around us, the better equipped we will be to handle some of the more loaded issues that peak in the schools, in our classrooms, and in our lives. Most importantly, by living social justice we stand up at all costs for others who may struggle to find their voices, who are dispossessed, or who are being oppressed, and we ally ourselves with those who need our support until justice is met.

If a preservice teacher is made aware of student-to-student sexual harassment, regardless of gender, the teacher should immediately report it to the school counselor, the Title IX coordinator, or the cooperating teacher, and write down the details: dates, times, places, and witnesses. Preservice teachers may follow up afterward with informal discussions but should not be involved in any entanglement that may lead to the courts. If the preservice teacher learns that the problem cannot be resolved at the school level, it is possible that it may be resolved by the U.S. Department of Education's Office for Civil Rights, but s/he should stay out of any legal entanglements and let it resolve through the proper authorities.

When a student has experienced sexual harassment, it is important to help the student re-stabilize in school. The preservice teacher and the cooperating teacher can check in with the student periodically, keep a watchful eye, let the student know that she/he may stay in the classroom during breaks if necessary, and encourage the student to also take small steps toward re-socializing. The preservice teacher may also address the problems through film, texts, and guest speakers from local rape crisis centers or peer counseling organizations. Careful planning must go into addressing sexual harassment and it would be imperative to involve the cooperating teacher and possibly the clinical supervisor.

In our methods courses we can discuss how to help our preservice students teach their own students about other ways to avoid putting themselves in positions that might lead to sexual harassment. We can also discuss with them how people express gender differently. Some of the following are examples that we can read and view together and which should be taught to adolescents with extreme care and careful planning.

Middle School Texts
Including Gay/Lesbian/Bisexual/Transgender Themes
Alice Alone, Phyllis Reynolds Naylor
Alice on the Outside, Phyllis Reynolds Naylor
The Eagle Kite, Paula Fox
I Feel a Little Jumpy around You: A Book of Her Poems & His Poems Collected in Pairs, Naomi Shihab Nye and Paul B. Janeczko
From the Notebooks of Melanin Sun, Jacqueline Woodson
The House You Pass on the Way, Jacqueline Woodson
Risky Friends, Julie A. Peters
The Misfits, James Howe
The Skull of Truth, Bruce Coville and Gary A. Lippincott

High School Texts
Heterosexual (*=made into a film)
Boys Lie, John Neufeld
Lucky, Alice Sebold
Out of Control, Shannon McKenna
Shattering Glass, Gail Giles
*Speak,** Laurie Halse Anderson
*To Kill a Mockingbird,** Harper Lee
Unexpected Development, Marlene Perez

Gay/Bisexual Themes
Alt Ed, Catherine Atkins
Am I Blue? Marion Dane Bauer and Beck Underwood
The Drowning of Stephan Jones, Bette Greene
Geography Club, Brent Hartinger
The Perks of Being a Wallflower, Stephen Chbosky

Rainbow High, Alex Sanchez
Rainbow Boys, Alex Sanchez
Shattering Glass, Gail Giles
Simon Says, Elaine Marie Alphin
What Happened to Lani Garver, Carol Plum-Ucci

Lesbian/bisexual themes
Am I Blue?, Marion Dane Bauer and Beck Underwood
Annie on My Mind, Nancy Garden
Color Purple, Alice Walker
Empress of the World, Sara Ryan
Keeping You a Secret, Julie Anne Peters
Kissing Kate, Lauren Myracle
Name Me Nobody, Lois-Ann Yamanaka
Out of the Shadows, Sue Hines

Transgender themes
Define "Normal," Julie Anne Peters
The Flip Side, Andrew Matthews
Luna, Julie Anne Peters
My Heartbeat, Garret Freymann-Weyr
"Standing Naked on the Roof," Francess Lantz
Written on the Body, Jeanette Winterson

Films: We encourage you to have discussions with your cooperating teacher, clinical supervisor, university instructor, and administrator if you intend to use any of these films. Some of these films are better suited for the methods classroom.

A Girl Like Me, Billy Elliot, Boys Don't Cry, Beautiful Thing, But I'm a Cheerleader, Camp, Confronting Date Rape: The Girl's Room, Date Violence: A Young Woman's Guide, It's So Elementary, This Boy's Life, Ma Vie En Rose, Normal, School Ties, Speak, You Ought to Know: Teens Talk about Dating and Abuse

Texts for Teachers
When the Drama Club Is Not Enough: Lessons from the Safe Schools Program for Gay and Lesbian Students, Jeff Perrotti

➡*Teaching Points*

∞Methods Courses and Secondary Classrooms

Questions That Align with the Texts and film for both Preservice teachers and classroom students (adapt as necessary for grade level)

How was the victim sexually harassed?
Did anyone try to help or intervene?
What resources were available to the victim?
After the harassment, what did the victim do?
Was there any moment when the victim could have acted differently, but did not? Why or why not?
Describe the situation leading up to the harassment. What could the victim have

done differently so as not to put her/himself in harm's way?
What happened to the perpetrators?
Did anything change in the school environment after the harassment?
If the victim were in the situation again, do you think s/he would likely act the same, why or why not?
How were genders portrayed in the text? Did language contribute to the victimization? If so, speculate how.

Furthering Inquiry for Social Action for Methods and Secondary Classes
•Invite in guest speakers from local rape crisis centers.
•Research which states have nondiscrimination laws.
•Research which states have laws that privilege homosexuals.
•Research which states discriminate against homosexuals.
•Research which state laws exclude homosexuals.
•Understand how nondiscrimination policies work by state.
•Do a critical discourse analysis of a TV show on gendered-language use.
•Do a discourse analysis of your own use of gendered language.
•Research Title IX, its past, and its future.
•Review the sexual harassment policy of your university and school sites.
•Determine if peer mediation is available at your university or school site and, if not, start one.
•Rewrite a scene or passage from the film or text and shift the use of gendered-language so it affirms the characters.
•Rewrite scene or passage from the film or text and change the outcome of the sexual harassment incident.
•Conduct an analysis of how language is used in a passage or scene. Review the number of positive or negative stereotypes that affirms/disaffirms gender differences.

Colleague Sexual Harassment

It is quite appealing to be a new teacher, fresh from a university. With that, the preservice teacher is somewhat vulnerable to those in power and authority over him/her. A preservice teacher should never put him/herself in a compromising position in order to please a colleague nor should s/he become romantically involved with someone at the school site while in the placement. Why not? Plain and simple, it is just not wise and it may turn into sabotage. When feelings become hurt or someone is rejected, it may cause the preservice teacher considerable duress and may even cost him/her a career.

If in fact the preservice teacher finds her/himself in a position that can be perceived as sexual harassment, or feels any type of coercion, s/he should immediately notify the clinical supervisor for support. It is then up to the supervisor to investigate the situation, determine if the preservice teacher is unsafe, discuss it with the supervising department of the university, and take necessary action. If the preservice teacher has endured psychological, physical, or emotional abuse, s/he should seek professional counseling.

In our methods courses we can discuss with our students what might occur and discuss possible scenarios with them. For instance, we can role-play and discuss the following scenarios to help them consider what to do if they are sexually harassed. By bringing this to their attention, we help to buffer them from a possible mishap.

•A colleague invites you out for a drink and you unsuspectingly accept. Once out at the bar, makes a blatant pass at you, how do you respond?
•A colleague admires your outfit and reaches out to touch the fabric and in so doing gropes you, how do you respond?
•You suspect your cooperating teacher has a crush on you, how do you handle it?
•Your principal invites you to participate on the curriculum committee, but you feel pressured to join because of the way she/he looks at you and because you fear losing your position in the school. What do you do?

We might also help our preservice teachers consider what to say to someone when unwanted sexual advances occur. We can urge them to say "No thank you," and let it end there.

➡Teaching Point
Brainstorm other statements with your student teachers for what to say if someone sexually, verbally, or physically harasses you.

Sexual and Physical Abuse

Each school district should have a written district policy for reporting child abuse and neglect (Wakefield, 2002). What should a preservice teacher do if a student discloses that s/he is being abused by someone outside of school? How can the university methods courses support the preservice teacher through this loaded issue? We must prepare ourselves to have these discussions in our methods courses to assist our students with what they may encounter in their teaching placements.

If a preservice teacher suspects that a student is being sexually and/or physically abused, as in the case with Beth, there are several options: tell the cooperating teacher, the school counselor, the clinical supervisor, or the university methods instructor. The preservice teacher should not push the student to disclose but rather let someone who has the proper reporting authority handle the situation. The preservice teacher may put him/herself in a compromising entanglement if s/he encourages the disclosure. If a preservice teacher suspects a student disclosure, s/he should interrupt the student and inform the student that if it is disclosed to the preservice teacher, the latter has a legal responsibility to report the abuse. Should the student proceed to disclose, the preservice teacher should listen closely to the student, reassure the student that there is help available, reassure the student that s/he has done the right thing by telling someone not make judgments, not interrupt, and take notes. The preservice teacher should also ask the student to name anyone else that has been told about the abuse, and inquire about the student's current level of safety at home. It is extremely difficult to walk away from a student knowing about the abuse and feeling disempowered to help in that immediate spacetime; however, that is what must happen save any legal entanglements. The preservice teacher must report the suspected evidence immediately as both a moral and legal responsibility to the school counselor, the cooperating teacher, and follow up with the student at school. The school then has an immediate legal and moral responsibility, or else becomes liable, to report the abuse (even if it is only suspected) to protective services and/or law enforcement. If in the case that a peer of a student who is being abused discloses information to the preservice teacher, she/he should follow the same instructions as above but explain that the report is secondhand. It is possible that the preservice teacher may also begin to experience feelings about the disclosure and may need to work through any possible discomfort.

When a student has experienced or is currently experiencing sexual and/or physical abuse, it is important to help the student re-stabilize in school. Students who experience such abuses may appear depressed, angry, withdrawn, gaunt, agitated, and injured. They may also suffer academically or perform below grade level, have psychosomatic illnesses, experience emotional outbursts, have low self-esteem, become antisocial, become self-destructive, be overly compliant, and manifest symptoms of an eating disorder (Wakefield, 2002).[7] Studies show a high correlation between those students who are either being physically or sexually abused and having an eating disorder (Hernandez, 1992). Some of the manifestations of an eating disorder regardless of gender include lower self-esteem, more stress, more anxiety, skipping meals, a ring around the outside of the lips, skin discoloration, more hopelessness, and more suicidal thoughts. It is important that both the preservice teacher and the cooperating teacher extend concern to the student periodically, pay attention to him/her, offer the classroom as a respite during breaks, provide a stable and predictable environment for the student, help the student feel a sense of belonging, and provide affirming feedback.

In methods courses, teacher educators can alert their students to the warning signs and help preservice teachers consider how to address sexual and physical abuse problems in lessons through film, texts, and guest speakers from local rape crisis centers or peer counseling organizations. It is important to understand that when addressing these topics in school, it can lead to disclosures and it might also save a life. Careful planning must go into addressing sexual harassment and it would be imperative to involve the cooperating teacher and possibly the clinical supervisor. The following resources address issues relating to sexual and physical abuse.

Middle School Texts
I Hadn't Meant to Tell You This, Jacqueline Woodson
Laurie Tells, Linda Lowery
Silver, Norma Fox Mazer
So Much to Tell You, John Marsden
When Jeff Comes Home, Catherine Atkins
When She Hollers, Cynthia Voigt

High School Texts (*=also made into a film)
A Child Called It, Dave Pelzer
America, E.R. Frank
*Bastard Out of Carolina,** Dorothy Allison
Chinese Handcuffs, Chris Crutcher
*Color Purple,** Alice Walker
Darkness before Dawn, Sharon M. Draper
Easy Connections, Liz Berry
Forged by Fire, Sharon M. Draper
Friction, E. R. Frank
Hold Me Tight, Lorie Ann Grover
I Know Why the Caged Bird Sings, Maya Angelou
I Was a Teenage Fairy, Francesca Lia Block
Margaux with an X, Ron Koertge
Mercy's Birds, Linda Holeman
My Aunt Is a Pilot Whale, Anne Provoost, Ria Bleumer (Translator)
Perks of Being a Wallflower, Stephen Chbosky
Push, Sapphire
*Speak,** Laurie Halse Anderson
Shattering Glass, Gail Giles
So Far from God, Ana Castillo
True North, Jim Harrison
When She Was Good, Norma Fox Mazer

Films: Most of these films are heavy in content and may not be suitable for classroom use. We encourage you to have discussions with your cooperating teacher, clinical supervisor, university instructor, and administrator if you intend to do a unit with any of these films. These films are better suited for the methods classroom:

Bad Education, Bastard Out of Carolina, The Boys of St. Vincent, Color Purple, L.I.E., Mommie Dearest, Mysterious Skin, Mystic River, Once Were Warriors, Thirteen, This Boy's Life, Woodsman

Bullying

Bullying is a serious problem in public schools.[8] In fact to date, twenty-three states have antibullying laws and sixteen states this year are trying to pass laws in their state legislatures. Though there is not one universal definition of bullying, according to H.R. 284 (House of Representatives),

> "Bullying and "harassment" include conduct directed at students that substantially interferes with their educational opportunities, specifically including conduct that is based on a student's actual or perceived identity with regard to race, color, national origin, gender, disability, sexual orientation, and religion (as well as other distinguishing characteristics that may be defined by the state or district). In addition, the term "violence," as presently defined in the Act, is modified to include bullying and harassment. (as on Bully Police)

Bullying can be in stages or take on different forms of violence—it can be one, two, or all of these and can begin or end with any of these—with taunting and making fun of someone or name-calling (often prompted by another peer to poke fun at someone or cause mental or emotional stress), to hurting someone physically (torture), to killing someone (like a drive-by shooting).

Although students may encounter harassment by peers, teachers, or other school personnel for perceived or actual personal characteristics, it can also occur for no apparent reason. According to the U.S. Department of Education: Office for Civil Rights (1999), harassment "can encompass a range of harmful conduct, from the most violent crimes of episodes of vandalism or persistent and abusive name-calling among grade school students that may deprive students of equal educational opportunities" (p. 1). It is important for our preservice teachers to be aware of these kinds of issues because it affects a student's ability to function emotionally, academically, and physically in school and it may provoke "retaliatory violence, damage the school's reputation, and exacerbate community conflict" (U.S. Department of Education: Office for Civil Rights, 1999, p. 1). School should not be about survival, it should be about learning; and preservice teachers, when made aware of the pervasiveness of bullying, can help students feel good about school. It is ironic that the Safe and Drug-Free Schools and Communities Act that is part of the No Child Left Behind Act provides federal support to promote school safety, but it fails to directly address the issue that is left to individual state legislatures and that is tied to federal funding.

The National School Safety Center identified different types of bullying, some of which involve direct action and indirect action. Direct action involves physical contact while indirect action involves "verbal, emotional, sexual, or passive-aggressive behaviors" (Ferrell-Smith, 2003, p. 2). Hate-motivated bullying in some cases can legally constitute a hate crime (see chapter 7 for a detailed discussion) when taunting is about race, national origin, ability, religion, sexual orientation; and physical or mental abilities.[9] Another kind of bullying that is invisible at school is *cyber bullying*, which is that although a student has left school, there are continued verbal, sexual, and even physical threats made against the student through any technological means. Some students receive threatening instant messages (IM) that can haunt them at home and follow them to school. Some students bully by posting information about other students to be read on their web pages and even post inappropriate photos.

Markow and Fein (2005), in their comprehensive study on school climates across the United States, found that girls are more likely to report feeling unsafe in schools that is generally based on personal appearance; girls experience more verbal harassment, white students generally feel safe in school, Latino/a students are more likely to experience racially based harassment, and Lesbian/Gay/Bisexual/Transgender (LGBT) students are over three times more likely than non-LGBT students to feel unsafe and experience acute harassment. While six out of every ten non-LGBT students experience harassment in some form, nine out of ten LGBT students experience harassment. Below are some of the alarming statistics from their study:

- 65 percent of teens have been verbally or physically harassed or assaulted during the past year because of their perceived or actual appearance, gender, sexual orientation, gender expression, race/ethnicity, disability, or religion,
- 39 percent of teens report that students in their school are frequently harassed because of their physical appearance,
- 33 percent of teens report that students in their school are frequently harassed because of their perceived or actual sexual orientation,
- 52 percent of teens frequently hear students make homophobic remarks,
- 51 percent of teens frequently hear students make sexist remarks,
- 69 percent of teens frequently hear students say "that's so gay" or "you're so gay"; expressions where "gay" is meant to mean something bad or devalued,
- 36 percent of teens indicate that bullying or harassment is a serious problem at their school, and
- 53 percent of secondary school teachers say that bullying or harassment is a serious problem at their school.

They also found that bullying or harassment varies by the type of school the students attend.

- Junior high school students are more likely to report harassment because of physical appearance or body size frequently occurs (48 percent versus 39 percent);
- Junior high school students are more likely to frequently have rumors or lies spread about them;
- Junior high school teachers are more likely to describe bullying and harassment as a serious problem at their school (64 percent versus 46 percent);
- Public school students are more likely than others to consider bullying or harassment to be a serious problem at their school (38 percent versus 14 percent);
- Public school students are less likely than private or parochial students to feel very safe at their school (44 percent versus 81 percent); and
- Public school students are more likely than private or parochial school students to report that harassment based on sexual orientation frequently occurs (34 percent versus 18 percent). However, private school students are much less likely to know a student in their school who identifies as LGBT (36 percent versus 57 percent), to have a close

> friend who is LGBT (10 percent versus 20 percent), or to identify as LGBT themselves (2 percent versus. 6 percent).

Bullying takes its toll on its victims. Victims tend to skip school more often, have lower self-esteem, lowered academic performance, and experience depression at rates higher than nonbullied students (Harris & Isernhagen, 2003). While most schools were found to have an antiharassment policy, only half of the schools reported protection on sexual orientation or gender expression. Those schools with sexual orientation or gender expression written into their antiharassment policy reported fewer problems with school safety. The pervasiveness of bullying in schools does require our attention in teacher education.

When a preservice teacher is made aware of some type of bullying in either his/her classroom or elsewhere, she/he should immediately report to two separate people: the cooperating teacher and the school counselor. Again, the preservice teacher should be absolved from any legal entanglements and by surrendering such information is resolved from possible redress. The preservice teacher may also want to discuss matters with the clinical supervisor or bring it up for discussion in the university classroom. Bullying is ubiquitous and is a topic that most of our student teachers will encounter in some form. By discussing the cycle of bullying with our student teachers we can help them recognize the warning signs and help them interrupt a possible bullying problem before it manifests.

First, we can discuss with them what causes bullying such as that bullies are likely to have suffered bullying themselves prior to an attack. Bullies are often socialized into bullying behavior by role models or peers and revenge against an individual or a group is often a motive that bullies attack others. Next, we can teach them about the different types of bullying that are visible and invisible in schools. We can also teach them about the consequences of bullying on the victim. It is also important that we help our preservice teachers teach their own students about how to critically use the Internet and recognize that bullying can occur there. We can then discuss reporting issues and when it is appropriate to step in. Lastly, we can encourage them to talk about nonviolence as an alternative to bullying.

We have compiled a list of some books and films that can be used in teaching student teachers about the pervasiveness of bullying in schools. Such lessons can be modified for age and grade level for their own classroom students. It is advisable to talk to others about these materials to assess what best meets your students' grade level needs. Prior to conducting a unit on bullying, it is advisable to discuss it thoroughly with the cooperating teacher and clinical supervisor.

Middle School Texts
*=also made into a film
*Holes,** Louis Sachar
*Hoot,** Carl Hiaasen
Kissing the Rain, Kevin Brooks

High School Texts
Black Boy, Richard Wright
*Chocolate War,** Robert Cormier
*Killing Mr. Griffin,** Lois Duncan
Monster, Walter Dean Myers
Probably Still Nick Swansen, Virginia Euwer Wolff
Project X, Jim Shepard
Shattering Glass, Gail Giles
*Speak,** Laurie Halse Anderson
Staying for Sarah Byrnes, Chris Crutcher
Stotan!, Chris Crutcher
Tears of a Tiger, Sharon M. Draper
The True Believer, Virginia Euwer Wolff
Who Will Tell My Brother? Marlene Carvell

These books can be paired with activist-type books about people who believed in nonviolence or who tried to stop fighting in some form.

Activist/Nonviolence Texts for Middle School
The Borrower's Afloat, Mary Norton et al.
Diary of Anne Frank, Anne Frank
Esperanza Rising, Pam Munoz Ryan
Francie, Karen English
House Made of Dawn, N. Scott Momaday
The Revealers, Doug Wilhelm
Roll of Thunder, Hear My Cry, Mildred D. Taylor
Watsons Go to Birmingham, Christopher Paul Curtis
Zlata's Diary, Zlata Filipovic

Activist/Nonviolence Texts for High School
*A People's History of the United States,** Howard Zinn
*The Bee Season,** Myla Goldberg
An Autobiography: The Story of My Experiments with Truth, Mahatma Gandhi
God of Small Things, Arundhati Roy
The Autobiography of Martin Luther King, Jr., Martin Luther King Jr., & Clayborne Carson
Poisonwood Bible, Barbara Kingsolver
*Razor's Edge,** W. Somerset Maugham
Siddhartha, Herman Hesse
*To Kill a Mockingbird,** Harper Lee
*Way of the Peaceful Warrior** (about a college athlete but suitable for older students), Dan Millman
Walking Stars, Victor Villasenor
Walden, Henry David Thoreau

*Zen and the Art of Motorcycle Maintenance,** Robert Pirsig

Middle School Films
Holes, Hoot, Let's Get Real, Mean Creek Speak

High School Films
Anatomy of a Hate Crime, Bowling for Columbine, Elephant, Jawbreaker, Glory Road, Heathers, Killing Mr. Griffin, Mean Creek, Mean Girls, Never Been Kissed, O, She's All That, Speak, The New Guy. Walking on the Moon, Whatever It Takes

These films can be paired with activist/nonviolent films from people who believed in nonviolence or who tried to stop fighting in some form.

Activist/Nonviolence
The Chocolate War, Gandhi, Long Walk Home, MLK, Paper Clips, Razor's Edge, Schindler's List, Way of the Peaceful Warrior, You Can't Be Neutral on a Moving Train

➡*Teaching Points*

∞Methods Courses and Secondary Classrooms

Questions That Align with the Texts and Film

What forms of bullying did you identify?
What do you think caused the bullying?
Were there any preventatives that were in place to stop the bullying? If so, what were they?
What were the consequences for the victim? For the bully?
How was the victim helped by others?
How did a teacher or school personnel respond to the incident?
Was the incident reported, why or why not?
Develop a plan for how to discuss bullying with your own students.
How did the protagonist respond to the bullying that was perpetrated on him/her?
Speculate why the protagonist did not retaliate.
Compare and contrast the protagonists in the films/texts and describe the differences in their reactions to the bullying.
Describe other ways the protagonist might have responded to the harassment.
What did you learn that you can apply to your classroom or to your lives?
What would a bully-safe school look like?
What can you do today to help stop bullying?

Other Suggestions for Combating Bullying in the Classroom

•Bring in a guest speaker to discuss bullying and its consequences.
•Bully proof your school by adopting a bully prevention program.
•Post antibullying posters in your classroom.
•Promote nonviolence.
•Model discourse that honors and validates all people.
•Have a well-balanced library of books that represents all aspects of humanity

and society.
•Do not tolerate or accept any put-downs in your classroom.

Other Resources about Bullying in the United States
Colorado Center for the Prevention of Violence
http://www.Colorado.EDU/cspv
Provides extensive violence prevention information produced by the Center for the Study and Prevention of Violence (CSPV).

National School Safety Center
http://www.NSSC1.org/
Provides information that helps combat school safety problems such as books, resources papers, films, and workshops on school safety–related topics.

National Center for Educational Statistics
http://nces.ed.gov
Provides data from several National Center for Educational Statistics (NCES).

Department of Justice
http://www.ojp.usdoj.gov/bjs/
Provides data from the Bureau of Justice Statistics such as: crime and victims; criminal offenders, special topics; law enforcement; prosecution; federal justice system; courts and sentencing; corrections; expenditures and employment; and criminal record systems.

National Resource Center for Safe Schools
http://www.safetyzone.org
Provides information for schools, communities, and state and local education agencies to help establish developing safe learning environments and preventing school violence.

Emotional (Mental or Psychological Problems)

There are a number of other manifestations of violence that can impact a student's ability to function well in school that may be less subtle such as a student who may struggle with an emotional problem that causes him/her severe duress. If a preservice teacher observes a student exhibit certain behaviors over a period of time, she/he should discuss such matters with the cooperating teacher and possibly the clinical supervisor or university methods instructor prior to making a referral to the school counselor. The following list of symptoms may necessitate a referral but does not necessarily indicate the presence of a problem:

> Difficulty paying attention, distracts other students, performs below grade level, talks incessantly, cannot sit still, drifts, appears distracted, forgetful, looks depressed, talks to self, looks tired often, argumentative or defiant, acts hyper or manic.

In our methods courses we can discuss symptoms with our preservice teachers that may indicate the presence of a mental or psychological problem so that our student teachers are more sensitive and attuned to the students in their classrooms.

Social (Substance Abuse)

Violence can manifest through drug and alcohol use. Students have access, regardless of class, to drugs and alcohol and may use these even right at school. I have known from reports where I used to teach that students would use in the bathroom, on the playground, in their vehicles, and even ingest through the food they eat, or the thermoses they bring. How do we know if our students' use of substances is a problem or if it is even habitual? The answer is if it is done in our schools, it is a problem because students are minors, bottom line!

What do we tell our preservice teachers about suspecting that a student is under the influence or is using a controlled substance while in class? Symptoms do not necessarily indicate that someone is under the influence but may include: being distracted more than usual, smelling like marijuana, dilated eyes, falls out of chair, slurs word, does not walk straight, is forgetful, and is outwardly defiant or argumentative. If any of these symptoms are present we must admonish our preservice teachers to alert the cooperating teacher and let the cooperating teacher handle it. There are proper procedures for suspected drug and alcohol use and schools must be careful about how students are searched and questioned.

Preservice teachers can address these issues with their students through films and texts to draw attention to the social and cultural pressures around substance abuse and the consequences of using. Although these topics tend to be addressed in health classes, a student may be more receptive and open in an English classroom. It is important that we help our students recognize that substance abuse can become addictive and it can interfere with academic performance, relationships with others and with the self, and can lead to life-long problems. Some texts and films that address drug and/or alcohol use for middle and/or high school students include:

Texts
Drugs
A Scanner Darkly, Philip K. Dick
Babylon Boyz, Jess Mowry,
Beauty Queen, Linda Glovach
Crank, Ellen Hopkins
Crosses, Shelley Stoehr
Go Ask Alice, Anonymous
Living at the Edge of the World, Tina S., Jamie Pastor Bolnick
Motown and Didi, Walter Dean Myers
Orfe, Cynthia Voigt

Pretty Little Devils, Nancy Holder
Rats Saw God, Rob Thomas
Scorpions, Walter Dean Myers
Smack, Melvin Burgess
Street Pharm, Allison van Diepen
Stoner and Spaz, Ron Koertge
White Oleander, Janet Fitch

Alcohol
A Door Near Here, Heather Quarles
Black Boy, Richard Wright
Crosses, Shelley Stoehr
Imitate the Tiger, Jan Cheripko
Moonlight Man, Paula Fox
Parrot in the Oven: Mi Vida, Victor Martinez
Rules of the Road, Joan Bauer
Smashed, Koren Zailckas
Song of Solomon, Toni Morrison
The Tenant of Wildfell Hall, Anne Bronte
Up Country, Alden Carter
We All Fall Down, Robert Cormier

Films
Dolphins, Girl Interrupted, Heathers, Homeless to Harvard, Igby Goes Down, Purgatory, Requiem for a Dream, 13, White Oleander

Again, it is important that these lessons be carefully planned, that discussions with the cooperating teacher occur in advance of the lesson and that goals and assessment outcomes are clear and detailed.

➡*Teaching Points*

∞Methods Courses

Questions for Discussion with Preservice Student Teachers

What are some of the reasons people use drugs or alcohol?
What are the symptoms of using drugs or alcohol?
How do you know if you have a substance abuse problem?
Where do you go if you need help?
Who can you turn to?
What is the difference between a problem and experimenting?
Did you ever have a problem with substance abuse? If so, how did you overcome it?
Did you know someone who had a problem with substance abuse? If so, how did it affect her/his life? Does she/he still use it?
What other behaviors might manifest if someone uses drugs or alcohol?
Is there a problem in your school? Community? Country?
What can you do in your school community to help others not use drugs?

Furthering Inquiry for Social Action

•Design a lesson to help students understand the problems associated with substance abuse.

•Identify the resources available to help teens in your community.

•Research a drug or alcohol company and determine its profits, if it outsources, who is the target audience, who is the vulnerable population, who is the guinea pig, what is the government stance, and what are the pros and cons of the drug.

•Inquire what the main substance abuse problems are in your school community and determine how you can support your students against using drugs.

•Seek out posters that are antidrug, antialcohol, and post them in your room.

•Consider what alternatives to substance using are available to your students and reflect on how you can convey that to them.

•Determine what populations in your school community are most vulnerable to substance using and consider ways you can support them.

Secondary Classrooms

Questions for Discussion with Classroom Students

What would your parents/guardian think if they knew you used substances?
Is there easy access to substances in your school or community?
Which students are vulnerable to using these?
What are some of the reasons people use drugs or alcohol?
What are the symptoms of using?
How do you know if you have a substance abuse problem?
Where do you go if you need help?
Who can you turn to?
What is the difference between a problem and experimenting?
Did you ever have a problem with substance abuse? If so, how did you overcome it?
Did you know someone who had a problem with substance abuse? If so, how did it affect her/his life? Does she/he still use it?
What other behaviors might manifest if someone uses drugs or alcohol?
Is there a substance use problem in your school? Community? Country?
What can you do in your school community to help others not to use these?

Furthering Inquiry for Social Action

•Design a lesson to help younger peers understand the problems associated with substance abuse.

•Identify the resources available to help teens in your community and be proactive in your school community.

•Research a drug or alcohol company and determine its profits, if it outsources, who is the target audience, who is the vulnerable population, who is the guinea pig, what is the government stance, and what are the pros and cons of the drug.

•Inquire what the main substance abuse problems are in your school community and determine how you can support your peers against using these.
•Consider what alternatives to substance using are available to you and make a commitment to not use.
•Determine what populations in your school community are most vulnerable to substance using and consider ways you can support them against.
•Review the online resources and books in the school or community library that discuss substance abuse and create an annotated reading list for your teacher's classroom library.

Additional Substance Abuse Sources for Youth
Teenspace
http://www.ipl.org/cgi-bin/teen/teen.db.out.pl?id%2BicO000
For access information about a wide range of topics relating to substance abuse

Al-Anon/Alateen
http://www.al-anon.alateen.org/
1-888-4AL-ANON- for problems with drinking

Drug Abuse and Addiction- Signs, Symptoms, Effects, and Testing
http://www.helpguide.org/mental/drug_substance_abuse_addiction_signs_effects_treatment.htm

Teens 411, Teens in Crisis
http://www.child.net/teenhelp.htm

Society against Self (such as Appearance, Beauty, Eating Disorders, Self-Injury)

We live in a world where our youth are vulnerable to interpreting messages about what the ideal female or male should look like. Some students as a result will manifest social and cultural pressures internally through eating disorders, by cutting themselves, or even inflicting injuries to their own bodies that cause bruises, cuts, burns, or rashes. As teacher educators we must draw attention to these issues for our preservice teachers and equip them with the skills and knowledge about how to be aware of and to be of service to their own classroom students.

How can we know whether a student manifests any of these symptoms, especially when some may seem obvious and others are hidden beneath clothes? Some of the possible symptoms of eating disorders for all genders but which do not necessarily indicate the presence of one may include lower self-esteem, more stress, extreme weight fluctuation, appearing to be losing weight, exhibiting anxiety, skipping meals, wearing baggy clothes, seeming lethargic, being moody, having a ring around the outside of the lips, skin discoloration, more hopelessness than usual, and having suicidal thoughts.

What is self-injury? Self-injury includes burning (or "branding" with hot objects), picking at skin or re-opening wounds, hair pulling (trichotillomania), hitting (with hammer or other object), bone breaking, head-banging, and multiple piercing or multiple tattooing. A student who injures her/himself may go to extreme lengths to cover up. How can we detect whether a student is causing self-injury? Symptoms may include but do not necessarily indicate that someone is self-injurious:[10] is hypersensitive, chronically angry at self, tends to wear long sleeves and long pants regardless of weather, has obvious injuries regularly, mood swings, inconsistent in relationships, has poor attachments, and has a sense of hatred toward many things.

If a preservice teacher suspects that a student may have an eating disorder or appears to be self-injurious, s/he should consult the cooperating teacher, the school counselor, the clinical supervisor, or the university methods instructor. We do not necessarily advocate teaching these issues directly to our students as it may inadvertently provoke a problem instead of preventing it. It truly depends on the environment of the school and the needs of the students. We have compiled a list that addresses eating disorders and self-injury. It is best that you screen the texts first to determine the age best suitable for the readings as you may determine that some texts are more appropriate for certain individuals.

Eating Disorders

Middle School Texts

Divine Secrets of the Ya-Ya Sisterhood, Rebecca Wells
Girl Power in the Mirror, Helen Cordes
Just Listen, Sarah Dessen
Like Mother, Like Daughter: How to Break Free from the Female Food Trap, Debra Waterhouse
Stick Figure: A Diary of My Former Self, Lori Gobblieb
The Best Little Girl in the World, Steven Levenkron

High School Texts

"Adios, Barbie," Ophira Edut (Editor)
Food Fight, Kelly Brownell, Katherine Battle Horgen
Bitter Ice, Barbara Kent Lawrence
Kim: Empty Inside the Diary of an Anonymous Teenager, Beatrice Sparks
Life Inside the Thin Cage: A Personal Look into the Hidden, Constance Rhodes
Life Size, Jenefer Shute
Ophelia Speaks, Sara Shandler
Perk!: The Story of a Teenager with Bulimia, Liza F. Hall
Reviving Ophelia, Mary Pipher
Second Star to the Right, Deborah Hautzig
Wasted: A Memoir of Anorexia and Bulimia, Marya Hornbacher

Films

Best Little Girl in the World, Eating, For the Love of Nancy, "Girl, Interrupted," Heathers, Interrupted, Karen Carpenter Documentary, Life Is Sweet, Models: The Real Skinny, Real Life Teens (MTV), Sybil, What's Eating Gilbert Grape

Self-Injury

Middle/High School Texts (in most of these cases, the books can be read at either level, but screen first)

Checkers, John Marsden
Crosses, Shelley Stoehr
Cut, Patricia McCormick
Cutting, Steven Levenkron
Define "Normal", Julie Anne Peters
Green Angel, Alice Hoffman
Keeper of the Night, Kimberly Willis Holt
Kyra's Story, Kyra Karadja
The Luckiest Girl in the World, Steven Levenkron
Saint Jude, Michael Aquilina
Silent to the Bone, E.L. Konigsburg
Skin Game, Caroline Kettlewell
So Much to Tell You, John Marsden
Speak, Laurie Halse Anderson
The Dream Where the Losers Go, Beth Goobie
The Earth, My Butt, and Other Big Round Things, Carolyn Mackler
Things Change, Patrick Jones
Wanderer, Sharon Creech, David Diaz
We're Not Monsters, Sabrina Solin Weill
You Don't Know Me, David Klass

Films

Dolphins, Donnie Darko, Girl Interrupted, My First Mister, Purgatory House, Skin Deep, 13

⇒*Teaching Points*

∞Methods Courses

Questions That Align with the Texts and Film for Preservice Teachers

What symptoms revealed that there was an eating disorder or an issue with self-injury?
What might you have done had you been working with the student?
What if a peer of the student brought to your attention that there was an issue with a friend, what would you do?
What kinds of discussions do you feel are appropriate with your own students?
What kind of support is available to students who self-abuse or who have an eating disorder?

Furthering Inquiry for Social Action

•Design a lesson that addresses eating disorders and that is both preventative and proactive.
•Create a journal about your own experiences or with others about eating disorders or self-injury.

•Consider what kinds of posters you can place in your own classroom that affirm body images.
•Compare and contrast images in the media (TV, film, magazines) of girls and boys to real life images by conducting an inquiry into how images are air-brushed, and how cosmetic surgery "enhances" people's looks.
•Research some aspect of the media and consider how images of girls or boys reinforce and construct binary understandings of identity.
•Keep a journal that details all of the kinds of positive and negative images you see or hear about men and women in society. Discuss in class with peers.
•Research the benefits of nutrition on adolescents and design a lesson for students.

Secondary Classrooms
Questions That Align with the Texts and Film for Classroom Students
With whom could you most identify and why?
What symptoms indicated that a there was a problem?
What might you have done had you been a friend of the person who had a problem?
What kinds of support are available to students who self-abuse or who have an eating disorder?
Do you know someone who suffers from an eating disorder or from self-abuse, if so, how does it affect him/her?

Furthering Inquiry for Social Action
•Research some aspect of the media and consider how images of girls or boys reinforce and construct binary understandings of identity.
•Research how a company markets a food product, what is its nutritious value, the politics of the company, who the target audience is, the cost of making the product versus selling it, whether the company outsources, who the vulnerable population is, and present the findings in class.
•What can you do to help a friend who has an eating disorder or who is self-injurious?
•What community resources are available to youth? Hold a community fair at school and invite different nonprofits to attend and distribute information to youth. Invite all students to attend.
•Compare and contrast images in the media (TCV, film, magazines) of girls and boys to real life images by doing an inquiry into how images are air-brushed, and how cosmetic surgery "enhances" peoples looks.
•Keep a journal that details all kinds of positive and negative images you see or hear about men and women in society. Discuss in class with peers.
•Review the online resources and books in the school or community library that discuss self-injury and create an annotated reading list for your teacher's classroom library.

Other Resources about Seeking Help for Eating Disorders
Eating Disorders: Facts for Teens
http://familydoctor.org/277.xml

National Eating Disorder Information Center
http://www.nedic.ca/

Other Resources to Help Bring Attention about Self-Injury
American Self-Harm Information Clearing House
http://www.selfinjury.org/indexnet.html

National Mental Health Association
http://www.nmha.org/infoctr/factsheets/selfinjury.cfm

S.A.F.E. Alternatives (Self-Abuse Finally Ends)
http://www.selfinjury.com

Institutional

One of the most egregious and insipid forms of violence is institutional. Institutional violence is the expression of dominant societal ideologies that have manifested as a mechanism of social control (Herr, 1999). On January 8, 2002, *No Child Left Behind (NCLB)* anthropomorphized into the most recent weapon against public schooling in the United States. It requires that school districts and schools achieve adequate yearly progress (AYP) toward universal student achievement of state standards (set by the state) each year. Fairclough reminds us that "policies define how we are to act and by what rules we must abide" (Woodside-Jiron, as in Rogers, 2004, p. 174) and this dynamic, to some extent controls our discourse, our pedagogy, our actions, and boxes us into particular binary ways of teaching—if we let it.

Such ideologies lock individuals into binary notions of history and perpetuate a myopic view of humanity. Teacher educators like us who are committed to social justice and who are committed to challenging these expressions, have done so in imaginative and innovative ways through curricular and pedagogical choices. This section examines how a dominant form of institutional violence, *NCLB*, perpetuates violence as a way of maintaining social control. We have a social and moral obligation to address how *NCLB* impacts schooling in our methods courses, although it is problematic. Preservice teachers are unlikely to recognize how they are being impacted, how their students are being impacted, and how identities are being co-constructed intercontextually during any spacetime unless we make it visible to them.

A current related issue in education to this is do we prepare our students for vocations through functional and skill-based literacies or do we prepare them for college with multiple literacies? Such a choice was presented to the New Orleans school board, even against contradictory research, when the lower ninth ward, an impoverished area with a large African-American population, which suffered greatly during the hurricane, was starting to be rebuilt in the aftermath of Hurricane Katrina. Proponents for the vocational-based literacy felt that it would help to rebuild the economy, while opponents thought this would be an ideal opportunity to improve the educational system in New Orleans (King, Miller, Scheurich, & Valencia, 2006). The issue is still at bay; however, it begets the larger question about the kinds of literacies that should be used in the public schools, whose agenda is being furthered by the kinds of literacies we use, and who benefits from the literacies we teach. In order to unpack this issue further, we present some background to *NCLB* that is covertly and overtly pushing toward the kind of acquired and procedural knowledge that is needed to best serve the U.S. economy and government.

Educational policy is driven by results and interpretations from quantitative studies that dictates and mandates standardized testing in our country. Consequently, policy reinforces binary concepts in education, and therefore perpetuates antiquated notions about education that reinforces the normalizing of hegemony. Standards are an attempt to try to level the academic playing field by suggesting outcomes for students by grade level. Because states have control over what standards are created, there is a lack of consistency across space and time of states' standards. Roth and Pipho (1990) tell us, "although almost all states developed their own standards, most have been influenced by the standards developed by NASDTEC" (p. 127), which have been around for close to thirty years. Standards do reinforce binary outcomes and box teachers into teaching to the expectations that others have set forth. As standards change in time, teachers and their students are impacted by the spacetime relationship.

Although states have a hand in developing and sustaining their own standards, if they expect to receive federal funds under *NCLB*, they must prepare their teachers to use standards because the standards are redesigned during the spacetime a policy is enacted. In other words, standards reflect national educational policy and impact the rewriting of standards in states. Teacher educators then, if they want to prepare teachers to prepare students for standardized testing, are obligated to help them understand standards and their applications in the classroom. We are reminded by Corrigan and Haberman (1990) that the individual states accredit teacher education programs and,

> Through this process the state establishes specific criteria for program standards, which the universities must meet. Second, the state establishes specific licensure requirements for individuals to be certified including mandated tests. Third, almost all states require individuals to pass tests of basic skills before they can even be admitted to university teacher education programs. (American Association of Colleges for Teacher Education, p. 200)

In sum, Shulman's (1983) following comment is consonant with the aforementioned, "indeed it might be very well argued that, although teachers are employees of particular school districts, it is the state that exerts the most pervasive controls over their practice" (as in Corrigan & Haberman, 1990, p. 206). Teachers are co-constructed therefore through the particulars of *NCLB* and those who accept it without critique pass on the values of those in power of constructing those policies during the spacetime of its enactment. The larger issue herein is that we are all being co-constructed relationally to *NCLB*, whether toward or in negotiation against. We can all benefit by engaging in postmodern thirdspace imaginings of how to prepare both our students and ourselves to think critically about the state exams and, in so doing, open up to nonbinary thinking during the spacetime of a policy's enactment.

The *NCLB* impacts states, which impacts teacher educators, who then impact student teachers, who in turn impact students (see *NCLB* conceptual policy framework). Government sanctioned, *NCLB* has the power to affect states' governance over teacher education programs and has both a direct and an indirect hand in co-constructing preservice educators, who in turn teach students (see figure 3.1). *NCLB* impacts the identity co-construction of everyone in its path and hence reinforces governmental control over our bodies and minds.

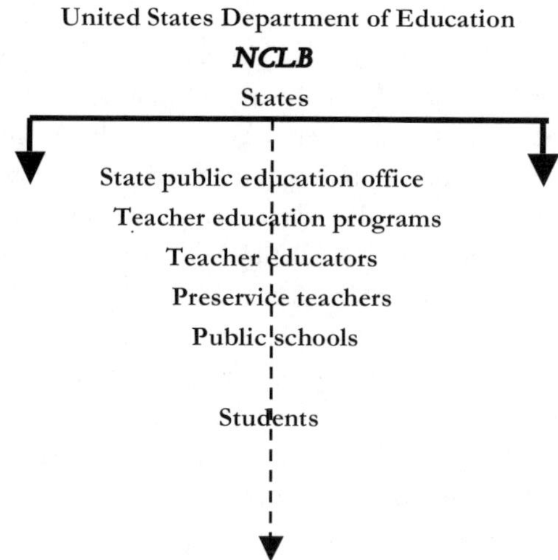

Figure 3.1 *NCLB* conceptual policy framework.

States and their school districts, if they expect to receive federal dollars under *NCLB*, must meet AYP and adhere to meeting the specifications of constructing "highly qualified teachers." Some states such as Utah have abdicated altogether from receiving funds from *NCLB* and are free to construct their own standards for local school districts. As a result of *NCLB*, teacher education programs in states that receive *NCLB* funding are expected to comply with the criteria of *NCLB*. Herein surfaces the quandary. If a teacher education program has left-oriented ideals and pushes a qualitative agenda, then the ideals of that program may be in opposition to the ideals of *NCLB*. If teachers are positioned to question educational policy and then teach from that perspective, they are taking a political stance. The stance is likely to be part of their pedagogy and may be in conflict with the ideals of state and national mandates. On the other hand, if they opt not to challenge *NCLB,* the silence is damaging to all of us because it normalizes what we are critiquing. Perhaps part of the hidden agenda of *NCLB* is that its success is so dependent upon students' success on standardized exams, and because states need federal funds to improve their schools that even teacher educators are powerless against the titanic force of the policy during the spacetime of its enactment. Perhaps leftist teacher educators have little choice but to repress or sublimate their beliefs because they recognize that states need funds, and without a larger consensus backing their position, their hands are bound to the policy. Perhaps herein is where the hidden agenda of *NCLB* has monolithic power. The way *NCLB* works is that it capitalizes on teacher educators as cultural capital. On one hand, policymakers recognize that states who seek federal assistance must use teacher educators to construct teachers who will help students succeed on standardized testing under *NLCB*, and on the other hand, teacher educators are contractually bound to prepare teachers in all aspects of the classroom. This is a lose-lose for leftist educators. Any silence or lack of information provided to teachers about *NCLB* in teacher education programs is part of the hidden agenda it seeks to normalize. *NCLB* uses teacher educators to carry out its mission.

We suggest that to not be conscientious about how individuals are impacted by *NCLB* is to reinforce values that perpetuate a status quo society and marginalize the marginal. So we ask, how can we create a balanced curriculum, educate to the left and to the right, but yet position our student teachers to challenge the status quo, and prepare them to meet the expectations under *NCLB*? Smith and Stock (2003) illustrate this by articulating how teachers' identities are impacted by policy through citing Hoffman who says (2000):

> The result of numerous educational policies legislated in the 1990's-mandates that control teachers' actions both directly and indirectly can be found in standardized testing plans that shape curriculum; state curriculum framework for reading and writing that produce detailed scripts and specifications for what is taught, and when it is taught; state-level legislation that requires specific methods of instruction; and federal legislation that defines the kind of research that can be used to prove programs "effective." (Hoffman, p. 620, as on p. 125)

Unfortunately there is even more. *Title II* from the Public Law print of Pl107-110, of the *No Child Left Behind Act of 2001*: Title II—Preparing, Training, and Recruiting High Quality Teachers and Principals (Sections 2101, 2102, and 2103), was designed to improve teacher quality. However, Altwerger et al.

(2004) tell us "this act has led to an unprecedented level of control by the federal government over the American public school system" (p. 119). Zancanella and Noll (2004) tell us that *NCLB* has new power in reshaping teacher preparation. They write that "because so much of the law focuses on literacy, those who prepare teachers to teach reading, writing, and language arts may well experience even more tumultuous changes in their programs than their colleagues in other disciplines" (p. 101). While student teachers are viewed as the agents to prepare students to take exams, their instructors have been pressured to negotiate between their values and government stipulations under *NCLB.* This predicament warrants further research and our field would benefit by examining how English educators grapple with their own values as they bump against standardized testing and how they are teaching student teachers to grapple with the complexities of standardized testing as it collides with their own values.

Analyzing *Title II* helps us see how teachers' identities are being co-constructed. Sec. 2101 PURPOSE reads:

> The purpose of this part is to provide grants to State educational agencies, local educational agencies, state agencies for higher education, and eligible partnerships in order to:
> (1) increase student academic achievement through strategies such as improving teacher and principal quality and increasing the number of highly qualified teachers in the classroom and highly qualified principals and assistant principals in schools; and
> (2) hold local educational agencies and schools accountable for improvements in student academic achievement.

The impact of this statement on preservice teacher identity is first seen from the perspective of the state. This policy has put pressure on states that want to receive federal funds for students to do well on high-stakes testing. Indirectly, states are pressured to co-construct preservice teachers to help students achieve competent marks on these mandated exams. Teacher educators are pressured to teach student teachers about best practices in reading and writing but at the same time must decide to either perpetuate or challenge the expectations of *NCLB* and come under possible reprimand and scrutiny from colleagues or others. Do we give our student teachers the tools to help their students do well on the exams or do we teach our student teachers how to be effective in teaching reading, writing, and other skills? *NCLB* holds us hostage to "dumbing" down our teaching and our teachers, and teaching to the status quo. If we want federal funds to help our students to ultimately succeed, we are in a pressure cooker being held down by *NCLB* state expectations. The pressure is needlessly unfair. Borman (1990) states, "whatever model students are encouraged to adopt not only influences their classroom instruction but also affects their orientations to career, colleagues, and supervisors" (p. 393). We have to ask ourselves are we going to "manufacture" preservice teachers or are we going to create preservice teachers who can think for themselves? Whether a university instructor agrees or disagrees with high-stakes testing, s/he is making a political statement by adopting either point of view.

Teacher programs are being hit to step up to meet the expectations and teach student teachers to be scientifically minded in the classrooms. *NCLB* recycles scientifically based teaching from the early 1900s through the early 1980s when teaching English was taught through a New Critics paradigm. McCracken (2004) agonizes, "those of us who prepare new teachers and support the development of experienced teachers face enormous ethical and tactical challenges working with teachers who are being required to act in ways that we, and they, know will be ineffective for many and harmful for some" (p. 106). Just as Zancanella and Noll articulated about the threat of *NCLB* to teacher education, so does McCracken describe that *NCLB* is a threat to the "credibility of the present work of teacher educators in the eyes of parents, students, publishers, and the business community" (p. 107). Further, she suggests that

> The effort to undermine the credibility of colleges of education is not only accomplished by painting colleges of education as bastions of ignorance. The Department of Education (2002) effectively erases educators, including those in colleges of education, in its Strategic Plan with a rhetorical sleight of hand in which the word "*customers*"(italics added for emphasis) is used consistently in places where one would expect to find the words, "teachers", "teacher educators," and "faculty". In the U.S. Department of Education Strategic Plan, for example, goals are established to "meet the needs of our customers." (p. 111)

We are not "educational customers" or "customers of education," nor are we supposed to be buying something—as the word customer implies. Unless the government is deliberately trying to "sell" us something, the word is an insult to the relentless work that teacher educators continue to stay committed to in the face of this new-found educational terrorism on our own soil. The conundrum of wanting student teachers to succeed and wanting the students they teach to succeed places teacher educators in a quandary of how to present material that will educate them in light of the terror that *NCLB* has unleashed on the education system in our country. How can we best meet the needs of each of these constituents, especially when *NCLB* has a finite life span and will be replaced with new "reform" when something "even better" replaces it? It seems that we are all puppets controlled by those who deem what is best at the time for our country. We owe it to ourselves and to our preservice teachers to consider ways that inform them to make critical choices about how they prepare their students for standardized testing. By keeping information from student teachers about *NCLB* and not informing them about key political agendas, instructors may be doing more harm than good. One of the struggles we face in educating our preservice teachers about the larger implications of *NCLB* is that it is difficult enough to be a preservice teacher who is marginally situated in two worlds, that of the inchoate educator who is making meaning of what a teacher is and does, and that of still being educated (Britzman, 1991) and to also take a stance on standardized testing positions him/her on a political continuum that s/he may not be fully ready to embody let alone understand. Here are some examples for how to open up conversations in our methods courses:

⇒*Teaching Points*

∞Methods Courses

•Provide history about different kinds of standardized testing.
•Review the significance, purpose, goals, and intended outcomes for standardized testing.
•Review the design of the test (multiple choice, limited response questions) and what it measures and discuss the different sections. We can also invite a critique of the test from a sociocultural and feminist perspective.
•Imagine what an ideal exam looks like and design questions.
•Practice attacking the stems of the questions.
•Examine who benefits from and what are the benefits of the exam.
•Design fair and equitable assessments for testing or liberatory assessment[11] that would align with a standardized question.
•Create an interview protocol for our classroom students and interview them about their concerns around testing.
•Encourage preservice teachers to think about how their teaching philosophy aligns with their beliefs on standardized testing.
•Help preservice teachers to understand that teaching is political and that their choices on pedagogy and curriculum are highly political acts.
•Review along with our students the U.S. Department of Education's vision and mission statements and review how they align/malign with your state's vision and mission; then consider how that affects test development.[12]
•Debate different points of view about standardized testing through a talk show panel, as a film review, or as a comedy routine (i.e., craft jokes).
•Study the *NCLB* government web site and critique the way the test is designed against what students are studying in their assessment courses, pedagogy, knowledge, and what studies reveal about new and emerging forms of literacies: "literacy now relates to a much broader set of texts including visual, multimodal, and digital texts" (Sanford, 2006, p. 304).
•Discuss multimodal designs with students and have them design a multimodal project that demonstrates the knowledge needed in a given standardized test question (see Albers, 2006 for ideas).

⇒*Teaching Points*

∞Secondary Classrooms

•Ask students about their concerns about taking standardized tests.

•Work on test-taking strategies by section (such as pacing and order of complexity).
•Deconstruct stems with students.
•Set aside one hour a week to work on test-taking strategies.
•Offer extra support outside of class if students need help.
•Practice taking tests by section in low-stress times.
•Have students create questions by writing stems, answers, and rationales for and then trade with peers.
•Ask them about what biases they perceive are present in tests and why.
•Affirm their concerns about taking tests.

Further Reading on NCLB and Related Topics

Apple, M. (2000). *Democratic education in a conservative age.* New York: Routledge.

Berliner, D. & Biddle, B. (1995). *The manufactured crisis: Myths, fraud, and the attack on America's public schools.* Reading: Addison-Wesley.

CELA. (2004, June 28). *Teacher Education and Professional Development.* Retrieved June 28, 2004 from the World Wide Web: http://cela.albany.edu/.

Coles, G. (2003). *Reading the naked truth: Literacy, legislation and lies.* Portsmouth: Heinemann.

Crawford, J. (1995). *Bilingual education: History, politics, theory and practice.* Los Angeles: Bilingual Education Services.

Dewey, J. (1916). *Democracy and education.* New York: The Macmillan Co.

Edmondson, J. (2000). *America reads: A critical policy analysis.* Newark: International Reading Association.

Garan. E. M. (2001). What does the report on the National Reading Panel really tell us about teaching phonics? *Language Arts, 79*(1), 61–70.

Gutierrez, K. (2001) So what's new in the English language arts: Challenging policies and practices, ¿y que?, *Language Arts Journal, 78*(6), 564–569.

Gutierrez, K., Baquedano-Lopez, P., & Tejeda, C. (1999). Rethinking diversity: Hybridity and hybrid language practices in the third space. *Mind, Culture, and Activity: An International Journal, 6*(4), 286–303.

Hagood, M. (2002). Critical literacy for whom? *Reading Research and Instruction, 41*, 247–266.

hooks, b. (1994). *Teaching to transgress.* New York: Routledge.

Katz, S., & Kohl, H. (2002, December 9). Banishing Bilingualism. *The Nation, 275*(20), 6–7.

Moje, E. B., & Sutherland, L. M. (2003). The future of middle school literacy instruction. *English Education, 35*(2), 149–164.

Moll, L., Amanti, C., Neff, D., & Gonzalez, N. (1992). Funds of knowledge for teaching: Using a qualitative approach to connect homes and classrooms. *Theory Into Practice, 31*, 132–141.

Morrow, R. A., & Torres, C. A. (1998). Education and the reproduction of class, gender and race: Responding to the postmodern challenge. In C. Torres & T. R. Mitchell (Eds.), *Sociology of education* (pp. 19–45). New York: State University Press.

National Reading Panel (2002). *Teaching children to read: An evidence-based assessment got the scientific research literature on reading and its implications for reading instruction.* Report of the subgroups. Washington, DC: National Institutes of Health.

Nieto, S. (2002). *Language, cultures, and teaching: Critical perspectives for a new century:* Mahwah: Lawrence Erlbaum Associates.

Yatvin, J. (2002). Babes in the woods: The wanderings of the national reading panel. *Phl Delta Kappan, 83*(5), 364–369.

Issue #2: Censorship

> Unless they have access to texts that challenge conventional knowledge, and unless they engage in deep reflection and serious dialogue (Freire, 1970) about their own knowledge and the curriculum they will teach (Apple, 1993), most teachers do not develop the practice of questioning mainstream knowledge. (Nieto, 2006, p. 58)

Nieto articulates a divisive issue in teacher education: instilling in student teachers the freedom to question and challenge mainstream knowledge. However, a problem facing teacher education is that a growing body of research indicates that teacher quality is "the most important school-related factor influencing student achievement (Rice, 2003, p. v). So while emphasis has been placed on preparing teachers with knowledge that can be imparted to students, other important factors such as pedagogical knowledge takes subservient status. Since teacher education programs must honor national accreditation standards, teacher education programs are forced to privilege teaching more content and knowledge than pedagogy.

It has been suggested that what student teachers need more than knowledge is pedagogical knowledge (Dudley-Marling, Abt-Perkins, Sato, & Self, 2006). In their study, Dudley-Marling et al. found that in the random sampled pool of 5,000 NCTE members (from elementary, middle, secondary, and the Conference on English Education) who were asked a series of questions about perceptions of what it means to become and to remain a highly qualified English teacher, while content knowledge was found important, pedagogical knowledge was the most important factor in becoming and continuing to be a highly qualified English teacher. We must ask ourselves and be truly prepared to answer to whom do we listen and who are the *real* experts; those in the trenches or those creating policy?

Once we have answered these questions, how do we as English educators then begin to teach teachers to question mainstream knowledge when our teacher education programs are shackled to national standards such as NCATE? Even more so, how do we best prepare our students for the controversial demands placed on them when they enter the spacetime of their student teaching placements? How do we teach them to honor venerable institutions and yet question mainstream society? There is a fine line no doubt. Yagelski (2005) reminds us that "we are not gatekeepers: we are gate openers, who help students imagine possibilities for themselves and for all of us" (p. 269), and his words can help guide us toward making a decision about teaching to our students' needs or in choosing to reinforce hegemonic discourse. If we opt to open gates, we must first look inside ourselves, at our own belief systems, where they come from, unpack antiquated beliefs that no longer serve us, and be willing to change and alter what we have outgrown so that it fits with newer spacetimes. We have a hand in creating systemic change or in perpetuating the status quo;

we cannot do this kind of work unless we do our own inner work first and allow our praxis[13] to truly activate our teachings.

First Amendment

> Congress shall make no law respecting an establishment of religion, or prohibiting the free exercise thereof; or abridging the freedom of speech, or of the press; or the right of the people peaceably to assemble, and to petition the Government for a redress of grievances.
>
> —Bill of Rights for the U.S. Constitution was ratified December 15, 1791

There has been much controversy over First Amendment speech rights in public schools and little wonder when we cannot even come to a truce on what it means in our American university system. While some see censorship as a form of academic harassment, others sustain it as necessary to the success of secondary and postsecondary schools. Recent examples include UCLA's infamous the "Dirty 30" professors who align teaching with leftist values and are anti-American. Topping the list is equity "pedagogist" Peter McLaren who has written extensively on critical pedagogy and critical theory. His beliefs about education on his web site read:

> This website is developed as a resource for students of critical pedagogy. The critical pedagogy which I support and practice advocates non-violent dissent, the development of a philosophy of praxis guided by a Marxist humanism, the study of revolutionary social movements and thought, and the struggle for socialist democracy. It is opposed to liberal democracy, which only serves to facilitate the reproduction of capital. It advocates a multiracial and anti-imperialist social movement dedicated to opposing racism, capitalism (both in private property and state property forms), sexism, heterosexism, hierarchies based on social class, as well as other forms of oppression. (McLaren, 2006)

The controversy surrounding the "Dirty 30" surfaces issues of autonomy and self-regulation into the limelight. With a proposed Academic Bill of Rights[14] on the horizon that challenges academic freedom's self-regulation and autonomy in the universities, it would seem that the First Amendment would be summoned to reconcile these divisive issues in schools in the not so distant future.

Academic freedom is an umbrella term that encompasses the constitutional and professional rights of teachers (Flygare, 1976). Freedom of teaching is one of the four elements that is embodied by academic freedom.[15] One of the plaguing questions of our time within education is can a teacher be dismissed for actions or discourse used in the classroom? One might ascertain that the First Amendment guarantees the teacher the right to say or behave according to her/his beliefs but this is not the case. The courts have never fully agreed that freedom of speech is absolute (Flygare, 1976). However, when a teacher is dismissed from a position the courts must assess each situation case by case "to determine whether the school board properly restrained the teacher's freedom of speech" (Flygare, 1976, p. 9). The courts examine several factors such as the age of the students exposed to the objectionable speech, the relevancy of the objection, whether policies or regulations about classroom expression exist, and whether any alternative for free speech exists in the school. The courts may also examine if the speech was symbolic, that is, if a teacher wore an armband, button, or badge.

As we unpack some of the issues facing secondary English teachers, it is also important to update where we stand now on censorship and think forward about how the First Amendment continues to affect teachers. Public school teachers need to understand that First Amendment rights of academic freedom accorded to university professors are much more limited in public elementary and secondary schools. It is unlikely that a public school teacher could say or post what McLaren posted on his web site without repercussions. It should be noted that while we are discussing preservice teachers' First Amendment rights, classroom students' rights are suspended when they enter public school domain. Tierney (2006) in his review of current texts on hate speech in American universities asked a poignant question: "Who decides whether speech is hateful or how academic freedom is defined?" (p. 33). Answers to these questions have yet to be fully reconciled because school districts vary on what can and cannot be said and on how the First Amendment is interpreted. In fact, demands vary from state to state, district to district, and school to school, which makes it all the more difficult to achieve consensus on how the First Amendment is upheld in particular cases. With only "fewer than 10% of postsecondary institutions that have adopted policies that challenge First Amendment principles" (Gould as in Tierney, 2006, p. 34), it is little wonder that English educators might feel hesitant to address loaded topics in their methods courses.

Preservice Teachers and the Law

In a review of the literature there were no basic laws outright protecting student teachers (Mack & Norwood, 1973). Rather, they *are* protected under the departments of education in which they are enrolled. As such, the laws and regulations of the state guide the individual departments of education in their own development and structure of regulations for student teachers. Student teachers have limited authority and their position in schools with regard to the law remains vague and implied. What we found pertaining to the law comes from research before 1975:

> 1. Legally, the student teacher has no authority in the classroom. He [sic] should not punish a child: he does not promote or fail pupils. He [sic] has, however, the same responsibilities of a teacher, within the areas of his functioning without the authority of professional status. (Haines, 1957, as in Mack & Norwood, 1973, p. 3)

> 2. The student teacher should avoid creating any situation which might eventually involve legal entanglements. The courts would no doubt construe the student teacher's legal rights as very limited in a case concerning pupil discipline. (Notle & Phillip as in Mack & Norwood, 1973, p. 3)

Under school codes, all fifty states have some statutory provisions or implied authority for establishing student teacher training institutions and within various school districts (Mack & Norwood, 1973). Some districts might have statutes that include the student teacher as part of "civil immunity" and as such they gain protection from the school district. In many states, student teachers are expected to have liability insurance to protect themselves as well as their departments of education should anything be mitigated. Some states require student teachers to hold a teaching certificate prior to their classroom teaching. In some cases, if a student is injured, the cooperating teacher is liable because s/he delegates authority to the student teacher.[16] With these statutes and vaguely worded laws in mind, it can therefore be implied that student teachers' First Amendment rights are assumed to be even more limited than a classroom teacher with the exception as in number two above that might involve the preservice teacher in "legal entanglements." It is also likely that if a preservice teacher violates the basic rights of teachers, then the different university education departments that supervise the preservice teacher will be held liable for noncompliance and the preservice teacher is subjected to disciplinary action as per university policy. Such actions and rulings will vary by school and department.

What then can a preservice teacher say without redress and about which issues should a preservice teacher be cautious? To begin, Rubin and Greenhouse (1983) in *The Basic ACLU Guide to a Teacher's Constitutional Rights* report on teachers' rights in the First Amendment through various law cases. From this guide we learn key rulings about public school teachers' rights.[17] We have summarized key rulings below.

1. A teacher can be dismissed or disciplined for public out-of-class statements that are critical of school officials if it undermines close employment relationships, interferes with classroom performance of duties, or interferes with the effective operation of the school system (See *Pickering v. Bd. of Education*, 391 U.S. 563 [1968]).

The kinds of out-of-class speech that are deemed to cause substantial disruption include: speech by public employee that exposes corruption in the workplace, making false statements, and demonstrating a lack of character and intellectual responsibility. It must be noted that statements cannot be the sole cause of dismissal, but if the teacher has an undesirable character trait, that is further argument for a teacher's dismissal (pp. 59–60). In other words, a teacher's out-of-class speech is not necessarily constitutionally protected.

2. A teacher can advise parents of policies or practices that the teacher perceives to be harmful to students if the district does not demonstrate that the interests of the school system are more significant than the teacher's free-speech. Along the same lines a teacher cannot use students as couriers in order to disseminate material that is critical of the public schools.

3. In the classroom a teacher can wear an armband, button, or other symbol identifying with a political or social cause unless "the interests of discipline or sound education are materially or substantially jeopardized, whether the dangers stems initially from the conduct of students or teachers" (p. 69)(see Second Circuit ruling based on the outcome of *Tinker v. Des Moines Ind. Comm. School Dist,* 393 U.S. 503 [1969]).

4. A teacher does not have to salute or participate in compulsory flag ceremonies but, if it is part of the prescribed curriculum to teach about the flag and patriotism and a teacher refuses to do so, the teacher may be dismissed (see *West Virginia State Bd. of Education v. Barnette*, 319 U.S. 624 [1943]).

5. A teacher has the right to read books and view films in his/her home. If, however, students are present at such events, teachers surrender their rights to privacy.

6. A teacher can be held liable for drug use in her/his home if it renders him/her unfit to teach.

7. A teacher can be terminated for her/his sexual preference (to be discussed in greater detail in chapter 7).

8. A teacher can be terminated for sexual practices if her/his "retention in the profession poses a significant danger of harm to either students, school employees, or others who might be affected by his/her actions as a teacher" (p. 154). This can include an extramarital affair at school with a colleague or student, molesting a student, posing in a magazine that is deemed pornographic, has inappropriately displayed him/herself in public, and for "conduct unbecoming a teacher" (p. 158).

9. A teacher's classroom is not a public forum and a teacher cannot say or post whatever s/he wants. This can include but is not limited to taking a stance on a political issue or convincing students to join a political party. Teachers cannot distribute flyers for a political campaign. The rationale is that students are vulnerable to indoctrination; therefore, a teacher must present political issues from a nonpartisan, nonbiased stance, and provide an opportunity for students to

decide their beliefs for themselves. A teacher must present all sides of a political issue so as not to be vulnerable to redress.[18]

A teacher should also find out if there is a state Hatch Act-type law that applies to teachers. This law limits teachers outside of school political activities. If there is no state law applying directly to teachers, they can assume that they may engage in political activities outside of school at will.

10. A teacher cannot refuse to teach curriculum even when it interferes with her/his personal beliefs.

11. Under the Establishment Clause teachers are expected to be neutral about religion while carrying out their teaching duties. If a student inquires about a teacher's religion, it is advisable not to discuss it. It is important that if a teacher should decide to reveal his/her faith, that the age of the pupil be taken into consideration and that no retribution or harm come to the student if the student takes issue with the teacher's faith. A teacher is entitled to wear unobtrusive jewelry such as a cross or the Star of David but cannot wear clothing with a proselytizing message.

12. A teacher should inform him/herself about what books have been banned by the school district. Teachers can also speak with other teachers at the school site, other experts in the district, or contact the American Library Association (www.ala.org), the NCTE Anti-Censorship Center (www.ncte.org/about/issues/censorship), and Banned Books Online (onlinebooks.library.upenn.edu/banned-books.html). Most commonly, books are banned for containing (1) vulgar or sexually explicit language; (2) "racist" language; (3) gay and lesbian themes; or (4) discussions of witchcraft and the occult. If a teacher teaches a banned book, s/he subjects him/herself to redress from the school site and the school board.

13. Although not written in the *ACLU* guide, if a teacher wants to teach by using film there are several precautions a teacher should take to ensure that no harm come to the teacher or the students (this topic is addressed in more detail in chapter 5). A teacher should familiarize her/himself with district and school policies for showing films. The teacher should also be able to provide a firm rationale, intended outcomes, and assessments for viewing. If the material contains loaded content, such as nudity, profanity, sexual, or substance abuse, it is advised that the teacher receive written permission from the appropriate person at the school site, such as an administrator, and send home a note to the parent or guardian detailing the rationale, outcomes, and assessments. There should also be a clause opting the student out of the viewing assuring that there will be no grade or emotional penalty or redress.

Other Loaded Issues

Preservice teachers should not teach about issues that might be potentially loaded without consulting with their cooperating teacher or their clinical supervisor as s/he may not be professionally prepared to regulate what emerges. Some of these issues may include but not be limited to:

•The war in/on Iraq;
•Gay/lesbian/bisexual/transgender/two-spirited[19]/questioning (GLBTTSQ);
•Sex;
•Defiance of the government;
•Words that might be perceived as offensive;
•Race;
•Hate crimes;
•The occult; and
•Religion

Even then, it is imperative that such units are carefully created, align with district, state, and national standards, have clearly stated outcomes and objectives, and well-developed assessment strategies. It is also important that there is a back-up plan for loaded issues so a preservice teacher can handle what might potentially emerge. Some strategies then for preplanning potentially loaded lessons include:

•Discussions with cooperating teacher, clinical supervisor, and possibly an administrator;
•Sending a letter home to a parent or guardian explaining the lesson with a clear rationale, which is signed by the cooperating teacher, administrator, and the preservice teacher. The preservice teacher might offer to invite parents in to observe the lesson or offer to respond to inquiries or concerns. There should also be a clause opting the student out of the lesson assuring that there will be no grade or emotional penalty or redress;
•Research is thorough and offers multiple viewpoints; and
•Fact-checking with others who have expertise on the issue.

The Constitution offers teachers limited protection. In sum, the First Amendment offers teachers academic freedom so long as it is objective, curriculum related, factual, and impartial (Spencer & Hoffman, 2001). Hartmeister (as in Spencer & Hoffman, 2001) reminds us that "student teachers should be given guidelines for protecting their own privacy, and they should be informed about behaviors that may make them vulnerable to privacy violations" (p. 3).

Conclusion

The advancement of the government is dependent on dumbing down curriculum, attempting to level the playing field through standardized testing and constructing teachers to be cogs who reinforce and manufacture their arsenal: human lives. Keeping teachers in the dark about whatever political agenda is active during the spacetime of their lives advances and serves the purposes of the government. Whoever is running teacher education programs is the pendulum upon which the lever of power rests.

In sum, *NCLB* reinforces the agenda of a right-wing government by manufacturing students who will later serve its purposes. As humans with inalienable rights, preservice teachers have the right to be informed and be political agents even though, to some extent, they must suppress these tendencies when teaching. To remember this more clearly, keep in mind the *NCLB* conceptual framework. *NCLB* reinforces homogenizing education and controls, to some extent, the what and the how of curriculum that advances its agenda. By making states achieve certain standardized test scores in order to receive federal funding, teachers must take time away from key curriculum and prepare students for exams. The robbing of curriculum time or teaching to the test steals time from possible critical thinking and essentially "dumbs down" curricular choices. In "dumbing down" curriculum, students are likely to graduate as "deskilled laborers" with poorer critical thinking skills. When it comes time for individuals to become arsenal or "cultural capital" (Bourdieu, 1986) for the government, their lack of key knowledge or skills that might help them question authority makes them vulnerable to serving the government's purposes.

An issue of concern about teacher identity co-construction posed by Apple and Oliver (1998) reminds us that the "'Christian Right' has become an increasingly powerful movement in the United States, one that has had major effects on educational policy deliberations, curriculum and teaching" (as in Torres & Mitchell, 1998, p. 92). Apple (2000) in *Official Knowledge* tells us that the agenda of the New Right is to

> Confront the "moral, existential, [and economic] chaos of the preceding decades" with a network of exceedingly well-organized and financially secure organizations incorporating "an aggressive political style, on outspoken religious and cultural traditionalism and a clear populist commitment." (p. 24)

Schools are essentially controlled by a "hidden curriculum" that controls a means to an end (Apple & Oliver, 1998, as in Torres & Mitchell, 1998, p. 122). Clift and Guthrie (1988) say that messages of a hidden curriculum for teacher education are transmitted from within,

> And between departments or colleges of schools of education, other university or college programs, and elementary and secondary (field-site). These sources of hidden curricular messages include the institutional and broader social contexts in which teacher education operates and the structure and processes of the teacher education program, including pedagogical techniques and texts and materials within the program. (as in Ginsburg & Clift, 1990, p. 451)

In other words, the "hidden curriculum" reinforces and sustains a capitalist economy and culture and prepares students to serve the needs of society of which they are becoming a part. In this light, students are cultural capital and the individual becomes part of the economic capital as s/he is schooled and therefore acquires a status that can be converted to support the economy. In that sense, school then is a reproductive entity that produces individuals who will serve its economy. Schools are situated within values steeped in the reinforcement of hegemony, and consequently, those who do not fit into the dominant culture are often disenfranchised and marginalized from acquiring the status of cultural capital and are therefore often silenced and alienated in and from society at large.

To teach only the ideals of the right preserves traditional values and tends to support the values and ethics of the government. If we teach our students to be prowar, exclusively proheterosexuality, or even antichoice, then we feed into and reinforce a conservative agenda. Teachers are impacted by such an agenda to then produce students who align with these values. Thus teacher educators face the concern of whether they should co-construct thoughtful and sensitive teachers who are open to everyone's needs or whether to "manufacture" teachers that exclusively reflect the agenda of the right. Liberal teaching ideals and values are seen as the nemesis to the government at this point in time because they run counter to the spacetime values of the country. Apple (2000) poses two related concerns associated with the right-wing agenda. The first concern is the "separation of conception from execution" and the second is known as "deskilling" (p. 116). The prior is when the person doing the job loses sight over the process and over her/his labor because someone outside of the situation has greater control over what is happening. The latter is when "employees lose control over their own labor, the skills that they have developed over the years atrophy" (p. 116). In the second case, it is easier for management to have control over one's job because the individual can no longer control his/her own skills. Teacher educators must be watchful for tendencies to perpetuate values already steeped in hegemony and move future educators toward a counter-hegemonic stance that models language of inclusion and not reinforce a model of exclusion that the right has already modeled and established.

Preservice teachers' identities are just forming and teacher educators have choices about the direction they want education to go through the way they shape and co-construct preservice student identities, especially through the texts and pedagogical practices and theories they use in their teaching. We can "manufacture" teachers or we can activate the entire body and mind of the teacher, in order to help transform education and, ultimately, society.

Concluding with Beth

Beth, under the First Amendment, did have permission to discuss the issue of her abused students with the proper authorities at school. It was her moral and legal responsibility to pass on the information she received from her students to those in charge of reporting at school to save her any legal entanglements. In retrospect, the situation was handled well but much more could have been done prior to her students' reporting. Although Beth had been taught about sexual and physical abuse in methods class, she lacked the inner confidence about how to best support the students. This begets a larger issue around fostering teacher identity in English education courses and helping preservice teachers to develop a sense of self that speaks to the mind and the body of the teacher but which recognizes that teacher identity is impacted by the spacetime of particular contexts. It is likely that Beth experienced lack of control and incompleteness preservice teachers tend to feel when they are not really in charge yet, when they are not yet being the teacher; and perhaps that is okay because it is part of their development in becoming the teacher. It is more important, we think, that they know they may experience these feelings of becoming and that it is right to look to a higher authority to confirm their legal responsibilities and to avoid legal implications. Actually, what Beth did was right—she called me and asked what she should do. It is not what Beth had been taught; it is what she does or how she acts in the secondary spacetime with what she learns during the university spacetime the semester before.

In retrospect, there was more I could have done. I could have told her that she could follow up with the students, keep her classroom available to them, and contacted our department of education for further information pertaining to her rights. No one, however, needs to be faulted in this scenario because the issue is part of a larger systemic problem of censorship and violence in schools and the difficulty in addressing them head-on in our university courses. We suggest that it is not a coincidence that neither Beth, Linda, nor I felt that we could have done more and that we were not fully informed about how to proceed or even what our legal rights were as English educators. The gaps in our actions are gaps in the system that speak to the larger violence that is perpetuated on all of us systematically and by not being informed about our rights as citizens, or being tentative to address them in methods courses, we are furthering the agendas of the government in charge during this spacetime. Our inactions, our ignorance, and our confusion about how to act on loaded topics makes our government victorious in their fight for manufacturing schooled identities. We, Beth included, now understand how to respond to some of the more loaded issues facing us, and by continuing to listen to our preservice teachers, we can subvert the attempt at the body/mind split and arm all of our students with tools that can help them navigate the matrix.

Notes

1 Private schools are self-governed and may set their own standards. Addressing private schools is beyond the scope of this research.

2 Social action is an aspect of critical literacy that links curriculum to social change and instills in students a sense of responsibility to act on and transform some aspect of the community around them.

3 For further explanations of these terms see Miller, 2005b, "Cycle of Oppression and Prejudice" in pp. 88–89.

4 The Greek god of love and sexual desire.

5 See Johnson's (2004) article for scenarios to be used with student teachers, pp. 27–29.

6 When searching high profile cases of male teachers who cross sexual boundaries with students on the Internet through Google, there were several pages of female cases that came up even though it was worded/oriented toward male teachers.

7 Sexual and physical abuse symptoms are similar and the presence of any one symptom does not indicate abuse but should alert the teacher to the possibility of abuse. It is important to observe symptoms over a period of time.

8 In the 1999 U.S. Supreme Court decision of *Davis vs. Monroe County Board of Education*, the Court upheld that a school board may be liable for damages for student-to-student harassment if the district receives federal funds and acts with indifference to the known acts of the perpetration. Schools can be sued for having knowledge of bullying and doing nothing about it.

9 For specific behaviors that constitute bullying, see Ferrell-Smith, 2003, p. 4.

10 More female than male adolescents tend to cut.

11 Liberatory assessment is a term for equitable assessment that aligns with liberatory teaching.

12 The *vision* statements, the overall intention, and *mission* statements, the overall goals of the vision statement, serve as tools to navigate teachers toward the expectations of the state and the country. Taken from the U.S. Department of Education's web site (1980), its mission statement for teacher preparedness states that in the United States: "The mission of the Department of Education is to ensure equal access to education and to promote educational excellence throughout the nation." On May 4, 1980, Congress established the U.S. Department of Education in the Department of Education Organization Act (Public Law 96-88 of October 1979). Under this act, the mission statement was established.

13 Praxis is the action that comes through our personal reflection of our teaching and can change and shift based on space and place (Freire, 1970).

14 The Academic Bill of Rights is a document that calls for universities to maintain political pluralism and diversity. The Bill requires that "no political, ideological, or religious orthodoxy should be imposed on professors and researchers through the hiring or termination process." It also seeks to enforce that "faculty members will not use their courses or their position for the purpose of political, ideological, religious, or antireligious indoctrination." This grows out of the Academic Bill of Rights originally drafted by David Horowitz and which has now been proposed as House Concurrent Resolution.318, 108th Congress, 2003.

15 Academic freedom also includes: freedom of research, freedom of outside utterance and association, and academic due process (Flygare, 1976).

16 Although beyond the scope of this book, it is important to keep in mind that state legislatures have delegated day-to-day responsibility for public elementary and secondary education to local school boards and these boards possess authority only of that delegated by the legislature (Flygare, 1976). As long as local school boards do not violate individual or group rights, courts generally uphold the policies of local school boards.

17 For more information on First Amendment Rights go to: http://www.firstamendmentschools.org/about/aboutindex.aspx

18 A teacher is accountable to the code of conduct in the school and the individual districts and has a responsibility to inform her/himself of what is deemed appropriate.

19 Two-spirited is a Native American term that honors a homosexual native as being blessed with two spirits: male and female.

References

Albers, P. (2006) Imagining the possibilities in multimodal curriculum design. *English Education, 38(2)*, 75–101.

Altwerger, B., Arya, P., Jin, L., Jordan, N. L., Laster, B., Martens, P., Wilson, G. P., & Wiltz, N. (2004). When research and mandates collide: The challenges and dilemmas of teacher education in the era of NCLB. *English Education, 36*(2), 119–133.

American Association of University Women. (1993). *Hostile Hallways: The AAUW Survey on Sexual Harassment in America's Schools.* Washington, DC: Harris/Scholastic Research.

Apple, M. (1993). *Official knowledge.* New York: Routledge.

Apple, M. (2000). *Official knowledge.* New York: Routledge.

Apple, M., & Oliver, A. (1998). Becoming right: Education and the formation of conservative movements. In C. Torres & T.R. Mitchell (Eds.), *Sociology of education* (pp. 91–119). New York: State University of New York Press.

Borman, K. M. (1990). Foundations of education in teacher education. In W. R. Houston (Ed.), *Handbook of research on teacher education* (pp. 393–402). New York: Macmillan.

Bourdieu, P. (1986). The forms of capital. In J. Richardson (Ed.), *Handbook of theory and research for the sociology of education* (pp. 241–258). New York: Greenwood Press.

Britzman, D. (1991). *Practice makes practice.* Albany: State University of New York.

Bully Police USA. Retrieved May 14, 2006, from http://www.bullypolice.org/national_law.html.

Clift, R. T., & Guthrie, J.W. (1988). *Ed school: A brief for professional education.* Chicago: University of Chicago Press.

Corrigan, D. C., & Haberman, M. (1990). The context of teacher education. In W. R. Houston (Ed.), *Handbook of research on teacher education* (pp. 195–211). New York: Macmillan.

Darling-Hammond, L. (2005). Educating the new educator: Teacher education and the future of democracy. *The New Educator 1*(1), 1-18.

Dudley-Marling, C., Abt-Perkins, D., Sato, K., & Self, R. (2006). Teacher duality: The perspectives of NCTE members. *English Education, 38*(3), 167–193.

felman, j.l. (2002). *Never a dull moment.* New York: Routledge.

Ferrell-Smith, F. (2003). *School violence: Tackling the schoolyard bully. Combining policy making with prevention.* Denver, National Conference of State Legislatures. Children and Families Program.

Fineran, S. (2002). Sexual Harassment between Same Sex-Peers: Intersection of Mental Health, Homophobia and Sexual Violence in Schools. *Social Work, 47*(1), 65–74.

Flygare, T. (1976). *The legal rights of teachers.* Bloomington: Phi Delta Kappa Foundation.

Franzak, J., & Noll, B. (2006). Monstrous acts: Problematizing violence in young adult literature. *Journal of Adolescent & Adult Literacy, 49*(8), 662–672.

Freire, P. (1970). *Pedagogy of the oppressed.* New York: Continuum Publishing.

Ginsburg, M. B., & Clift, R. T. (1990). The hidden curriculum of preservice teacher education. In W. R. Houston (Ed.), *Handbook of research on teacher education* (pp. 450–462). New York: Macmillan.

Glenn. C. (2002). Educational freedom and the rights of teachers. *Educational Freedom, 76*(1), 30–33.

Gorian, B. (2002). *School law. Trends and issues.* Eric Clearinghouse of Educational Management. Washington, DC: Office of Educational Research and Improvement.

Haines, A. C. (1957). Role dilemmas in student teaching. *Journal of Teacher Education, 8*(4), 365-368.

Harris, S., & Isernhagen, J. (2003). Keeping bullies at bay. *American School Board Journal,* November, 43–45.

Hernandez, J. (1992, March). *Eating disorders and sexual abuse among adolescents.* Paper presented at the Annual Meeting of the Society of Behavioral Medicine Scientific Sessions. New York.

Herr, K. (1999). Institutional violence in the everyday practices of school: The narrative of a young lesbian. *Journal for a Just and Caring Education, 5*, 242–255.

Hoffman, J. (2000). The de-democratization of schools and literacy in America. *The Reading Teacher, 53*(8), 616-623.

Johnson, T. S. (2004). It's pointless to deny that dynamic is there. *English Education, 37*(1), 5–29.

King, J., Miller, R., Scheurich, J., & Valencia R. (2006, April). *Unpacking the Hurricane: Educating the Nation after Katrina: Part A: Unpacking the Hurricane in Our Own University Classrooms: Analyzing Race and Class after Katrina.* Paper presented at the annual meeting of the American Educational Research Association, San Francisco: CA.

Mack, M., & Norwood, E. (1973). The student teacher and the law. Southern Illinois University, Speech Department, U.S. Department of Health, Education, & Welfare.

Markow, D., & Fein, J. (2005). *From teasing torment: School climate in America—a survey of students and teachers.* Gay, lesbian, and straight educational network. New York: Harris Interactive.

McCracken, N. M. (2004). Surviving shock and awe: NCLB vs. colleges of education. *English Education, 36*(2), 104–118.

McLaren, P. Peter McLaren's homepage. Retrieved May 11, 2006, from www.gseis.ucla.edu/faculty/pages/mclaren/.

Miller, S. (2005a). *Geographically "meaned" preservice secondary language arts student teacher identities.* Ann Arbor, Umi Dissertation Publishing, www.lib.umi.com/dissertations/fullcit/3177097.

Miller, S. (2005b). Shattering images of violence in young adult literature: Strategies for the classroom. *English Journal, 94*(5), 87–93.

Morrow, J. (2004). Safety and excellence: Safety in the schools. *Educational Horizons, 83*(1): 19–32.

Nieto, S. (2006). Schools for a new majority: The role of teacher education in hard times. *The New Educator, 1*(1), 27–43.

Notle, M. C., & Philip, L .J. (1963.) *School law for teachers.* Danville: Interstate Printers and Publishers.

Pittsburgh Public Schools. *Sexual harassment policy.* Retrieved May 13, 2006, from http://www.pps.k12.pa.us/Sexual_Harassment.asp#2.

Rice, J. K. (2003). *Teacher quality: Understanding the effectiveness of teacher attributes.* Washington, DC: Economic Policy Institute.

Ripple Effects. Retrieved May 16, 2006, from http://www.rippleeffects.com/aboutus/mediakit/statistics.html.

Roth, R. A., & Pipho, C. (1990). Teacher education standards. In W. R. Houston, M. Haberman, & J. Sikula (Eds.), *Handbook of research on teacher education* (pp. 119–135). New York: Macmillan.

Rubin, D., & Greenhouse, S. (1983). *The rights of teachers: The basic ACLU guide to a teacher's constitutional rights.* New York: Bantam Books.

Sanford, K. (2006). Gendered literacy experiences: The effects of expectation and opportunity for boys' and girls' learning. *Journal of Adolescent and Adult Literacy, 49*(4), 302–315.

Shulman, L.S. (1983). Autonomy and obligation. In L. S. Shulman & G. Sykes (Eds.), *Handbook of teaching and policy.* New York: Longman.

Smith, K., & Stock, P. L. (2003). Trends and issues in research in the teaching of the English language arts. In J. Flood, D. Lapp, J. R. Squire, & J. M. Jensen (Eds.), *Handbook of research on teaching the English language arts* (pp. 114–130). Mahwah: Lawrence Erlbaum Associates.

Spencer, R. C., & Hoffman, D. H. (2001). Protecting teachers' privacy rights. *The Educational Forum, 65* (3), 214–220.

Tierney, W. (2006). Hate speech and academic freedom in the academy. *Educational Researcher, 35*(3), 33–37.

Torres & T. R. Mitchell (Eds.) (1998). *Sociology of education* (pp. 143–153). Albany: State University Press.

U.S. Department of Education: Office for Civil Rights. (1999). Protecting students from harassment and hate crime. National School Boards Association. Washington, DC, National Association of Attorneys General.

U.S. Department of Education: Office of Elementary and Secondary Education. (2002). *No child left behind: A desktop reference.* Retrieved June 21, 2004, from the World Wide Web: www.ed.gov/offices/OESE/reference.pdf.

Wakefield, C. (2002). *Preventing and reporting child abuse and neglect: Guidance for school personnel.* Colorado State Dept. of Education. Denver: Prevention Initiatives Unit.

Woodside-Jiron, H. (2004). Language, power, and participation: Using critical discourse analysis to make sense of policy. In R. Rogers (Ed.), *An introduction to critical discourse analysis in education* (pp. 173–205). Mahwah: Lawrence Erlbaum Associates.

Yagelski, R. (2005). Stasis and change: English education and the crisis of sustainability. *English Education, 34*(4), 262–271.

Zancanella, D., & Noll, E. (2004). Teacher education in language arts and literacy in the era of "No child left behind". *English Education, 36*(2), 101–103.

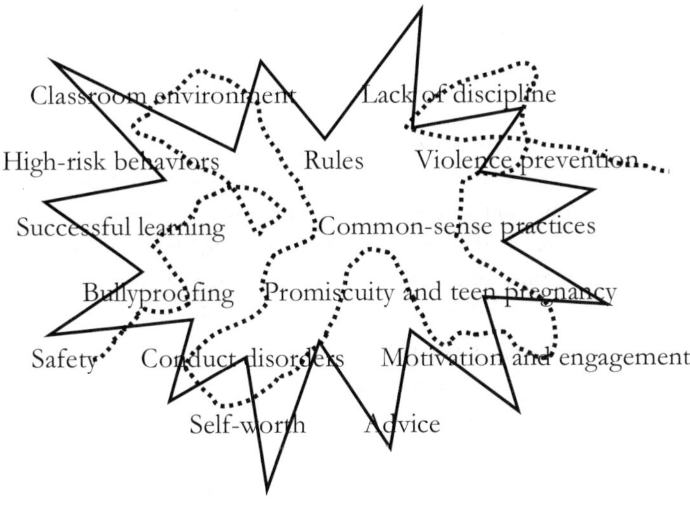

4

Do We Need Rules in the Loaded Matrix?

Introduction

This chapter presents critical issues that impact classroom management including violence with an emphasis on bullying (cyber and in-space), drugs, and sexual promiscuity. We discuss transactional, proactive pedagogies that minimize behavioral inappropriateness and tensions among preservice teachers and all the constituents in the schools, not just their own students.

Loaded Matrix Chapter Context

Going into her student teaching at Doverville Middle School, Acazia felt fortunate that she would be working with a seasoned teacher who had established a great reputation with students over the years. Taking a team-teaching approach with him for the first days of the semester, Acazia had very few discipline problems among her energetic and creative seventh-grade classes. But after the first two weeks, when she began leading the classes by herself, Acazia encountered two students who posed very different classroom management dilemmas for her that she was not fully prepared for from her previous university clinical experiences and course work—one male student who simply would not do anything, no matter how hard Acazia tried to reach him, and a female student who seemed to want to learn but was quite verbal, proclaiming to the rest of the class that she was a failure at everything she did.

Focus questions for chapter 4:

1. **Why do preservice teachers consider classroom management one of their most worrisome and problematic challenges in today's schools?**
2. **How do new teachers manage classes that are eighty–ninety minutes long with thirty or more students, all with differing abilities, some of whom may exhibit hyperactivity, inattentiveness, conduct disorders, and impulsivity on a regular basis?**
3. **What specific strategies can teacher educators and cooperating teachers provide so that preservice teachers can better engage students and minimize classroom disruptions, creating a win-win situation for themselves and their students during student teaching and beyond?**

> The top three problems facing our public schools today include drug abuse, violence such as gangs and fighting, and lack of discipline … Amongst teachers with three or fewer years of teaching in the United States in 2000, approximately half of these teachers indicated that they were not at all well prepared to manage their classrooms … Ninety-five percent of teachers in another study said that they learned their classroom management skills on the job rather than from their university education. (Kumarakulasingham & Harrington in Harrington & Holub, 2006, p. 25)[1]

Issue#1: Classroom Management Is a Real Concern

When our preservice teachers come to the methods class the semester before student teaching, one of the questions I ask is "What do you want to know more about before you begin student teaching?" The most frequent response is always classroom management. Our students feel the most underprepared in that area, and I think they believe that this final methods course before student teaching will magically reveal all of the deep, dark secrets for how to make their classes perfect somehow. While there really is no substitute for learning about classroom management or any aspect of pedagogy besides the actual experience of being in school and interacting with all of the components that impact that particular space and time, the university preparation program can and should do more to make the transition to the school site more tangible.

Taking in the Classroom Environment

In every methods class I teach, several semesters before student teaching, I incorporate a brief partnership with a competent experienced teacher at a local school so that students are able to sense the classroom environment, engage with secondary students in a specific way, and reflect on those interactions, even if those early experiences are only a small part of what we do in the course and are not yet a full mirror of the student teaching experience. For example, second-year student teacher candidates in my methods for reading and literature class taught Neal Shusterman's *The Dark Side of Nowhere* (1997) to rural seventh graders. When they go to a school site to teach a smaller unit of study, they can absorb the climate created by a competent and creative lead teacher, see first-hand how she designed her classroom from the seating arrangement to the bulletin boards, and learn more about students—in this case, junior-high students' responses to adolescent literature. It is no surprise that invariably on my student evaluations, preservice teachers will remark that the school experiences are the highlights of the methods classes and that they learned the most from them. Just seeing and working in a secondary school classroom space even for a short time creates the initial awareness of the multiple aspects of classroom management in new teachers.

Creating a Classroom Environment

Can we create an ideal classroom environment, and if so, how? Some of our preservice teachers' greatest fears are that they will lose control of their classrooms and that they will not be able to reverse the chaos. Most of them come with horror stories of the screaming teacher who cannot quiet the noise level, or the teacher who strong-arms a student up against the lockers in the hall, or the teacher whose students roam the halls, or the teacher who does not know how to counter a smart-mouthed answer, or worse, the teacher counters with another smart-mouthed reply. Preservice teachers ask tough questions like What if a fight breaks out? What if there is a bomb threat? What if a student threatens to kill me? What if my students do not do their homework? What if my students refuse to participate? New teachers often worry more about classroom management than they do about their content area knowledge, not realizing that the two are undoubtedly interwoven. And it appears that new teachers are not the only ones concerned about this issue. In fact, "One of the topics most requested for teacher in-service training is classroom management" (Harrington & Holub, 2006, p. 121).

Despite preservice teachers' qualms about student misbehavior and how they will handle it, the great majority of secondary students (at least 80 percent according to Burden, 2006) want to come to school and do respect their teachers. Other researchers agree with Burden that the overwhelming majority of students "believe in the importance of school" (Smith & Wilhelm, 2006) and want to achieve.

> Educators are induced to believe that classroom-management problems are inevitable, are intractable...What they miss is the fact that 94 percent of school-age students are not conduct-disordered at all—they are "normal"... This does not minimize the

> adverse effects that these aggressive students have on school climate. The range of behaviors that these students display includes lying, cheating, stealing, bullying, sexually acting out, bringing weapons to school, running away, being truant, setting fires, displaying offensive behaviors (such as swearing), refusing to comply, and arguing and complaining about school. The fact of the matter is, however, that most students are behaving just fine and are achieving at a very high level of performance in school. (Harrington & Holub, 2006, pp. xxi–xxii)

So do new teachers have to have rules, or will students just automatically do what teachers require? We think all teachers have the primary responsibility to create a classroom environment where students can learn and want to come to school. We know that many adolescents still drop out, and parents change schools or choose home schooling because the institution of school does not provide a safe, equitable, or challenging climate for students to study and grow. Discussion points worth raising in teacher education classes might include whether school should be compulsory for students over sixteen who want to drop out and who have consistent discipline problems; students who drop out and return as adults; alternative choices including private schools; and comparisons with other countries like Japan that have very few disciplinary issues because school is voluntary and more closely related to employment opportunities (see Volokh, A. with Snell, L. [1998], *School Violence Prevention: Strategies to Keep Schools Safe*).

In this chapter of the loaded matrix, however, we focus on some of the reasons for the range of behaviors students display currently and how we help preservice teachers recognize that the classroom management choices they make come from what Alfie Kohn refers to as "different points of departure" and the questions they ask that drive their practices (in Harrington & Holub, 2006, pp. 96–97). Preservice teachers will choose very different management strategies, rules, and interventions depending upon whether or not their basic objectives are compliance-based and therefore more authoritarian, or beliefs in what students need, encouraging self-actualization. We agree with Kohn that "the question of how a classroom is 'managed' is inextricably linked to the theory of learning that informs curriculum content and instruction.... No matter how much progress is made in that field [classroom management], it can never accomplish meaningful goals if it is divorced from pedagogical matters" (in Harrington & Holub, 2006, p. 99). Good teaching is the integration of thoughtful classroom management with proficient or advanced subject matter knowledge, dispositions, and skills.

From our own classroom practices in the schools, from teaching methods courses and observations during student teacher supervision, and from team-teaching we have done in workshops, we first advocate some general principles for creating an optimum classroom learning environment, and later, backed by student examples, we share more discipline-specific ways to obtain and retain the attention of our secondary students, minimizing and often eliminating classroom disruptions and disengagement, while reaching and even surpassing appropriate teacher performance standards. We describe in detail practical methods for autonomous classroom management we have witnessed firsthand that work.

Issue #2: Establishing Successful Learning Environments

We know that the choice of classroom-management approaches that teachers use vary from the most assertive (e.g., Skinner, Canter and Canter, and Jones in Burden, 2006, p. 31) to more subtle instructional integration (e.g., Glasser, Kagan, and Coloroso in Burden, 2006, p. 31) depending upon how acceptable those approaches are with what they know about their students, what their philosophy of education is (Burden, 2006; Alsup & Bush, 2003; Harrington & Holub, 2006), and whether their philosophy is manifest in their words and actions (Dickson et al., 2006, p. 315). Our key purpose in this chapter targets beginning teachers who strive to establish successful and effective learning environments. But what exactly is such an environment and would we know it if we saw it?

The requirements for teacher certification may provide a guide for an acceptable classroom environment. For example, our teacher candidates are expected to meet or exceed the seven Pennsylvania Department of Education Category II: Classroom Environment standards listed below (See figure 4.1) in order to be certified in our state. Teacher educators should question whether these seven points reflect sound teaching practices and principles, and they should discuss these points in teacher training. I find it helpful to talk about these points with student teachers and their cooperating teachers, asking them whether they feel these are reasonable and appropriate measures of a productive learning environment. We question what might be left out and whether we need to change or add anything. We also consider what would be visible evidence of meeting each of these points, that is, how can we really see a well-managed classroom environment take shape? The Pennsylvania standards serve to remind teacher educators who train preservice teachers to cultivate "a purposeful and equitable environment for learning, in which students feel safe, valued, and respected" (PDE-430, 2), but examples of exactly how a new teacher might do this are not provided in the state forms. If we examine the seven bulleted points in Category II more closely, we recognize a model of both Assertive Discipline (Canter & Canter, 2002) centered around clear requirements, continuous feedback, and a hierarchy of sanctions for rule breaking (as in bullets 4, 5, and 6), and one of more humanistic notions including student responsibility, dignity, and cooperation (bullets 1, 2, 3, and 7) such as those advocated by Kohn (in Harrington & Holub, 2006, pp. 96–101). Can both of these management styles coexist in a new teacher's classroom and in today's schools, and more importantly, should they? Can mutual respect among students and teachers be achieved when teachers take the lead by setting up rules for students to obey, or is assertive discipline incompatible with unconditional support and establishing proactive, student-centered learning communities? If we believe that the best new teachers meet or exceed these seven points, then we are agreeing to the coexistence of differing management theories and practices that are necessary and valuable in order to prepare today's teachers for the majority of well-meaning and respectful students and for those who need interventions in order to stay and succeed in school.

Category II: Classroom Environment— **Student teacher/candidate establishes and maintains a purposeful and equitable environment for learning, in which students feel safe, valued, and respected, by instituting routines and setting clear expectations for student behavior.** **Alignment: 354.33. (1)(i)(E), (B)**
Student Teacher/Candidate's performance appropriately demonstrates: • Expectations for student achievement with value placed on the quality of student work • Attention to equitable learning opportunities for students • Appropriate interactions between teacher and students and among students • Effective classroom routines and procedures resulting in little or no loss of instructional time • Clear standards of conduct and effective management of student behavior • Appropriate attention given to safety in the classroom to the extent that it is under the control of the student teacher • Ability to establish and maintain rapport with students

Figure 4.1 Pennsylvania Department of Education Category II: Classroom Environment.

High-Risk Behaviors in Adolescents

The following are some of the major problems affecting the classroom environment our student teachers confront in the public schools; these issues must be addressed if new teachers want to be best prepared for classroom spacetime challenges and what to do about them. We provide some insights on the status of each issue and what teacher candidates can gain from reading current publications, checking credible web sources, and learning from other experienced practitioners.

Drug Abuse

At least once a month 50 percent of high school students use alcohol, 40 percent admit having used an illicit drug including cocaine, marijuana, inhalants, and PCP at least once, 24 percent say they use drugs at least once a month, and 20 percent grow up in alcoholic families (Burden, 2006, pp. 178-179). The National Institute on Drug Abuse (http://www.nida.nih.gov/NIDAHome.html) provides the latest information for teachers, parents, and teens about substance abuse prevention and where to find help. In cooperation with Scholastic Publications, the NIDA provides materials such as *A Day in the Life of a Teen: Decisions at Every Turn* (http://teacher.scholastic.com/scholasticnews/indepth/headsup/) and other features that provide statistics on drug abuse, inform students about symptoms of drug overdose, and show students how to act and speak if they are pressured to take drugs. *A Day in the Life* reports findings from a 2005 Monitoring the Future survey that 84 percent of eighth graders, 70 percent of tenth graders, and 62 percent of twelfth graders did not try any illicit drug in the past twelve months. It may not be surprising that fewer middle school students try illicit drugs, but the percentages increase from 16 percent to 38 percent as students get closer to graduation. These findings also include race and ethnicity differences, but they do not provide information about the underlying sociocultural reasons for these statistics; for example, African-American students have lower rates of smoking cigarettes than white or Hispanic students; negative trends such as the continued concern in the rise of prescription drug abuse--25 percent increase since 2001 in annual abuse of sedatives and barbiturates among twelfth graders; and gender differences including "prevalence of use of anabolic steroids and smokeless tobacco, which are both more likely to be used by males than females" and "Use of 'any illicit drug other than marijuana' is slightly higher among females than males in the 8th and 10th grades, but is higher among males in the 12th grade" (http://www.nida.nih.gov/infofacts/HSYouthtrends.html).

Other Links about Seeking Help for Drug Abuse

inhalants.drugabuse.gov
smoking.drugabuse.gov
hiv.drugabuse.gov
clubdrugs.org
steroidabuse.gov
Marijuana-info.org

Other Recommended Reading on the NIDA Website

Preventing Drug Use among Children and Adolescents: *A Research-Based Guide for Parents, Educators, and Community Leaders, 2nd edition*

Public Service Announcements: *Send the Message (Drugs and HIV), Game Plan (Steroids) and others.*

Substance abuse of both students and parents can profoundly affect the behavior of the student, those around him or her, and the teacher. The new teacher's job is to be aware of signs of behaviors (also see chapter 3) related to alcohol or drug abuse such as irregular attendance, tardiness, class disruptions, and lower grades, then refer the students to the school counselor, nurse, or support personnel and be sure they get professional help (Burden, 2006).

Violence

In chapter 3 sj first addressed the issue of violence and its many manifestations in relation to school safety. Taking this issue further, we can also help preservice teachers to recognize warning signs and steps they can take toward violence prevention in and outside of their classrooms. In 2004 the National Youth Violence Prevention Resource Center published the document *School Violence*, reporting that students are more likely to experience violent acts away from school than in school and that schools are safer now than they have been in recent years. Feelings of increased safety may stem in part from heightened security in the presence of guards, cameras, elimination of lockers, mandatory dress codes or uniforms, weapons detectors, teacher phones or intercoms in classrooms, and other authoritarian measures used to get students to comply with school policies. On the other hand, some schools report that tightened security measures only tighten the tensions between young people and adults and prefer conflict resolution, cooperative learning, student mediation, and character development methods that "rely on education instead of discipline as a way of preventing violence"; we are cautioned, however, that "violence-prevention or conflict-resolution programs only work if properly done, and since there is currently no universal consensus on what constitutes doing violence prevention properly, we have every reason to expect empirical results of such programs to be highly mixed" (Volokh with Snell, 1998). It is evident that no two schools or school districts have the universal panacea for violent behavior in schools. School violence still occurs in several forms and is a major concern for preservice teachers who question their well-being during student teaching and the first years of employment.

> While the media has focused on school shootings, school violence includes a range of activities, including assaults with or without weapons, physical fights, threats or destructive acts other than physical fights, bullying, hostile or threatening remarks between groups of students, and gang violence. The data about these types of violence present a mixed picture of school safety. (*School Violence Fact Sheet*, http://www.safeyouth.org/scripts/facts/school .asp)

New teachers, without sufficient preparation for anticipating or managing acts of violence including physical acts and verbal threats of bodily injury and intimidation, are especially vulnerable when students become violent toward them or with one another.

> School violence affects teachers as well as students. On average, in each year from 1995 to 1999, about 3 out of every 1,000 teachers were the victims of serious violent crime at school. Additionally, teachers face threats of violence and intimidation. In the 1993–94 school year, 12 percent of all teachers were threatened with injury by a student from their school, and 4 percent were physically attacked by a student. (*School Violence Fact Sheet,* http://www.safe youth.org/scripts/facts/school .asp)

We can prepare preservice teachers by reassuring them that they cannot always predict where or when a violent incident may occur, but we can help them to recognize warning signs of violent behavior, including changes in personality, physical appearance, achievement, activity level, health, and socialization (Burden, 2006, p. 241). We can also discuss ways they could respond in advance to a potentially incendiary situation. "For example, if there is a physical fight, you may tell students to stop, disperse the other students, do not physically intervene, and get help" (Burden, 2006, p. 256). Preservice teachers need to seek out information about their school's violence prevention plan and to discuss these plans with their cooperating teachers. Student teachers should also know that their actions might be dramatically different in cases of bomb threats, natural disasters, or school shootings. The Departments of Education and Justice and the American Institutes for Research developed a report titled "Safeguarding Our Children: An Action Guide" outlining that

> ...[A]n effective school violence prevention plan must include three tiers.
>
> 1. Schools must build a school-wide foundation for all children. This involves: supporting positive discipline, academic success, and mental and emotional wellness through a caring school environment; teaching students appropriate behaviors and problem solving skills; positive behavioral support; and appropriate academic instruction with engaging curricula and effective teaching practices.
>
> 2. Schools must identify students at risk for severe academic or behavioral difficulties early on and create services and supports that address risk factors and build protective factors for them. Approximately 10 to 15% of students exhibit problem behaviors indicating a need for such early intervention. It is important that staff be trained to recognize early warning signs and make appropriate referrals. Once students are identified, they must receive coordinated services that meet their individual needs. A number of approaches have been developed for interventions at this stage, including anger management training, structured after-school programs, mentoring, group and family counseling, changing instructional practices, and tutoring.
>
> 3. Schools must identify and provide intensive interventions for the few children who are experiencing significant emotional and behavioral problems. This involves providing coordinated, comprehensive, intensive, sustained, culturally appropriate, child and family-focused services and supports. Such interventions might include day

> treatment programs which provide students and families with intensive mental health and special education services; multi-systemic therapy, focusing on the individual youth and his or her family, the peer context, school/vocational performance, and neighborhood/community supports; or treatment foster care, an intensive, family-focused intervention for youth whose delinquency or emotional problems are so serious and so chronic that they are no longer permitted to live at home. To be effective, these approaches generally require the collaboration of schools, social services, mental health providers, and law enforcement and juvenile justice authorities. (*School Violence Fact Sheet*, http://www.safeyouth.org/scripts/facts/school.asp)

Additional Websites for Violence Prevention
SAVE (Students Against Violence Everywhere)
http://www.national save.org/main/statistics.php

The Hamilton Fish Institute on School and Community Violence
(*http://hamfish.org/cms/*)

Mentors in Violence Prevention (MVP) *http://www.sportinsociety.org/vpd/mvp.php*

Peace Education Foundation (*http://www.peace-ed.org/*)

Family Violence Prevention Fund, Teens and Partner Violence Page
(*http://endabuse.org/programs/teens/*)

Bullying and Bullyproofing

To add to sj's discussion about bullying in chapter 3, "Bullying continues to be a serious problem, particularly in middle schools. In 1999, about 10 percent of students in grades 6 and 7 reported being bullied, compared with about 5 percent of students in grades 8 and 9 and about 2 percent in grades 10 through 12" (*School Violence Fact Sheet*, http://www.safeyouth.org/scripts/facts/school.asp). This problem is not just about students and does not begin with students; it begins with those who claim to be role models for students and is perpetuated in advertising and consumerism, popularized even in the latest videogame, "Bully" (http://www.usatoday.com/tech/gaming/2006-08-09-bully-preview_x.htm). Bullying is a learned behavior that children observe and try to follow; they see it in their homes, on the playing field, and in their classrooms. Bullies can be peers but they are also brothers and sisters, parents, coaches, teachers, administrators, and anyone who "uses an imbalance of power to repeatedly aggress against and harm another through physical, emotional, and social means" (Parsons, 2005, p. 88).

> Students aren't the only ones bullying in schools. Teachers, principals, and parents bully too. Together they create a bullying culture, with students occupying the lowest spot in the pecking order. Anti-bullying programs that focus solely on student-on-student bullying are bound to fail. Until all the elements in a school's bullying culture are addressed, the problem of student bullying won't be resolved. (Parsons, 2005, p. 5)

Cyber bullying, or threatening by any electronic means including computers and cell phones, is an everyday occurrence. "[O]ne student in four reports receiving bullying messages; 14% of young people have been threatened on the Internet, 16% have admitted to posting bullying messages, and 44% possess an e-mail account without their parents' consent" (Parsons, 2005, p. 22). Parsons advocates that schools must enforce clear antibullying policies, including electronic, that inform everyone at school and at home that it is a criminal offense to cause someone to fear for their safety or the safety of others. Teachers and parents have to work in tandem to supervise and react swiftly to unacceptable face-to-face harassment and inappropriate online behavior both at school and at home (p. 23).

According to Parsons (2005), homophobic torment is the most pervasive form of bullying in schools today. "A U.S. Department of Justice report disclosed that 97% of students at Lincoln-Sudbury School in Boston, Massachusetts, had heard anti-gay comments from other students and 53% revealed that they had heard them from teachers…. A typical secondary school student, for example, hears antigay slurs an average of 25 times a day" (p. 23). Even more shocking is Parsons' finding that only 3 percent of teachers actively intervene and provide only slight reprimands when they observe harassment; one in three gay students drop out before graduation (pp. 23–24). Parsons provides a detailed plan of steps we can take in antihomophobia education including normalizing the GLBT language and providing resources in the classroom and school libraries. The website http://youbigbully.com/ provides a Bully Survey, describes physical, verbal, and incidental bullies, and answers FAQs about bullying. According to the Bully Police web page (http://www.bullypolice.org/ retrieved August 10, 2006), twenty-six states have antibullying laws and fifteen more are taking action for laws to be in place.

➡*Teaching Points*

∞Methods Courses

Students can become more empowered by their teachers to combat bullying if teachers will model the courage to challenge any and all forms of bullying and have a no tolerance policy for bullying in their classrooms. Parsons includes the following steps teachers should take in bullyproofing their classrooms:

- Address every incident of harassment including name-calling and electronic intimidation by sending a clear message that harassing behavior is wrong and must stop and that victims have done nothing wrong and are supported;
- Deconstruct general examples of bullying episodes to develop greater understanding and empathy;

- Explore books, film, and other media with bullying themes, the negative effects and outcomes of bullying, and what can be done to prevent and stop it;
- Know what to expect in support from the school administration and behavior codes;
- Do not allow students to trivialize bullying behavior as playing or fooling around;
- If students request help, respect their privacy and keep their situations confidential;
- Goals should be to raise self-esteem for all students, to involve all students, to foster trust and cooperation, and to banish stereotypes. (Parsons, 2005, p. 28)

Promiscuity and Teen Pregnancy

> Ninety-four percent of adults in the United States–and 91 percent of teenagers–think it important that school-aged children and teenagers be given a strong message from society that they should abstain from sex until they are out of high school. Seventy-eight percent of adults also think that sexually active teenagers should have access to contraception … .A majority of both girls and boys who are sexually active wish they had waited. Eight in ten girls and six in ten boys say they wish they had waited until they were older to have sex. (http://www.teenpregnancy.org/resources/data/genlfact.asp)

Regardless of society's views on abstinence or teens' opinions that they wished they had waited to have sex after they were promiscuous, as of May 2005, The National Campaign to Prevent Teen Pregnancy states that one out of every three girls has had sex by age 16, two out of three by age 18; and two out of three boys have sex by age 18. The United States has the highest rate of teenage pregnancy with 34 percent of young women under age 20 becoming pregnant at least once, costing at least $7 billion annually. Of these 820,000 pregnancies per year, 8 in 10 are unintended and 81 percent are to unmarried teens. Only one-third of teen mothers complete high school and only 1.5 percent receive a college degree by age 30. Almost 80 percent of unmarried teen mothers receive welfare and 22 percent of teen daughters are more likely to become teen mothers themselves.

USA Today recently reported (July, 2006) that over 49 percent of males who do not finish high school will father a child out of wedlock in contrast to less than 5 percent of males who graduate from college fathering illegitimate children. One of the reasons that males drop out of school is because we are not engaging them in what Smith and Wilhelm (2006) refer to as "flow" activities (based on Csikszentmihalyi's 1990 work, *Flow: The Psychology of Optimal Experience*) that provide "an immediate experience, an appropriate challenge, the ability to control literacy and a feeling of competence" (Smith & Wilhelm, 2006, pp. 5–11). Their research with boys also includes the importance boys place on relationships and "an implicit social contract with their teachers" including that "teachers would get to know them as individuals, care about them, be attentive to their interests, help them to work hard and make sure they learned, and be passionate about what they are teaching" (pp. 14–15). Our experience has been that girls also place a high value on social contracts with their teachers, as our example with Acazia who had to build a trusting relationship in order for Karen to learn illustrates later in this chapter.

More teens prefer information on birth control to come from their parents than their friends:

> One in two teens say they "trust" their parents most for reliable and complete information about birth control, only 12 percent say a friend ... Seven of ten teens interviewed said that they were ready to listen to things parents thought they were not ready to hear. When asked about the reasons why teenage girls have babies, 78 percent of white and 70 percent of African-American teenagers reported that lack of communication between a girl and her parents is often a reason teenage girls have babies. (http://www.teenpregnancy.org/resources/data/genlfact.asp)

Discussions about homosexuality, safe sex practices for manual, oral, and anal sex, and sexually transmitted diseases are often limited or excluded even in schools that claim comprehensive sex education.

> Supporters of comprehensive sex education programs argue that abstinence-only curricula that advocate that youth should abstain from sex until marriage ignore and marginalize lesbian, gay, bisexual, and transgender youth, who might not be able to marry their partner due to legal restrictions. Proponents of abstinence-only education often have a more conservative view of homosexuality and are against it being taught as a normal, accepted lifestyle, or placed on the same platform as heterosexual relations, and so they generally do not see this as a problem... .
>
> [E]xcluding discussion of these issues or the issues of homosexuality, bisexuality, or transgenderedness, feelings of isolation, loneliness, guilt and shame as well as depression are made much worse. Supporters of including LGBT issues as an integral part of comprehensive sexuality education argue that this information is still useful and relevant and reduces the likelihood of suicide, sexually transmitted disease, acting out and maladaptive behavior. In the absence of such discussion, these youths are said to be de facto forced to remain in the closet, while heterosexual youth is left without guidance on dealing with their own possible homosexual attractions and with their homosexual classmates. (http://en.wikipedia.org/ wiki/Sex_education)

Aside from health and physical education classes that may still be lacking in critical information about sexuality for today's teens, adolescents are not or rarely asked about sexual health issues and rarely have input about sex education in schools. "Few sexual health interventions are designed with input from adolescents. Adolescents have suggested that sex education should be more positive with less emphasis on *anatomy* and scare tactics; it should focus on *negotiation skills* in sexual relationships and *communication*; and details of sexual health clinics should be advertised in areas that adolescents frequent (for example, school toilets, shopping centres)" (http://en.wikipedia.org/wiki/Sex_education).

Teenagers want to be heard and want to hear from adults, especially their own parents, about topics concerning sex. Teachers can provide information to parents and guardians from sources such as the ones we have mentioned in this chapter in order to help students become more aware of sex education; they can share this information to help families recognize how important talk about sexuality is to their teens and to make parents more comfortable with topics they often feel uneasy or unprepared to discuss. As with other issues like drugs and violence that adolescents are curious about and/or need someone to dialogue with, secondary students may approach preservice teachers, often because of their closeness in age to teenagers or because they can relate to other adolescent interests like music and clothing, with questions about sex. And sometimes students will test preservice teachers by asking inappropriate questions or making provocative remarks, just to see how a new teacher will react. During student teaching, preservice teachers can defer to the cooperating teacher, supervisor, and other qualified personnel if and when students act inappropriately or approach them with personal matters about their or their peers' sexual behavior. In the secondary English classroom, reading adolescent literature that deals with issues relating to sex (see examples in chapter 3), and writing and discussing the characters and circumstances in those novels, often provides avenues for teens to work through their opinions and stances on promiscuity, teenage pregnancy, sexual attraction, and relationships in a nonthreatening, more productive way.

Motivation and Engagement

Current research supports the idea that behavioral disruptions minimize when students actively engage (Antinarella & Salbu, 2003; Burden, 2006; Golub, 2000; Strickland & Strickland, 2002). More than ever, teachers in today's classrooms must consider sure-fire strategies that keep students engaged in order to create a productive learning community and to eliminate behavioral problems (Alsup & Bush, 2003; Ebbers & Brant-Kemezis, 2002; Firek, 2003; Meeks & Austin, 2003). New teachers who are just forming their identities and developing their teaching repertoires must test, often by trial and error, which interventions match the specific management issues in their classes.

> Behavior management that works considers that interaction of dynamic variables that can affect behavior, including genetics, home life, aptitude, prior academic history, classmates, classroom rules, curriculum, instruction, physical environment of the classroom, and temperament. Good behavior management involves a problem-solving approach in which the final decision about intervention is made only after all reasons for the behavior are carefully considered. (Harrington & Holub, 2006, p. xxv)

When their students are motivated to learn, new teachers feel accomplished and are less likely to leave the profession within the first three years, the most critical time to consider whether or not they have made the right choice to be an educator (Wong & Wong, 1998). Rather than wasting valuable minutes correcting and disciplining inattentive and unwilling adolescents, secondary teachers can create a win-win classroom situation where students become more self-directed, teachers become facilitators and co-learners, and both spend more time appreciating the deeper meanings and joys of learning.

> Many classroom-management texts wrongly suggest that the goal of behavior management is to get students to desist and to correct them. When educators correct students, they are generally using compliance-managing skills … they are manipulating consequences … (A) student may be successfully managed to "stop hitting his neighbor," but he may still not be working at the instructional task at hand. Classroom management that works generally focuses on positive replacement behaviors … and reinforces students on a regular basis. (Harrington & Holub, 2006, p. xxiv)

Standard #1 outlined by the National Board of Professional Teaching is "Engaging and supporting all students in learning." Teachers who commit to this standard "build on students' interests to achieve learning goals; use a variety of resources that respond to students' diverse needs; facilitate challenging learning experiences that promote autonomy, interaction, and choice; actively engage all students in problem solving and critical thinking within and across subject areas; and assist all students to become self-directed learners who demonstrate, articulate, and evaluate what they have learned" (Burke, 2003, p. 19). When we believe in supporting all students in learning, we develop a trusting relationship with them and build a constructive rapport that can be sustained over time, especially after students are reprimanded for wrongdoing or when they receive poor evaluations or failing grades on their work. It is the teacher's responsibility to make students want to learn. We can promote the desire to study, inquire, or achieve and dissuade classroom confrontations and clashes in the following ways:

1. Types of off-task behavior and misbehavior such as hyperactivity, inattentiveness, conduct disorder, and impulsivity (Burden, 2006) can be avoided or eliminated through managing and facilitating intellect-building instructional activities that make students want to come to school and learn and that assist teachers in sustaining student engagement for entire class periods (see Acazia's literature circles lesson on the following pages).

2. Offering classroom management techniques to prevent misbehavior through illustrations of "withitness" (Kounin, 1970) practices in context such as Constructivist Activities, Station Lessons, Literature Circles, and Differentiated Instruction that (1) appeal to auditory, visual, and kinesthetic learners, and apply

Howard Gardner's (1999) theory of multiple intelligences, (2) offer students choice, (3) satisfy both independent and collaborative learning, (4) monitor student behavior and communicate this regularly to the students, and (5) encourage peer and self-assessments.

Teacher educators must provide preservice teachers with sources of evidence from formal classroom observations, informal visits, and interviews with both experienced and novice teachers, resources, materials, and teacher identity concepts that align with performance criteria to engage students and to dissuade classroom management difficulties.

Issue#3: Rules in the Loaded Matrix, or What Do We Do on Day One? Although what we suggest may not be new, it bears repeating that no matter what discipline we teach, students in a win-win classroom know that we have high expectations for them to learn and achieve to the best of their abilities in our classes. From the first day, we let our students know that as their teachers we are approachable and accessible if they need our assistance; but a key goal in our secondary classrooms is that they become autonomous—self-reliant, self-aware, and self-disciplined.

In my methods seminars many preservice teachers remark that they do not think rules are necessary, or if they have to have rules, they only need one, respect. We talk about whether their definition of respect would match their students' definitions. We discuss whether social justice educators would believe in rules at all or if rules would be contradictory to a liberatory pedagogy. Emmer, Evertson, and Anderson researched that "effective managers had clear rules for general conduct as well as procedures or routines for carrying out specific tasks. Furthermore, (they) spent much of the first few days teaching these rules and procedures to students—as carefully as they taught academic content—and they continued to review during the first three weeks of school" (in Weinstein & Mignano, Jr., 2007, p. 101). Note that what they term "effective classroom managers" did not just post or go over rules the first day, but they reinforced positive classroom practices and behaviors constantly for three full weeks, approximately the amount of time it takes for anything to become a habit; in other words they demonstrated PDE Category II: Clear standards of conduct and effective management of student behavior that we earlier categorized as an assertive discipline strategy. If we are true to our teaching philosophy, it should determine how we feel and what we do about rules, but often the day-to-day classroom experience modifies the ways teacher candidates manage their classrooms, thereby also changing the teaching philosophy in action.

Rules may not be the most important classroom management consideration since, according to Burden (2006), 80 percent of our secondary students rarely break the rules, 15 percent do somewhat regularly, and 5 percent will consistently cause classroom disruptions (p. 237). Preservice teachers may, however, take time during the initial days to explain their policies and to enforce them fairly and often. Students may assist in creating the rules, as long as the rule is reasonable, sensible, and appropriate for all students. Student teachers could reserve the right to veto a student-suggested rule if it is not.

If teachers choose to have classroom rules, Burden explains the ideal number is about four–six short and simple ones, so students will remember them and not be overloaded with information. We suggest choosing rules carefully, making sure students understand what is expected of them by asking them to help us define a community of learners and what we all mean by respect, property, and civility. We explain that we follow the policies outlined for the entire school as well as our own classroom rules and procedures, and we reserve the right to create new rules if we find that a particular class warrants them. Some of the areas we feel are important to consider in creating classroom guidelines include students showing respect for themselves, their peers, and all employees and visitors in the school as well as their property and the property of others: peer's property, the school's property, intellectual property (i.e., the ideas and written work of others), and following the Student Code of Conduct.

Burden's text states that the number one school crime is theft. We believe that discussing school offenses like stealing money or property and cheating as stealing the ideas or work of another assists students to become more aware of and more responsible for their actions. Some students think nothing of taking a pen from another student's desk or copying the definitions of vocabulary homework from a friend during homeroom. We believe that talking about why these actions are infringements on other students' rights and property raises our students' awareness of fairness and civility. Letting students know well in advance that there are consequences for violating the rules is proactive and serves to avoid major confrontations if they do commit an offense against another student or school property.

If we as teachers are going to have rules for our students, then we should include rules for ourselves, for example, that we will be prepared for classes and that we will return graded assignments within a reasonable amount of time. We can ask students and their parents or guardians to read and sign our rules as a contract along with us. We can assist our students by being organized including having spaces like crates, shelves, and folders for them to place and to receive their materials each day. Another strategy that has worked for us from the beginning of the school year is calling home just to ask if there are any questions or sending an email, postcard, or note of praise when a student has done something well.

Lack of Discipline: "Won't Do" versus "Can't Do"

Teachers who have high expectations and approval for students who exhibit behaviors they condone are likely to also believe in consequences for not following the rules. Students need to be reminded that when they disrupt the class, they are interfering with the learning of others around them who want to learn. We agree with Jabari Mahiri (1998) when he writes, "Citizens of the twenty-first century are being educated right now. The challenge of new century schools is to teach them knowledge, skills, and values to collectively create rainbows of productive, non-oppressive human interactions that increase the prospects of individuals finding their own personal gold" (p. 159).

Before any student receives a reprimand for negative behavior, however, that student's teacher must be able to distinguish between students who "can't do" the task due to lack of knowledge and skills and "won't do" the task due to compliance behavior problems (Harrington & Holub, 2006, p. xxvi). Some of the measures that have worked for our preservice teachers, depending on the individual reasons for breaking a rule and the level of the infraction, include explaining to students that they disapprove of the behavior, not the person; quiet one-to-one conversations in or outside the classroom to communicate the reasons why the rules are for their benefit; reminding students of the guidelines by pointing to a place where they are visible in the room; meeting with students after school for tutoring, computer assistance, helping with tasks like reorganizing books or displaying student work; giving a "double load" of homework (homework for that night and an additional assignment on a previous lesson linked to the current assignment); and calling or meeting with parents or care-givers to seek out additional information. In the case of severe disciplinary action, the school's policies should be followed for behavior modification.

Are Acazia's Students Problematic, or Does the Problem Begin with Acazia?

During student teaching, Acazia had a consistent rule breaker, Anthony, who constantly tested his limits with her from the first day to close to the last. An example of a "won't do," Anthony blurted out inappropriate comments during direct instruction, ignored his group members during activities, or even walked around the room to disturb other groups. One day he thought that leaving the room without permission and returning thirty minutes later would be a good choice. After Acazia's early attempts at subtle techniques of "the teacher eye" and proximity control, followed by the more obvious change of seat, deemed ineffective, Anthony moved up the discipline ladder, first having a one-on-one discussion with Acazia, then getting a "double load of homework" (a review sheet to be handed in at the beginning of the next period in addition to his regular assignments), next phoning home, and finally finding himself in the discipline office with multiple detentions to be served. When Anthony saw that there were snowballing consequences to his actions that were supported by the larger school management plan, he began to turn around and take Acazia's English class seriously. As a new teacher, Acazia realized that doling out minor consequences to escalating negative behaviors like Anthony's were just not enough to create any real change in behavior. Chronic rule breakers need more than static negative stimuli to keep them from acting out; their teachers must understand that the intervention strategies available to them span a range of offenses and that, when necessary, all personnel in the school must be behind the teacher in helping the student to modify behavior in order for learning to occur.

Ensuring the Student's Self-Worth

The best way of keeping our students' attention and minimizing disruptions is to be as proactive as possible right at the onset of getting to know our students, letting them see that our classroom is a place where they are encouraged, safe, and where we are accountable to each other. "(T)he primary obligation of a behavior manager is to ensure the emotional and physical well-being of the student. Behavior management that works ensures that the self-worth of the student remains intact even during the intervention and even after it is completed" (Harrington & Holub, 2006, p. xxix). This is especially true for students like Karen, an example of a "can't do," in Acazia's third-period class. When the first writing assignment was returned, Karen broke into tears, sharing loudly, "I'm so stupid; I will never be able to write anything." Acazia tried to comfort her by setting up a meeting to go over her grading rubric and her written comments on her paper thoroughly and reminding her of weekly tutoring after school, or peer tutoring in the mornings, if Karen preferred. But on Karen's next portfolio writing assignment, little work was completed; instead the entire paper was flooded with statements like, "I am so clueless," and "I'm sorry that I am this dumb." On the advice of her cooperating teacher, Acazia called home and referred Karen to the Student Assistance Program at school. Karen's mother willingly came in for a conference and was very open about the fact that Karen had been abused as a child and never fully recovered. Acazia realized that Karen was completely lacking in self-confidence as a writer and would need more opportunities to revise her portfolio pieces. Only after seeking professional help and realizing that Acazia's classroom was a safe place where she could practice writing with chances to improve did Karen begin to turn her attitude—and her grades—around. We must be preparing our preservice teachers to understand that creating an environment where students believe they can achieve is the first step to engagement and an instrumental part of successful teaching. Before she could reach Karen, Acazia had to begin to apply PDE Category II: Appropriate attention given to safety in the classroom to the extent that it is under the control of the student teacher and ability to establish and maintain rapport with students.

Common-Sense Practices and a Teaching Scenario

We believe in thoughtful lesson and unit preparation and teaching for the whole class period (PDE Category II: Effective classroom routines and procedures resulting in little or no loss of instructional time). This may seem a common-sense practice, but we have witnessed many models of current pedagogy where experienced teachers and teacher educators do not lead, connect, or communicate well from the beginning to the end of the class period and allow opportunities for students to become disruptive in especially the last five–ten minutes of a class or during a rocky transition from one point, lesson, or unit to the next. There is simply no substitute for a competent and caring teacher who knows her/his goals and how to match them with the students' learning styles, who is prepared to move on to the next learning opportunity, and who considers and uses possible alternatives when a lesson is not working for whatever reasons. To use Jeffrey Golub's astute metaphor, "'If the horse dies…dismount!' Sometimes lessons or activities don't work out. Your instructional 'horse' dies… .You can reflect later on the problem when you have some time available to make needed revisions. The important thing is to 'dismount' and jump on a different horse. That is why it is so essential to have backup plans available" (Golub, 2000, p. 16). So often we are quick to blame our students for their actions, but we must remember to examine and reexamine what we are doing, that is, either nurturing or interfering with the learning process. Kohn reminds us, "Some teachers respond with fury when they have a conflict with a student, and some respond with understanding, but few teachers have the courage to reflect on how they may need to reconsider their own decisions" (in Harrington & Holub, 2006, p. 98).

Literature Circles Example

One method that works for a variety of differentiated classrooms (King-Shaver and Hunter, 2003) in grades six–twelve has been literature circles (Daniels, 2002). Students discuss literary texts by taking on specific roles as the Summarizer, Discussion Starter/Director, Passage Finder, Illustrator, and Investigator/Connector. When class size is large and class periods are long, students can react by becoming hyperactive or inattentive. In longer eighty–ninety-minute blocked-scheduled classes, literature circle activities hold the interest of even the students with the shortest attention spans by giving specific responsibilities to each class member, followed by asking the students to share their expertise with the other members of their group. These small groups then present what they learned to all members of the class. We know that we really learn something when we have to teach it to someone else; in this dynamic, students have multiple opportunities to share what they know. The organization for an eighty to ninety-minute class of approximately thirty students could be similar to the one we have witnessed in Acazia's classroom. She used a modified version of Daniels's concepts to promote high engagement (PDE Category II: Effective classroom routines and procedures resulting in little or no loss of instructional time). Class begins immediately with a short writing exercise to get students focused:

1. *Quick Write*—ten minutes. Students enter the classroom and take their seats in small clusters of four or five. Acazia calls attention to the question of the day on the board, "What do you think about poetry?" She adds subquestions verbally or in writing such as, "Do you like poetry? Why or why not? Where have you seen or heard poems? Do you have a favorite poem? Are songs poems? How are they poems and not poems? Do you write poetry? If so, what do you write about? If not, do you know anyone who does?" Students are encouraged to write whatever comes to mind on this question. Acazia does some writing with her students and monitors students by walking around and assisting those who may have trouble getting started.

2. *Read-Alouds and Modeling*—fifteen minutes. Just before the first ten minutes have passed, Acazia tells students they have about a minute to finish their quick writes and to hand in their responses. In this class, students like being read to aloud, so she reads several responses to the question as students listen. Their responses are varied with many opinions and experiences. This activity sparks students' interest in the genre of poetry and uses the students' voices to explain what they already know about the subject. Acazia shares what she has written as part of the learning community. They then begin the main activity of the day, the study of a published poet. In this particular seventh-grade language arts class, Acazia selects six poems by Sara Holbrook. Each cluster will be responsible for reading and interpreting one of the six poems for the rest of the class. She models how each cluster of students will be asked to read one of the poems, take on a literature circle role to analyze the poem (students have used literature circles in the study of other genres, so they are comfortable with the roles and how they function), and suggests ways students might present the poem dramatically to the class. Students are provided with copies of all six poems, four–five questions of varying difficulty about each poem with additional space for students to write their own questions about the poem (Holden & Schmidt, 2002), transparencies, and marking pens to write and draw their interpretations. Students are then assigned which poem they will be working with in their groups, either randomly or by level of difficulty, or by student selection, depending on Acazia's knowledge of the students (PDE Category II: Attention to equitable learning opportunities for students).

3. *Discussion of teacher-prepared and student-formulated questions and carrying out roles*—twenty minutes. Students in their clusters choose their roles and begin the poetry analysis. Acazia moves from group to group, making sure that each student has a specific task, listening to students' interpretations, and offering assistance only when needed. One student reads the poem out loud and makes a short statement about what he thinks it might mean. Another checks for difficult vocabulary and looks up words they are not familiar with in the dictionary. Another uses the transparency and colored markers and begins to draw what she thinks the poem means. Another takes one of the lines that stands out and reads it again, explaining why it might be the key line of the poem. Still another goes to one of the classroom computers to check for further information about this poem. As each team member selects a task that appeals to his or her learning style and brings something new to the group, students begin to put the pieces of the poem together for better understanding and appreciation. They read the poem a third or fourth time and decide how they want to stage it in front of the whole class; maybe everyone will read a line, or maybe two people will read together, or perhaps they will do a full choral reading. They decide if they will sit, stand, have someone play dead, do the poem as a rap, which words they will emphasize, and negotiate several other considerations in the performance. If students become disorderly, Acazia intervenes with proximity, eye contact, a finger to her lips, a verbal reminder about how much time is left, or asks if there is a problem. Any or all of these signals work for returning the team members to their tasks. She lets them know when they have about three minutes before they begin the presentations. (PDE Category II: Clear standards of conduct and effective management of student behavior.)

4. *Presentations*—thirty minutes. Before the presentations begin, students are reminded that they have copies of all of the poems, so high visual learners can follow along with the readings; everyone may take notes if they wish. To deter inappropriate conduct or impulsivity, Acazia reminds them to watch and listen to one another since they will have to explain a poem from another group at the end of the class. Students volunteer to come to the front of the room to read and interpret their poems for the large group. Each team takes about five minutes to dramatize the selection out loud, to discuss what they think the poem means, and to show their transparencies of their interpretations to the whole class. Students are riveted to what is going on in the front of the room because it is their peers, not the teacher, teaching the class. Acazia encourages students to applaud each team as they return to their seats. (PDE Category II: Appropriate attention given to safety in the classroom to the extent that it is under the control of the student teacher.)

5. *Peer summary and reflections*—ten minutes. When all of the presentations are completed, students from one group are asked to summarize what another group told them about the poem to see what they have retained. Students are then asked to write their reflections about the activity on a 3 x 5 index card, paying particular attention to what they learned from the group work as well as about the poems themselves. Acazia collects the index cards and awards class participation points to all those who willingly completed the task (PDE Category II: Expectations for student achievement with value placed on the quality of student work).

The seventh-grade suburban students in Acazia's classroom experience multiple forms of literacy and apply multiple intelligences through reading, writing and drawing, research, creative dramatics, and collaboration, all in just one class period. Students make choices that match their visual, auditory, or kinesthetic learning preferences and are encouraged to move around the room and use all available classroom resources to improve comprehension (Beers, 2003). Acazia acts as a co-learner, mentor, monitor, and facilitator rather than lecturer or disciplinarian (PDE Category II: Ability to establish and maintain rapport with students). Students participate in active learning for the entire class period (PDE Category II: Effective classroom routines and procedures resulting in little or no loss of instructional time). They work in teams, pairs, and individually; they then share information and knowledge with the whole class. There is visible evidence that they are accountable for and reflective about what they have learned. They engage in genuine activities that real readers, writers, and investigators might do on a daily basis.

Implications for Teacher Education

Milner and Milner (2003) state that "amid all of their uncertainties, our prospective teachers worry most about control of the classroom" (p. 419). Ironically perhaps, when teachers like Acazia allow students to be more in control, they empower both their students and themselves. Our observations indicate that beginning teachers can engage secondary students much like successful experienced practitioners by breaking traditional instructional habits of teacher-centered, lock step, inflexible, and only compliance-managing behaviors. "Good behavior management does not stifle independence, creativity, divergent thinking, originality, or giftedness in the name of compliance…Behavior management that works is respectful to the needs of the student and the teacher" (Harrington & Holub, 2006, p. xxv). Those of us who educate new teachers currently must complete required assessment instruments like the PDE-430 a minimum of two times per student teacher per semester with clear evidence that our student teachers are demonstrating appropriate practices and performance, not the least of these is classroom management. We can help new teachers to succeed in this evaluation, particularly in the area of establishing and maintaining a productive classroom environment, in the following ways:

- Provide preservice teachers with general education and discipline-specific reading, online materials, and videos to better understand classroom management issues and how to deal with them by proactive, consistent, ethical, and fair means.

- "We should examine effective programmes designed to prevent other high risk behaviours in adolescents. For example, Botvin, et al. found that school based programmes to prevent drug abuse during junior high school (ages 12–14 years) resulted in important and durable reductions in use of tobacco, alcohol, and marijuana if they taught a combination of social resistance skills and general life skills, were properly implemented, and included at least two years of booster sessions" (http://en.wikipedia.org/wiki/Sex_ education).

- Help beginning teachers to become "star teachers" (Haberman, 1995) whose "normal teaching involves them in a great deal of personal interaction with students that revolves around learning tasks and natural relationships that allow (them) to 'anticipate, prevent, or ward off many emergencies'" (in Milner & Milner, p. 420).

- Have them read several school-wide building plans and observe other experienced teachers' classes from the beginning of the school year to see how they create, establish, and maintain a classroom environment in the first weeks of school.

- Anticipate and talk about real management concerns and play out possible scenarios in methods classes as they surface in pre-student teaching and student teaching experiences.

- Remind teacher candidates that if students write or say anything that constitutes a threat to their well-being or the well-being of others, they are protecting the student by reporting it to the proper authorities.

- Study the seven bulleted points for PDE Category II: Classroom Environment (or equivalent) prior to and during student teaching and discuss how teacher candidates' performances could demonstrate or exceed each of those requirements with specific examples. Ask preservice teachers, student teachers, and cooperating teachers how they would document their sources of evidence for all of those points.

- Talk with cooperating teachers in person or through emails about their classroom rules and procedures and what has worked and not worked for them.

- Be mindful of common-sense practices that include strong subject matter knowledge, preparation and organization, teaching for the whole class period, student involvement and motivation, student choice, constructivist methods, mentoring, a sense of humor, and enthusiasm.

- Take genuine interest in students both in and outside the classroom. Learn as much as possible about students' cultures and home lives and apply that knowledge in the classroom.

- Continue to advocate reflective practice, interactive classrooms, support from the whole school and larger community, and meeting the learning needs of all students.

- New teachers need to self-reflect regularly on each of their classes, questioning whether the classroom management style and techniques they are choosing is working or whether they need to modify their strategies to promote a better classroom climate. Asking a mentor teacher to observe a class now and then may provide another pair of eyes to see what a newer teacher cannot see.

Concluding with Advice from Other Teachers

One of the most helpful things we can do to prepare preservice teachers about classroom management is to invite current student teachers and their cooperating teachers into the methods class to answer questions about classroom management and what works for them. What they tell my preservice students varies depending upon what has been successful for them. Secondary students respond differently to different teaching personalities, techniques, and strategies, so what works for one teacher may not work for another. However, often student teachers make a list of practices they find successful and share those lists with my methods class students who will begin their student teaching the next semester. Some of those practices have included ones like student teachers Jamie and Renee[2] shared with my teaching methods class last semester:

- Be prepared and organized.
- Proximity and verbal cues are more effective than you think..

- Avoid confrontations, but ask students to stay after class or meet with them in the hallway. Ask, "What can I do for you?"
- Do not bribe students.
- Try to handle the problem as much as possible yourself before going to the administration. But send kids out if they seriously will not back off.
- Variety and choice are important. Never do the same thing three days in a row.
- Be patient with your students; do not expect them to be university students.
- Always try to be fair and consistent.
- Find student advocates and allow them to help you with classroom disruptions. Sometimes a student peer can turn another student away from misbehavior more quickly than the teacher can.
- Ask students to self-assess their behavior.
- Try a direct appeal to the class. "I would like to see everyone's eyes up here, please."
- Call out the names of students randomly to arrest their attention.
- Try sudden sustained silence or physical gestures rather than speech to get students to be quiet.
- Remember that students are resilient and forgiving for the most part.
- Be friendly but not their friend.

I added a few of my own observations to their lists:

- Classroom management is learned by gaining experience with what works from class to class and on an individual-to-individual basis.
- Every class has its own personality, a different dynamic that can change from day to day.
- Classroom management may be more or less successful depending upon how aware the teacher is of the nuances and subtleties of the classroom environment including but not limited to time of day, temperature, light, color, seasonal changes, student relationships that can change on a daily basis, who is present and who is absent, seating arrangement, uses of technology, and what the focus of instruction will be.
- I would post the slogan written on the front of the House of Blues in Atlantic City in my secondary classroom: "Help Ever, Hurt Never."

My preservice students tell me that they feel relieved and more confident after these seminars because they realize that there are a range of techniques they can try to make classes most productive, there is a cooperating teacher to mentor them, a school system to support them in most cases, and a network of peers they can call or email if they have a particular dilemma they cannot solve on their own.

We hope that our reflections and suggestions will assist both students and teachers to stay focused and to enjoy and appreciate being in school. Methods like these serve more often than not to resolve classroom management issues in the secondary classroom, or more importantly, they circumvent disciplinary issues to begin with. Students in well-managed classes often remark to us how quickly the time passes; they often enter the room smiling, asking their teachers what they will be working on that day. They know that they will have more to do with their class time than to become disruptive. We all win.

Notes

* Parts of this chapter were first published in Norris, L., & Norris, K. J. (2006). Creating a win-win situation: Engaging students and minimizing behavioral disruptions in the secondary classroom. *Pennsylvania Teacher Educator, 5*. Harrisburg: The Pennsylvania Association of Colleges and Teacher Educators.

1 We recognize that knowledge is never neutral and is generative based on the space and time in which it fortifies. We also recognize that some textbook companies that share particular concepts have close ties to Right-Wing agendas. While we think it is important for preservice teachers to use materials of all sorts so as to present a well-balanced curriculum, we do not condone teaching myopically. For our research, then, we draw upon texts that have ties to knowledge and political parties that, for some, they may not be partial to. We feel that it is important that we draw upon sources where we can either critique or affirm our own thinking.

2 I am grateful to current first-year secondary English teachers Jamie Lee and Renee Brown, Renee's cooperating teacher Larry Nath for additional classroom management tips, and all of the student teachers and cooperating teachers over the years who have graciously given their time to come to my methods classes to share their advice and experiences with preservice teachers.

References

Alsup J., & Bush, J. (2003). *But will it work for REAL students?* Urbana: National Council of Teachers of English.

Antinarella, J., & Salbu, K. (2003). *Tried and true: Lessons, strategies and activities for teaching secondary English.* Portsmouth: Heinemann.

Beers, K. (2003). *When kids can't read: What teachers can do*. Portsmouth: Heinemann.

Burden, P. (2006). *Classroom management: Creating a successful K-12 learning community*. Hoboken: John Wiley & Sons.

Burke, J. (2003). *The English teacher's companion: A complete guide*. Portsmouth: Heinemann.

Canter, L., & Canter, M. (2002). *Assertive discipline: Positive behavior management for today's schools* (3rd ed.). Bloomington: Solution Tree.

Daniels, H. (2002). *Literature circles: Voice and choice in book clubs and reading groups*. Portland: Stenhouse.

A day in the life of a teen: Decisions at every turn. (2006). Retrieved August 4, 2006, from http://teacher.scholastic.com/scholasticnews/indepth/headsup/.

Dickson, L., & Smagorinsky, P., with Bush, J., Christenbury, L., Cummings, B., George, M., Graham, P., Hartman, P., Kynard, C., Roskelly, H., Steffel, S., Vinz, R., & Weinstein, S. (2006). Are methods enough? Situating English education programs within the multiple settings of learning to teach. *English Education, 38,* 312–328.

Ebbers, F., & Brant-Kemezis, A. (2002). *Supervisor/student teacher manual.* Villa Maria: The Center for Learning.

Firek, H. (2003). *10 easy ways to use technology in the English classroom*. Portsmouth: Heinemann.

Gardner, H. (1999). *Intelligence reframed: Multiple intelligences for the 21st century*. New York: Basic Books.

General facts and statistics. (2005). Retrieved August 7, 2006, from http://www.teenpregnancy.org/

resources/data/genlfact.asp

Golub, J. (2000). *Making learning happen: Strategies for an interactive classroom.* Portsmouth: Boynton/Cook.

Haberman, M. (1995). *Star teachers of children in poverty.* West Lafayette: Kappa Delta Pi.

Harrington, R. G., & Holub, L. (2006). *Taking sides: Clashing views on controversial issues in classroom management.* Dubuque: McGraw-Hill/Dushkin.

Holden, J., & Schmit, J. (2002). *Inquiry and the literary text: Constructing discussions in the English classroom.* Urbana: NCTE.

King-Shaver, B., & Hunter, A. (2003). *Differentiated instruction in the English classroom.* Portsmouth: Heinemann.

Kounin, J. S. (1970). *Discipline and group management in classrooms.* New York: Holt, Rinehart, and Winston.

Mahiri, J. (1998). *Shooting for excellence: African American and youth culture in new century schools.* Urbana: NCTE.

Meeks, L., & Austin, C. (2003). *Literacy in the secondary English classroom: Strategies for teaching the way kids learn.* Boston: Allyn and Bacon.

Milner, J. O., & Milner, L . F. (2003). *Bridging English* (3rd ed.). Upper Saddle River: Pearson.

Parsons, L. (2005). *Bullied teacher: Bullied student.* Portland: Stenhouse.

Pennsylvania statewide evaluation form for student professional knowledge and practice (PDE-430). Commonwealth of Pennsylvania. Department of Education. 333 Market St., Harrisburg, PA 17126-0333.

School violence fact sheet. (2004). Retrieved August 10, 2006, from http://www.safeyouth.org/scripts/facts/school.asp

Sex education. (2006). Retrieved August 8, 2006, from http://en.wikipedia.org/wiki/Sex_education.

Shusterman, N. (1997). *The dark side of nowhere.* New York: Starscape.

Smith, M. W., & Wilhelm, J. D. (2006). *Going with the flow: How to engage boys (and girls) in their literacy learning.* Portsmouth: Heinemann.

Strickland, K., & Strickland, J. (2002). *Engaged in learning: Teaching English, 6-12.* Portsmouth: Heinemann.

Volokh, A., with Snell, L. (1998). *School violence prevention: Strategies to keep schools safe* (Unabridged). Policy Study No. 234, January. Retrieved August 4, 2006, from http://www.reason.org/ps234.html.

Weinstein, C. S., & Mignano, Jr., A. J. (2007). *Elementary classroom management: Lessons from research and practice* (4th ed.). New York: McGraw-Hill.

Wong, H. K., & Wong, R. T. (1998). *The first days of school.* Mountain View: Harry K. Wong Publications.

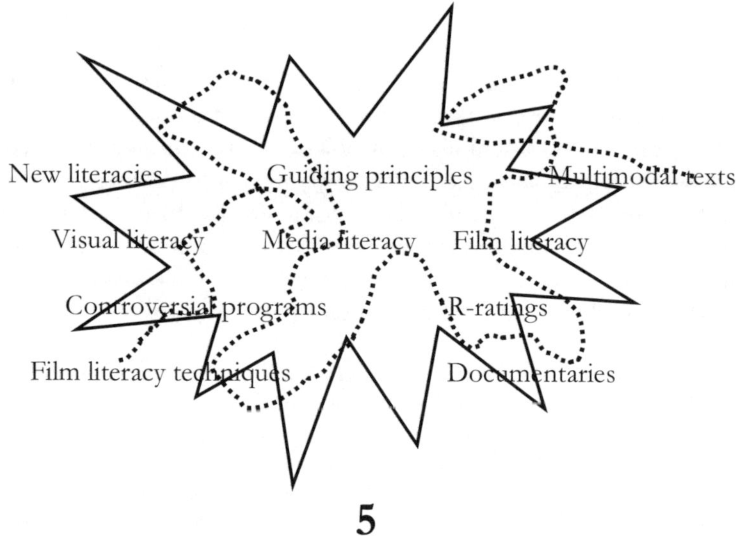

5

How Film and Critical Media Studies (Re)shape the Loaded Matrix: Critical Visual Literacy

Introduction

In this chapter, we describe ways for preservice teachers to tap into image, language, and sound messages and promote visual literacy as a key component for learning in today's schools. One of our most important goals is to help new teachers expand their own and their students' thinking about both print and non-print fiction and nonfiction in engaging ways. As Meg Callahan advises in her 2002 *English Education* article, "If we truly are embracing a broader notion of text in the English classroom, then we need to face all that this implies. If we want students to be savvy viewers/readers/listeners and to analyze critically the multimodal texts around them, then they need to experience the production of multimodal texts—just as we want students' experiences as readers and writers to intersect in meaningful ways" (p. 64). Today's youth must be provided with opportunities to explore how media are produced and to produce different forms of multimedia texts in the classroom. Some of our preservice teachers have a background in and bring with them experiences in making short films from their secondary and university course work or just from learning how to use their own digital cameras and camcorders; and for those who have little expertise in this area, there are more and more resources readily available to assist students in both meaning-making of existing multimodal texts and designing their own quality mixed-media compositions (e.g., Firek, 2003; Kenny, 2001; http://www.diynetwork.com/diy/shows_dmhm/episode/0,2046,DIY_16162_31168,00.html). Just as we continue to teach better comprehension of more traditional print texts, we must help today's secondary students acquire discernment and analytical ability for viewing movies and television because the majority of their daily information comes from non-print sources not limited to the news, MTV, commercials, ESPN, soaps, cartoons, and documentaries. Students also benefit from the auditory, visual, kinesthetic, intra- and interpersonal experiences of designing their own audio and video projects either on their own or in collaboration with their peers.

> One of the things that many of us have noticed about our culture and especially our students is the reliance they have on the visual for information and entertainment through film, television, computer monitors, and their cell phones. And many would prefer to spend hours in front of the "screen" than reading a book. However, this reliance on the visual does not have to take students away from reading but can also be used to complement the study of literature, as a bridge to the classics, and as a text in the classroom. The use of movies especially can enhance the teaching of reading, writing, and thinking in the English/language arts classroom. The NCTE/IRA standards challenge us to expand our idea of literacy to include non-print text. (Norris & Johnson, 2002)

Much as Joan Kaywell has integrated the classics with adolescent literature (Kaywell, 1997, 2000), we encourage teachers to use visual literacy strategies for creating thematic and interdisciplinary lesson plans and units by integrating media and literature in ways that their students can readily identify with and relate to. In the following pages, we share theories, techniques, and examples of how media, particularly movies, can work alone or with other kinds of texts to challenge students and promote higher critical literacy in our classrooms. We do not claim to be experts in visual literacy; however, we add our ideas to the media resources educators may already have, and we demonstrate some additional ways to teach what are now referred to as "models of new literacies pedagogy" (Kist, 2005; Lankshear & Knobel, 2003; Miller, forthcoming) including the "pedagogy of multiliteracies" suggesting that "students should be able to both read critically and write functionally, no matter what the medium" (Kist, 2005, p. 11). We write this chapter to recharge teachers and students who feel there is little or no connection between what they are watching and "reading" outside of school and what they do in school.

Loaded Matrix Chapter Context

This chapter originated when Ethan, in methods class one semester prior to student teaching, expressed concerns about observing a teacher in his first urban clinical experience showing *Scream 3* (2000) to her eleventh-grade students on one of the last days of school while other students completed their vocabulary workbook assignments. Ethan noticed students talking, sleeping, and doodling during the film while others tried to tune the film out, occasionally looking up when the music or noise got loud, as they reluctantly filled up the pages in their workbooks. When I questioned him about this experience further, he recounted that the teacher did not give the students anything specific to observe or to write about this film and that it was a film students requested to watch as a reward after the majority had completed their workbooks. From these observations, Ethan and his preservice teacher peers raised questions in my methods class about whether or not teachers should use movies and other forms of pop culture media as incentives or fillers, for example, for students who complete other tasks early, whether class time should be taken to watch whole films, and whether or not R-rated films like this one are ever appropriate for secondary students in an English language arts classroom.

Focus questions for chapter 5:

1. **What are the new literacies and why should they be promoted and even privileged in the secondary English classroom?**
2. **How do we train teachers to engage students in school with the familiar visual, electronic means they use to learn outside of school?**
3. **How and why do film and other forms of nonprint media work often more effectively (but may also be more abused) than printed texts in the secondary English classroom?**
4. **Should teachers be allowed to use R-rated or controversial films in their classes?**

Issue #1: Promoting Critical Visual Literacy in the Classroom

Today's youth understand media culture better than most of their teachers.

> Constantly changing, media has exploded into a world that is interpreted by youth entirely differently than by adults. Driven by MTV, clubbing, music, video, advertising, television, video games, Manga and Anime, instant messaging, cellular phones, the World Wide Web, Disney, and the relentless kinderculture of adolescence, today's youth are experts on the operation and purposes of media....Unfortunately, many school curriculums are determined to avoid or ignore youth media culture, isolating students and reinforcing their belief that adults really are *out* of it. (Steinberg, Parmar, & Richard, 2006, p. xvii)

Little wonder students fall asleep in class, cause disruption, or don't attend; we aren't challenging a highly visual, multisensory, multitask oriented population with exciting ways to explore these genres because we aren't thinking innovatively about how to use them. Callahan (2002) provides a thorough example of how one classroom teacher empowered his students by asking them to study radio documentaries and then create their own intertextual compositions; and Firek's (2003) book provides guidelines and assessments for teachers whose students want to create their own multimedia projects. Learning through and with media shouldn't become a contest where students try to outwit their teachers by watching the video version the night before to pass the book test. Unfortunately, we know this kind of schooling ritual has gone on in the past; and one of our objectives is to get teachers and students away from this kind of competition. We do not advocate showing films, television, or music videos as rewards or filler, or see the necessity of always showing an entire film to go along with the same book or play. We like the idea of film clips and other media including newspapers, magazines, music CDs, screenplays, or any vehicle communicating information that complements other books and books that enhance other movies, radio, and television excerpts rather than just the traditional book and film comparison.

Importance of Media Literacy

> Media is the most voraciously consumed product in America, besides food and air. If you have generations of children not understanding the importance of that in their everyday lives, you've got a problem. (Humphrey as quoted in O'Driscoll, 2006, p. 19)…But the subject [media literacy] is not widely featured in U.S. school curriculums, and funding for extracurricular programs can be hard to find. (O'Driscoll, 2006, p. 19)

Critical media literacy must become a priority in American classrooms as it is in other countries, including India, Canada, Australia, and Great Britain; it cannot be an extracurricular activity where only some students choose to participate, and it cannot be taught just by guest lecturer experts who can be afforded only by some of the privileged schools. We must train all preservice teachers about the essential role that "new literacies," as defined by Kist as "the plethora of communication media available today" (Kist, 2005, p. 12), play in their classrooms and that without these key components, many students will simply not learn anything from and with them.

We define visual, media, and film literacies—three terms often referred to separately but closely aligned and frequently used interchangeably. Our definitions come from the current experts and alliances on critical literacy studies and from those who write the foremost pedagogical texts in these areas (Beach, 2004; Considine & Haley, 1999; Golden, 2001, 2006; Hobbs, 2000, 2003, 2004, 2005; Teasley & Wilder, 1997; Worsnop, 1999). Perhaps one way to think about these terms is to envision and unpack these literacies, imagining visual literacy as the largest in a set of nesting boxes, media literacy as the second largest, and film literacy as the smallest of the three (figure 5.1). Because this pedagogy of multiliteracies is so vast, we can only scratch the surface of this subject in this chapter. However, we include some of what we do in our preservice methods courses to promote this pedagogy, with an emphasis on teaching film literacy, as a way for our readers to consider reshaping their own secondary English teaching philosophies and repertoires.

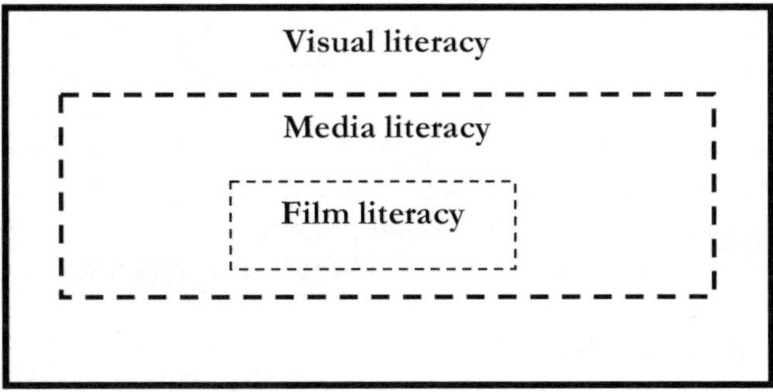

Figure 5.1 New literacies diagram.

Defining Visual Literacy and Its Importance in the Loaded Matrix

Visual literacy is a set of skills used to interpret and critique images. Visual literacy, visual rhetoric, and critical media literacy are part of what we now call new literacies since the mainstream increased different usages of technologies in the early 1990s. Literacy has expanded to include diverse technology and its communicative processes. Visual literacy as an overarching umbrella "is the ability to comprehend and create images in a variety of media in order to communicate effectively" (www.boydsmillspress.com/poetry3.tpl). To be more specific, visual literacy, defined originally by the International Visual Literacy Association, is

> (A) group of vision competencies a human being can develop by seeing and at the same time having and integrating other sensory experiences. The development of these competencies is fundamental to normal human learning. When developed, they enable a visually literate person to discriminate and interpret the visual actions, objects, and/or symbols, natural or man-made, that are [encountered] in [the] environment. Through the creative use of these competencies, [we are] able to communicate with others. Through the appreciative use of these competencies, [we are] able to comprehend and enjoy the masterworks of visual communications (Fransecky & Debes, 1972, p. 7). (International Visual Literacy Association, 2002, www.ivla.org/organization/whatis.htm)

Visual literacy is a key component of several NCTE Standards, particularly 1, 8, 11, and 12 (NCTE/IRA, 1996). The cognitive and aesthetic benefits of visual literacy (e.g., see *Four aspects of visual literacy* for Messaris' four propositions at http://www.siue.edu/~jandris/it590002/messaris1.html) are unquestionable. Yet as preservice methods instructors, student teacher supervisors, and in-service workshop facilitators who have visited hundreds of classrooms, it has become obvious to us that many teachers have little idea about or are just beginning to understand how to promote new literacies effectively to enhance curriculum as tools that lead to oral and written proficiency. We offer teachers, librarians, reading specialists, and parents help in teaching their students to become more visually literate and to recognize that visual literacy is not only a necessary teaching tool but also a survival tool today. We explore all types of media as text; we use film as a strategy for teaching reading, writing, speaking, listening, and viewing; and we develop curriculum that integrates media and literature and film as literature. We advocate that teachers become familiar with texts and websites such as Richard Beach's at the University of Minnesota Twin Cities for models of how current theory and practice in these new literacies are integrated (http://www.tc.umn.edu/~rbeach/teachingmedia/index.htm).

Defining Critical Media Literacy

Critical media literacy is the application of a deconstructionist framework to media images that attempts to understand the subtext of sociopolitical agendas as they attempt to construct identities. Media literacy lessons benefit students with access, analysis, evaluation, and creating skills. Like visual literacy, critical media literacy crosses into academia through technology, history, mass communications, journalism, foreign languages, women's studies, and English. According to Diedra Downs, Executive Director, Downs Media Education Center, Santa Fe, NM:

> Comprehensive media education is the most exciting trend in school reform today. It leads our children, and eventually our society, to become media literate. Media literacy is defined as the ability to access, analyze, evaluate and produce information through a variety of mass media forms. Mass media includes radio, television, film periodicals and books (including text books), newspapers, computer on-line and interactive technologies, cultural environments (shopping malls, freeways, cereal boxes, etc.), popular music, and emerging technologies up to and including Virtual Reality. (http://www.chamisamesa.net/time2.html)

Our secondary English methods courses require that preservice teachers incorporate media and media instruction into their lesson and unit plans; media literacy is an integral part of our English education program and standards. Students in our program are encouraged to visit the Alliance for a Media Literate America (AMLA) website[1] and study examples of plans developed by this organization to promote critical media literacy skills. A current example I used in my methods class was the unit provided on Hurricane Katrina developed by Faith Rogow with the AMLA Board of Directors (http://www.amlainfo.org/home/resources/hurricane-media-literacy). This unit includes strategies and techniques we value in teacher preparation: a solid rationale for teaching this unit, media literacy teaching tips, critical thinking questions, grade-level appropriateness, and cross-disciplinary instruction. We believe in strong models like this one for how our students should be designing unit plans. We concur with the AMLA that

> Media literacy empowers people to be both critical thinkers and creative producers of an increasingly wide range of messages using image, language, and sound. It is the skillful application of literacy skills to media and technology messages. As communication technologies transform society, they impact our understanding of ourselves, our communities, and our diverse cultures, making media literacy an essential life skill for the 21st century. (Alliance for a Media Literate America website)

A similar unit sj has taught in preservice methods was designed to help students develop cultural and critical lenses by viewing images of people from Hurricane Katrina. sj projected an image from a PowerPoint slideshow of eight African-Americans, without a caption, exiting what appeared to be a sporting goods store in downtown New Orleans—a place traditionally habited by a large African-American population. sj then asked students to create a chart and reflect on what they suspect the caption might read if written by the media. sj then asked them to consider what other captions might read had the people all been senior citizens, Asian, queer, firefighters, teens, or white. Students inferred negative captions about African-Americans and teens using such adjectives as "stealing" and "looting." For senior citizens and firefighters they inferred positive phrases such as "helping others" and "getting necessities." For homosexuals they inferred stereotypical yet lighthearted terms such as "shopping" or "decorating." They were stumped on what terms the media would use for Asians but said it would likely be positive. For white people they inferred such adjectives as "taking" or "obtaining." Upon hearing each other's answers and how similar they were to one another, the class became infuriated at how images in the media perpetuate stereotypes of individuals. It was obvious to sj that there was something here that merited more attention and that students had expert knowledge on media distortions that sj could build upon throughout the remainder of the course. In fact, most students referred to the Katrina exercise throughout the course as a touchstone to reference how they were viewing images in the media and interpreting texts.

➡*Teaching Points*

∞Methods Courses and Secondary Classrooms

Relevant and Controversial Media

We would encourage all teachers to select something relevant and controversial in the media and attempt to duplicate such an activity. This will build tools instantly as students share their answers and listen to each other's mostly already informed impressions. The answers shared will spark conversation and open up the floor for students to challenge each other. The English educator should be prepared to work with all of the stereotypes that emerge and build them into their curricular units.

We see a unit such as this in several phases. In the first phase, some key questions will set the tone for unpacking the media images. The instructor might ask students about Where do they think stereotypes begin? How are they reinforced? What stereotypes affect people negatively? How are they disseminated? How can we interrupt the cycle? The class can then move to more complex issues with other film clips such as asking what is the media's role in perpetuating stereotypes? How does the media challenge stereotypes? What positive examples can you think of that show how the media attempts to subvert the status quo? In the last phase, students can do a project that builds upon some of these questions by looking for examples in the media and presenting it to the class. Additional considerations for a project such as this might include the following: describe the ethics of the clips, describe the intended audience, describe who you would be careful about viewing such a clip and why, explain the appeal of the clip, describe what audience is marginalized from such a clip, why might the clip be seen as detestable, and describe the sociopolitical messages of the clip.

Websites with Pictures and Resources from Hurricane Katrina

http://www.amlainfo.org/
http://www.noahswish.org/Hurricane%20Katrina.htm
http://www.icfj.org/ http://www.allianceonline.org/katrina.page

Film Literacy

We also require that our preservice teachers have more than a rudimentary knowledge of how to use film in their classrooms:

> What do we mean when we talk about film literacy? When we talk about "literacy" we usually mean a certain level of decoding skills, comprehension skills, vocabulary, and an ability to apply a wide range of reading conventions from knowing we read left to right, top to bottom, to the use of literary metaphor and symbol to make meaning from a written text. Also context and purpose often determine the levels at which we do this. So it seems logical to think about visual literacy as using certain decoding skills, comprehension skills, vocabulary, and certain conventions to get meaning from a text. When we read film then, what might be the decoding skills we need? Comprehension skills? Vocabulary skills? Conventions? Yes, all of these are necessary for a student to learn to be film/visually literate. Visual texts call for a different type of literacy, since they have the power to manipulate viewers through multisensory images. (Norris & Johnson, 2002)

Teaching Film Literacy and Why It Needs to Be Taught

Most of us need a methodology for showing movies in our classrooms for several reasons, probably the most important of those being that film is exciting to watch and/or fun to create. Our students are often more enthusiastic about engaging with film than they are with traditional texts like books and plays. We know that adolescents spend hundreds of hours glued to HBO and spend hundreds of dollars going to the movies or renting them. They now have digital cameras in their cell phones. Clearly, bringing film into the classroom is a great way to connect with them and their world. That said, we also have the responsibility as teachers to educate students to see movies as much more than entertainment or much less, as an opportunity to zone out in class. Therefore, we also need to share strategies and tools for making meaning from movies just as we teach our students to think, write, and speak critically about the literature they read. The possibilities for teaching films in the classroom are now as wide and endless as they are for teaching books or plays. Film adds another dimension to the problem posing and solving that is often connected with reading and writing. Students also like to make movies, so we encourage our preservice teachers to know as much as they can about film study and filmmaking so that they can provide this as a choice or an alternative when evaluating secondary students' literacy progress.

Issue #2: Training Teachers to Use Film

Introducing Students (and Their Teachers) to Film Study

Our readers might be familiar with Teasley and Wilder's *Reel Conversations* (1997), Golden's *Reading in the Dark* (2001), or Costanzo's *Great Films and How to Teach Them* (2004). We suggest these as starter texts for educators like us who want to gain a finer appreciation for integrating film alone or with literature and composition. We also strongly suggest the use of documentaries and John Golden's latest book, *Reading in the Reel World: Teaching Documentaries and Other Non-fiction Texts* (2006), for teaching the elements of nonfiction film in the secondary classroom.[2] We've witnessed too many classrooms where film and literature are juxtaposed in unproductive ways, for example, as a reward for plowing through a hard text like *Hamlet*, or as a filler when they are winging it that day, or as the ever-popular read-the-book-then-see-the-movie comparison tactic. We insult our students' intelligence when we tell them that they should read the book because it's better than the film, and we deceive ourselves when we think our students won't rent the DVD version instead of reading the novel or play anyway.

One of the best responses a teacher can receive from a student is "I'll never view a film the same way again." We hear this reply from many of our students after a very short time of instruction on the basic vocabulary and screening of film clips. As other educators such as Golden point out, most high school students (and their teachers) have a familiarity with the basic literary vocabulary of plot, setting, character, and theme; but when we expand students' literacy to include film study with new terminology including types of angles, shots, lighting, sound, and mise-en-scene, we can write and discuss at another intellectual level if not a higher one. And as students (and teachers) become comfortable with film terms and seeing these terms come alive on the screen, they actually use them as well if not better than traditional literary definitions.

➡*Teaching Points*

∞Methods Courses

Here are a few basic ways I ask preservice teachers to begin thinking about how to use film differently in their classrooms and to actively start incorporating movies and film clips into their existing or new curriculum.

Guiding Principles

1. *Watch current and classic movies and television.* This is what our students are doing with much of their out-of-class time, and it is one of the ways we can best relate with what's happening in their world. When we know about their favorite media including films, songs, and television shows, we can better connect with them.
2. *View films actively and with goals in mind.* This is what we do when we are preparing to teach selected literature. It is easy to be a passive receptor of a film, and sometimes that's a good purpose for going to the movies or reading a book, to escape from our daily routines and concerns. But when we are using film as a method of instruction, we need to ask ourselves questions while watching the film and think about other films we have seen that might be challenging matches for the one we are currently considering for classroom study, just like we coordinate other kinds of texts for our students to read.
3. *Play with combinations of ideas.* Sometimes one film is enough to see and discuss in its entirety, just like one novel may be sufficient for examining a variety of literary terms, techniques, and devices. But other times we need two or three entire films or five film clips from five different movies to get to our goal, just as we might select a collection of short stories or poems to expand our students' thinking.
4. *Come up with a solid plan.* Our lesson, unit, or course plan has to include meaningful core questions, rich assignments that are worth doing and that push students to higher levels of thinking, and fair assessments with sensible grading rubrics.

➡*Teaching Points*

∞Methods and Secondary Courses

We might also use the framework of an overarching topic question or inquiry that could explore different combinations of films, for example:

Topic: Based on true stories—*Walk the Line, Hotel Rwanda, The Elephant Man, Saving Private Ryan, Glory, The Right Stuff*
Topic: Special Effects—any of the superhero films: *X-Men, Spiderman, Superman Returns; War of the Worlds*, any *Harry Potter*, any *Lord of the Rings*
Topic: Study of culture or time period—*Gosford Park, Shakespeare in Love, Sense and Sensibility, Bend It Like Beckham*
Topic: Death—*The Green Mile, Gladiator, Titanic, My Girl, The Andromeda Strain*
Topic: Gender Roles or Role Reversal—*Freaky Friday, Whale Rider, The Color Purple*
Topic: Kevin Spacey [or insert favorite actor here] films—*The Life of David Gale, Shipping News, Pay It Forward, K-Pax, American Beauty, A Bug's Life*

Topic: Parental Influences on Children—*Mrs. Doubtfire, Ordinary People, Dead Poet's Society*

This kind of framing, working with a pool of films and/or books and some different approaches to inquiry, is just the beginning of an endless list of ways we might see any number of quality media being used in the classroom. For example, when I was watching the film *Run, Lola, Run* (1998) recently, I was inspired to think about how that film could be paired with Alan Lightman's novel *Einstein's Dreams* (1993) and the film *The Lake House* (2006) for a unique unit about time and different scenarios for the same story. All of these works do that, and this combination would be a strong one for teaching students how they can begin with an image in their thinking or writing and come up with different combinations of plots or endings on their own. I explain to our preservice teachers that whichever way they choose to use film as a teaching tool, keep these four guiding principles in mind:

➡*Teaching Points*

∞Methods and Secondary Courses

Guiding Principles

1. *Know your students.* What are your students' passions? What do they do for fun? What are their hobbies? What school activities to they participate in? I provide a survey (see appendix A at the end of this chapter) on the first day of class so that I can get to know students better and plan my course with what students are familiar with so they become engaged and successful right away. This helps us to build a community of learners who know each other and who have common interests or who can learn from others with different backgrounds and hobbies.

2. *Know your parents and community.* What film ratings will be allowed in your school and which might you have to have a letter of consent for? For example, in the Teasley and Wilder book we learned that the state of North Carolina will not permit the showing of any film rated R in any school situation. They advise educators to know federal, state, and local board of education rulings on fair use provisions and copyright laws. Keep the lines of communication open with your students' parents/guardians so they understand why you have chosen to show films in your classroom and why their teenagers may want to discuss them further at home.

3. *Know your curriculum parameters.* Before incorporating films into your curriculum, beginning teachers especially may want to discuss the use of movie clips just as you would the use of other texts with your department coordinator or principal.

4. *Have a sound, meaningful rationale.* If we teach our preservice teachers anything in our methods courses, it is to always, always ask themselves,

Why am I teaching this? What are my goals and purposes for using this film or film clip in my class? Would anything else work as effectively? Is the movie clearly connected to the concepts I want to teach? Does it make sense and is it worth the class time to show it?

5. *Consider the best way to introduce texts.* My student teachers, when comparing a book with a documentary or contrasting two film clip versions of the same Shakespearean play, will often naively go from the more difficult to the easier one instead of the other way around. When I question them on why they want to do this, they often don't readily know; some suggest that it is the way their teachers taught them, or they say we have to get through the written text first or do the correct chronological progression followed by the movie version or the newer version as the back-up for what students didn't understand in the printed text or older film. It is our responsibility to help them to know the best ways to use media, film, and print texts, so we challenge them to reconsider their choices and goals. Why do we have to do it the harder way and turn students off? Why can't we as twenty-first century educators facilitate learning the ways our students understand communication best and connect with right away, then work with them on texts that are less familiar and more difficult to comprehend?

All these principles will help new teachers to plan and implement meaningful, productive, and appropriate uses of films as texts in their classes. The following pages will reveal how to plan more specific units or courses using these basic techniques.

Issue #3: Designing a Unit or Course around Film Study

I encourage teachers to attend workshops, speak to other university professors and media specialists like Renee Hobbs and Elizabeth Thoman, and to read Bishop (1999), Considine and Haley (1999), and Wilhelm and Smith (Smith & Wilhelm, 2006; Wilhelm, 1997, 2004) who write about the successes they have had with designing courses and workshops around movie themes and messages. In the loaded matrix, school culture is a fascinating visual literacy topic for training teachers in secondary English education, especially since there are so many movies available that include school settings. Considering film as text, I designed a course for preservice and experienced teachers called "The Culture of School in American Film." I was curious about how Hollywood presents American school culture, which brings us to a key point in our methodology for promoting critical media skills: teachers should choose a film and literature exploration that they and their students are really curious about, something they really want to understand on a deeper level with their students, such as school culture, family relationships, heroism, or leadership. I chose Golden's *Reading in the Dark* (2001), Teasley and Wilder's *Reel Conversations* (1997), and Sharon Crowley's *A Teacher's Introduction to Deconstruction* (1989) to help teachers analyze film and to develop a vocabulary to talk about film. I posed several questions and ideas to explore with my fellow teachers, for example, Are male and female teachers equally in control of their classes in school culture films? How is lighting used in the comedy genre of school culture film versus another genre like horror? Do we see patterns in the groups of students in school culture films from the 1960s to the 1990s? What is an "inspirational teacher film" and how does it compare with your notions of an inspirational teacher?

One goal in examining American school culture films with our preservice teachers is to introduce them and their students to a range of schoolteachers, students, administrators, and staff and have them discuss what is being promoted and marginalized in these texts. Teasley and Wilder (1997) suggest a unique way to help students begin to see or to read film. They suggest that teachers help students first look at film using literary conventions (plot, theme, characterization, setting, motif) that they already know. Then they move to looking at dramatic conventions (dialog, costuming, directing, makeup, casting), and finally those conventions that are called cinematic (type of shots, camera angles, camera movement, duration of shots, sound) and represent those aspects, which can only appear in film (Teasley and Wilder, 1997). I ask my preservice teachers to look at the literary, dramatic, and cinematic elements in these films besides paying attention to camera shots and special visual and sound effects similar to directing them to examine textual conventions of dialog, description, characterization, symbols, and themes in the books they read. I integrate films and books that span different decades to show contrasts in how teachers and students dress, act, and what their main issues and concerns are. Students also can compare book and film versions of the same text like *Dangerous Minds* by Louanne Johnson (1995) with the film version (1995) to consider what is marginalized in these texts. I also select different school locations and try to get both male and female lead teachers and students and as diverse groups of teachers and students as possible. For that, I use clips and chunks of the following films:

Boyz 'N the Hood, 1991, Columbia Pictures, Dir. John Singleton, R, 107 min.
Carrie, 1976, United Artists, Dir. Brian De Palma, R, 98 min.
Dangerous Minds, 1995, Buena Vista Pictures, Dir. John N. Smith, R, 99 min.
Dead Poet's Society, 1989, Touchstone Pictures, Dir. Peter Weir, PG, 128 min.
High School High, 1996, TriStar Pictures, Dir. Hart Bochner, PG-13, 86 min.
Higher Learning, 1995, Columbia Pictures, Dir. John Singleton, R, 127 min.
Lean On Me, 1989, Warner Bros., Dir. John G. Avildsen, PG-13, 104 min.
Matilda, 1996, TriStar Pictures, Dir. Danny DeVito, PG, 102 min.
Renaissance Man, 1994, Touchstone Pictures, Dir. Penny Marshall, PG-13, 128 min.
Stand and Deliver, 1988, Warner Bros., Dir. Ramon Menendez, PG, 102 min.
Teachers, 1984, United Artists, Dir. Arthur Hiller, R, 106 min.
The Breakfast Club, 1985, Universal Pictures, Dir. John Hughes, R, 97 min.
The Substitute 2, 1998, Live Entertainment, Dir. Steven Pearl, R, 89 min.

To Sir, With Love, 1967, Columbia Pictures, Dir. James Clavell, NR, 105 min. (This British film, rated PG in the United Kingdom, takes place in a London high school with a lead African-American actor [Sidney Poitier] playing a Guyanese teacher.)
Up the Down Staircase, 1967, Dir. Robert Mulligan, NR, 124 min.

Encouraging students to raise questions about what they observe creates an awareness in preservice teachers of teaching practices and philosophies and what kinds of teaching and learning communities are promoted in and outside of Hollywood.

Student teacher candidates become very adept at analyzing film as text very fast, but they don't necessarily have to analyze everything at once. For example, I could introduce a concept like camera angles and make sure students understand what the angles are and why they might be used before they studied a film clip with close-ups or long shots. Or we might talk about films they have already seen that they recognize as examples of high and low lighting techniques before I show another for them to analyze. At the conclusion of each class, we all write a one-page response to anything we learned about visual literacy and the portrayals of school culture we see in the film clips we watch and discuss in class. Later, I require that they choose a film about school culture and share a twenty-minute presentation including a film clip they thought was powerful to demonstrate what they learned.

Lighting and What Acazia Taught Us

In one class with preservice teachers, we discuss different effects produced by high and low lighting. We watch two scenes from *Psycho* (1960), for example, one shot in broad daylight and compare it to an indoor night scene. Students recognize the differences in mood and tone right away. In the next class, Acazia decided to use a film clip from *A Beautiful Mind* (2001) to show us what she learned about the value of lighting. She played for us the opening scene where we see mathematician John Nash (Russell Crowe) for the first time in a classroom at Princeton. It is evident in this scene that half of Nash's face is easy to see because it is lit from the sunlight coming from the window to his left; the right side of his face, in stark contrast, is hidden in shadow. The light splits his face into two distinct halves, sending us a subliminal but powerful message about his split personality, even before we know anything about Nash's life or what will unfold as the film progresses. Many of us who saw this entire film, before Acazia decided to use this clip to teach us something about lighting, were positively awestruck when she pointed out this subtle yet dynamic clue to John Nash's personality. We now saw something we didn't see at first glance. Just as revisiting a favorite book teaches us something new each time we read it, so do films bring new insights when we take time to examine them more deeply. We are always amazed at what our students can teach us when we give them a few simple tools to be more aware of visual cues themselves.

Camera Angles and Sound

In teaching any methods class about ways to use film more critically, I begin with a hands-on technique that Golden advocates: roll up a piece of paper and look through it, rolling the hole bigger and smaller, to see different camera angles—the close-up, long shot, and medium shot. The paper lens can also illustrate high angle and low angle shots by standing on a chair looking down and by sitting on the floor looking up, respectively. When students do this for themselves, they immediately understand why cinematographers use different shots for different effects besides the fact that they are engaged and have fun trying this. Right after this mini-lesson, I show the class a film clip from *Matilda* (1996) where Matilda goes to school and meets the principal, Miss Trunchbull, for the first time. Students were immediately able to not only point out which camera angles were used, but they understood readily why the director chose a low angle shot to represent Miss Trunchbull's ominous and dreadful nature and why a close-up of her grimacing face made the students fear her. It is important to teach a film technique and then show an example right away so students can apply what they have learned (Golden, 2001). Students will see other things besides what you ask them to look for in the film clip. For example, in this five-minute scene in *Matilda*, there are lots of other great things to watch such as the metaphor of school as a prison and a dungeon illustrated by the school rooms and buildings, the innocence of the children by the colors they wear (lots of white and pink) contrasted with the prison warden uniform of Miss Trunchbull, and the way the camera uses high angles and low lighting on Matilda suggesting her helplessness and timidity.

Another method I have used to teach angles and what they can mean is to show a short film of a baby climbing steps from a video I obtained from the nmec.org entitled *Know TV* (Hobbs, 1996, video clip number 4). We watch the different high and low angle shots of a child climbing the stairs, and we talk about what we observed. Right away the discussion centers on the huge task climbing from the bottom of the stairs to the top is for the child from the low angle point of view of the child. When the baby looks back down the stairs at the end of his climb from the high angle shot, students notice the sense of achievement and relief the child experiences. So they begin to see that camera angles hold the message of a film and that they are important and deliberate for a reason. From this short example, we turn immediately to a more popular mainstream film they may recognize, *About Schmidt* (2002), starring Jack Nicholson, and ask them to watch the opening scene before any credits come up. In about two minutes of film, students observe the high and low angle shots of a dreary industrial city, buildings towering over the landscape, and a giant sign on one of the towers, "Woodmen," where Nicholson's character is about to retire at 5:00. They make immediate connections that the angles used express the cold, hard, power-hungry, and impersonal world of the city and that buildings are more important than people. I mention to the students that it is not necessary to know what a film is about or to have to watch the entire movie to appreciate one aspect of film and what it can reveal. I explain that it is not important whether they like it or want to see all of it, either. What matters most is that through these short models, students can apply this basic knowledge to other films and recognize the intentionality of certain cinematic techniques.

Next, we listen to sound and consider why it is an essential cinematic element. Again I select clip number 5 from the *Know TV* video, "Music and Emotion," which contains a scene of two monkeys in the trees. First we watch the thirty-second clip that has no sound while I invite students to imagine what they heard in the background. Some describe jungle sounds that might be close to something we'd hear on the Discovery channel; some select a popular song like "Jungle Boogie," which is upbeat and humorous. A majority of students see this film as jovial, light, and playful, so they select sounds that match that mood. But occasionally I have a student who questions the action of the scene and suggests that the actions of the two monkeys may not be amusing but could be signaling danger or evil. I ask how the sound would differ in that case. We then listen to two soundtracks as the same scene plays again twice through; the first is as most have predicted, a flute that makes a light and airy melody as the two chimps frolic in the jungle. But the second, a heavy, piercing string melody, suggests the monkeys are escaping quickly from some kind of danger in the rainforest. Students immediately understand the value of a soundtrack and what it contributes to mood setting.

➡Teaching Points

∞Methods Classes and Secondary Classrooms

Generating Questions to Talk about Film

One of the most important skills a new teacher can learn to engage secondary students, yet one of the most difficult for them to initiate and sustain, is how to have a good discussion (Holden & Schmit, 2002; Meeks & Austin, 2003). In our teaching literature and reading methods class, we talk about how students can generate questions about what they are reading or viewing and how teachers can model questioning to help students raise questions that range from recall to synthesis to application. Using the film *Good Will Hunting* (1997), an activity we try is to watch the DVD clip that takes place in the Harvard Bar (about five minutes); I ask the class to focus on what Will (Matt Damon) and his rival Clark are saying that reflects their views about education. After viewing the clip, students are handed index cards and asked to write one or two questions for discussion that they think would be important to talk about with other members of the class concerning this part of the movie. I collect the cards and have them form small groups where their questions are distributed at random; students can choose one or two questions to which they would like to share answers with the rest of the class after they have had time to talk in their groups. The teacher can make a handout from the questions students raised and bring it to class the next day so that students can see the range of questions other students posed or possibly use those questions for a writing response the next day. A sample of some of the questions my students had after viewing this clip were these:

- Will seems to come off very well read but doesn't seem to care about getting a degree. Why do you think he feels this way?

- Matt Damon's character is the smarter one, but because he is not wealthy, he does not have the same chances. How does a family's income relate to the quality of education they receive?

- What is your opinion on whether or not a degree is a measure of success in life?

- What are the different meanings of education in this scene? Who is education more important to, Will or Clark? Does having a degree necessarily mean you are an intelligent person?

- Will is obviously a very knowledgeable person having gained information from various sources. He chooses to show this off while in the bar yet hides it otherwise. Why do you think he struggles to let himself be known as intelligent around his friends? Why would he not further this knowledge with a formal education?

- Why does Will ask Clark to step outside after he was done verbally humiliating him? Wasn't his intelligence enough to embarrass Clark? Why does he still feel the need to use physical violence?

- Will seems to struggle between his upbringing and his intellectual potential. Do you think that is why Skylar is attracted to him?

- How do you think Clark felt as a college student being outsmarted by a noncollege student? How would you feel?

- Why didn't Will step into the discussion between Clark and Chuckie earlier instead of when he did?

- What does the title *Good Will Hunting* have to do with this scene? Was Will "hunting" for something at the bar, or was he just trying to be "good" helping his friend out?

We can also model examples of discussion questions to help preservice teachers learn how to promote in-depth thinking and response by using five short scenes from the movie *American Beauty* (1999). In this lesson, we also read excerpts from Alan Ball's screenplay (Ball, 1999) that match the film clips either before or after viewing the scenes. In my experience, asking students to read whole or parts of screenplays along with viewing the film is a novelty most have never tried in a secondary classroom. I strongly advocate using screenplays for their value in teaching about dialog, stage directions, and camera techniques, and they often include photographs from the movie and storyboards that are especially interesting for high-visual learners and students who may want to create their own storyboards.[3] Note that this Best Picture is R-rated, but teachers could choose another picture for secondary students like *What's Eating Gilbert Grape?* (PG-13, 1993) and generate similar small-group discussion questions. Small groups can then share their responses with the larger class to obtain different perspectives and points of view.

1. What are the parents like in these scenes? What are their children like? If the saying is true that "the apple doesn't fall far from the tree," what predictions could we make about how these children might turn out? Do you think it's possible that these parents could change from the way we see them in these scenes? Why or why not?

2. The film was clearly named *American Beauty* on purpose. These two words take on many connotations throughout this film. In the short scenes we've seen and read from the screenplay, what did you observe that seemed American or anti-American? And what did you think about how beauty is being defined so far and how it is contrasted with things that are ugly?

3. This film might be described as a "dark comedy" or tragic-comedy. Point to places in the screenplay that your group thought were strangely comic or funny yet also sad or even tragic. Steven Spielberg said that he was amazed at the "raw truth" of this screenplay. What do you think the raw truths in these scenes are?

4. What do you think the white bag represents? Why do you think Ricky says that there is no reason to ever be afraid after he films the bag? See if you can find other examples in the screenplay excerpt where "fear" words are mentioned. What is the "fear" (or "fears") that this screenplay is about?

5. Of these five short screenplay scenes, which one was the most believable and which was the most unrealistic in your group's opinion? You might look at factors like the use of language and say whether you have ever heard people talk like this or not. Or you might look at the setting and say whether people actually live like this or not. Or you might also look at the characters' behavior and say whether people would really act like this or not. Do people really talk, live, and act like this? If not, why do you think screenplay writer Alan Ball wrote this play? And if so, show us which scene is the most real.

Designing a Lesson Using Film Study

⇒*Teaching Points*

∞Methods Courses

We also use film clips in secondary English methods courses when a short scene really captures a teaching technique or point better than any other visual method like PowerPoint or a transparency can. In reading methods, sj introduced literary criticism through film by showing a clip from *Legally Blonde* (2001). The idea behind such an activity is that it promotes awareness about how dominant culture reads and sees images in the media so that preservice teachers can challenge dominant views and images that perpetuate hegemony and reinforce stereotypes. Additionally, it hones several lenses at once so that we no longer see the world myopically but have other tools to critically read images in the media. Reading with several theories in mind can help us broaden our scope and recognition about how others view or read the world. The scene shows Reese Witherspoon's video application to Harvard Law School in which she challenges how people are admitted to law school by using a video application and challenges an application committee's beliefs through how she uses "valley-girl-like" discourse that sits outside of the normative expectations that one might expect from someone who is applying to a school of prestige.

sj showed the clip once and asked students what their initial reading of the clip was in the tradition of Rosenblatt's reader-response theory. After each student made some type of connection or contestation with the clip, sj then asked what stereotypes they observed about blonds and asked how the main character, Elle, played by Witherspoon, also challenged dominant stereotypes. sj then handed out explanations about different kinds literary criticisms and had a lengthy discussion about what each meant.

Literary Criticism

Reader-Response Criticism

- examines reader's reaction to text as central to interpretation;
- examines author's interactions with outside world.

Sociological Criticism

- work cannot be separated from social context in which it was created;
- literature reflects society and derives existence from social institutions to which it responds.

Feminist Criticism (late 1960s)

- focuses on negative female stereotypes in books (and constructed in relation to patriarchal values) and points out alternative feminine characteristics suggested by women authors;
- focuses on woman as the reader and the author and *her* response to the text.

Marxist Criticism

- readings on social and economic theories of Marx and Engels;
- looks at class struggles, power, and money.

New Historicism

- focuses on texts in relation to historical and cultural contexts of the period in which it was critically evaluated.

Psychoanalytic Criticism

- focuses on inner workings of the mind by focusing on character or author analysis.

Deconstruction

- begins with the assumption that texts are social constructions;
- argues that every text contains within it some ingredient which undermines its purported system of meaning ... in other words, it is unstable because it depends on conclusions of a particular theory to hold the text together;
- helps individuals make meaning of how systems oppress them.

Post-Modernism and Post-Structuralism

- began around the 1920s;
- meaning is fluid and changes in space and time;
- meaning can be found in negotiation toward or against something.

They watch the clip again, and this time sj hands out a chart (see appendix B) and asks students to insert an answer about how the clip can be viewed through these eight lenses. For preservice teachers, this is an effective tool that instructs them on how to introduce their students to different ways of reading texts. sj encourages them to find clips that the students can understand on a literal level. Once they've established an understanding of these lenses, they can apply them to text.

Speech and Communications

In my Speech and Communications for Secondary Teachers course, preservice teachers study and discuss Deborah Tannen's gender theories on how men and women communicate with one another (Tannen, 2001, 2004). We also read Virginia O'Keefe's work (O'Keefe, 1995) on how to teach students to communicate, and we observe various forms of verbal and nonverbal communication including metamessaging, codes, and gestures. Students write a short paper analyzing the style and techniques from a conversation they are able to observe either live or from a movie or television clip.

After they explore some of Tannen's notions about how women and men communicate, I model one way to complete the assignment by asking the class to watch a short scene from Sofia Coppola's Academy Award winning screenplay *Lost in Translation* (2003). The husband (Giovanni Ribisi) and wife (Scarlett Johannsen) meet a young starlet in a Tokyo hotel where they are both staying; the wife is ultimately ignored by the starlet until close to end of the conversation with the husband. After the class watches this scene together, we pair up and talk about the language and body movements they observed, and I ask them to interpret what they've seen. I note that it is not important that they know about this picture in terms of the plot or setting, or that they have seen it in its entirety; what matters most is that this particular three-minute conversation is interesting and relevant to the purposes of analyzing speech and gesture to better comprehend communications, the main goal of this lesson and an integral part of this course. Students become thoroughly engaged in their pair discussion and are able to respond in meaningful ways to the large group session that follows the pair share for several reasons, not the least of which are that they identify with the people in the film clip by dress, age, manner, and conversational style. They are able to see and recall techniques we have discussed previously with regard to Tannen's assumptions; and they are empowered to draw conclusions about both the obvious and more subtle nuances of the characters' interactions. For a follow-up assignment, Ethan designed an effective lesson on characterization using the opening scene from *Falling Down* (1993) by asking our class to follow the body movement, gestures, and facial expressions of Michael Douglas's character before he speaks and as he speaks.

Issue #4: R-Rated Films and Is a Rating Really the Issue?

Visual literacy and critical media studies including film, television, and music videos can work effectively in the secondary English classroom because they are an integral part of our students' cultures and identities. Providing new teachers with multiliteracy skills and tools empowers them to connect with students' interests and lives outside of school and allows them to create innovative lesson plans, units, and assessments that students will find demanding, yet worthwhile and connected to the world. Even though secondary students have seen many current films and television programs that we may or may not be familiar with, they are probably not the best judges of what should be watched at home or in the classroom, until they learn to view film and other media with an educated eye. The teacher Ethan observed may have had the best intentions attempting to appease and reward her students by allowing them to watch a film of their choice; but Ethan observed that most of them were not "actively" watching it, probably because they had already seen everything they thought they knew about it before. The teacher in this class did not require anything from her students that would help them to advance intellectually. Ethan reflected that if we do not help students to (re)see films and other forms of media in new ways, we are wasting their time and ours. Furthermore, we may do harm to our students intentionally or not when we allow them to view certain genres or subjects that may be beyond them developmentally or that may negatively affect them physically, emotionally, or psychologically.

In our methods class we discussed what Ethan observed and if *Scream 3* could have been an acceptable choice, although the majority of Ethan's peers felt that they would not show this film in a secondary classroom because of its rating, language, and violence and because it was the third film in a trilogy of horror spoofs that students may not have been previously familiar with or have had any prior knowledge about. Other class members did not want to rule out the value of using possible clips from the film if they provided proper background information and were illustrating points about the horror genre and why this film mocked it, or if they were comparing other films by director Wes Craven, or comparing Craven's directing style to another director like Tim Burton. These preservice teachers brought up the notion of the horror genre's popularity with adolescents and that other films like Burton's *Edward Scissorhands*, *Beetlejuice*, or *Nightmare Before Christmas* (rated PG or PG-13) or Golden's suggestions to use the original *Frankenstein* and *Bride of Frankenstein* (Golden, 2001, p. 123), both Not Rated, might be alternate choices. We concluded with a short discussion about how important it is to take risks and incorporate the popular culture into the secondary English classroom, but only when teachers have reasonable and appropriate goals and their or their students' selections raise students' awareness and capabilities to comprehend media and why and how it is constructed. We agreed that we have seen R-rated films and television programs that are milder in persistent violence, drug use, sexually oriented nudity, and harsh language than some PG-13 rated movies, so a rating cannot be the main reason a teacher would choose to show or not show a film in class. We also agreed that where there might be any debate about why a new teacher would use any print or non-print text in a secondary classroom, the selection should be discussed with a mentor teacher or department chair and a permission form should be sent home to be signed and returned before teaching the lesson or unit with alternatives ready if a parent has any objections to the teacher's choices.

Conclusion

It is our duty as teacher educators to train teachers to make students more aware of and more thoughtful about the familiar digital and electronic means they use to learn in and outside of school. Similar to book clubs, teachers can encourage students and their parents to form film or media study groups or clubs with them in which they could attend a screening together and visit a local restaurant, coffee house, or home afterwards to talk about what they viewed (Lehman & Luhr, 1999; McNulty, 1999; Vanderveld, 2004; Vaux, 1999). Secondary teachers should be permitted to use any and all applicable media in their classes, but PG-13 and R-rated film clips and controversial media must be used carefully, when teachers are informed about the state laws that apply, when they have secured permission to show them from the secondary students' parents or guardians if the subject matter is questionable, and most importantly, if they have a sound rationale for teaching them.

Appendix A

Sample Student Interest Survey

Name

Grade or Semester/Year

City, State, Country

What are some of your interests?

What do you do for fun?

Why are you taking this class?

What are one or two of your favorite books and/or favorite movies and why are they your favorites?

How do you learn best? And least?

What do you plan to do after high school (college)?

Can you do word processing? Use PowerPoint? Use a video camera?

Have you ever had a film or media study class? If yes, please describe it.

What films have you seen that have school culture in them (e.g., *Dangerous Minds*, *Dead Poet's Society*, *Carrie*, *High School High*, *Billy Madison*, *Harry Potter and the Sorcerer's Stone*, *Grease*, *Lean on Me*, *Stand and Deliver*, etc.)?

Choose one school film you've seen and write something you learned from watching it.

Appendix B

Literary Criticism Chart

Text title:

Reader-response criticism	Socio-logical criticism	Feminist criticism	Marxist criticism	New historic-ism	Psycho-analytic criticism	Decon-struction	Post-modern and post-structural-ism

Notes

1 http://www.amlainfo.org/ "The Alliance for a Media Literate America (AMLA) is committed to promoting media literacy education that is focused on critical inquiry, learning, and skill-building. This national, grassroots membership organization is a key force in bringing media literacy education to all 60 million students in the United States, their parents, their teachers, and others who care about youth." (Retrieved July 17, 2006 from the AMLA website.)

2 I learned about this text from the "High School Matters" session at the 2005 National Council of Teachers of English (NCTE) Convention in Pittsburgh, PA. John Golden presented our roundtable (Alan Teasley was also present) with a preview handout of his book on teaching documentaries. One of the best suggestions I can make to those in our profession is to attend sessions like these and talk directly with those who are making an impact in secondary English film pedagogy.

3 Other Academy Award winning screenplays I recommend in whole or in part are *The Green Mile* (Darabont, 1999), *A Beautiful Mind* (Goldsman, 2002), *Shakespeare in Love* (Norman & Stoppard, 1998), and *Good Will Hunting* (Damon & Affleck, 1997).

References

Arndt, S. (Producer). Tykwer, T. (Director). (1998). *Run, Lola, Run* (*Lola rennt*) [Motion Picture]. Germany: Bavaria Film International.

Ball, A. (1999). *The shooting script: American beauty.* New York: Newmarket Press.

Beach, R. (2004). Researching response to literature and the media. In A. Goodwyn & A.W. Stables (Eds.), *Learning to read critically in language and literacy.* Thousand Oaks: Sage Publications.

______. (2006). *CI5472 Teaching film, television, and media.* Retrieved November 10, 2006, from http://www.tc.umn.edu/~rbeach/teachingmedia/index.htm.

Bender, L. (Producer). Van Sant, G. (Director). (1997). *Good Will Hunting* [Motion Picture]. United States: Miramax Films.

Besman, M., & Gittes, H. (Producers). Payne, A. (Director). (2002). *About Schmidt.* [Motion Picture]. United States: New Line Home Entertainment.

Bishop, E. (Ed.). (1999). *Cinema-(to)-graphy: Film and writing in contemporary composition courses.* Portsmouth: Boynton/Cook.

Blomquist, A.C. & Hallstrom, L. (Producers). Hallstrom, L. (Director). (1993). *What's eating Gilbert Grape?* [Motion Picture]. United States: Paramount Pictures.

Bregman, M., & Peyser, M. (Producers). DeVito, D. (Director). (1996). *Matilda.* [Motion Picture]. United States: Jersey Films.

Bruckheimer, J., & Simpson, D. (Producers). Smith, J. (Director). (1995). *Dangerous minds* [Motion Picture]. United States: Buena Vista Pictures.

Callahan, M. (2002). Intertextual composition: The power of the digital pen. *English Education, 35*(1), 46–65.

Cohen, B., & Jinks, D. (Producers). Mendes, S. (Director). (1999). *American beauty.* [Motion Picture]. United States: DreamWorks.

Considine, D. M., & Haley, G. E. (1999). *Visual messages: Integrating imagery into instruction* (2nd ed.). Englewood: Teacher Ideas Press.

Coppola, S., & Katz, R. (Producers). Coppola, S. (Director). (2003). *Lost in Translation* [Motion Picture]. United States: Universal Pictures.

Costanzo, W. V. (1992). *Reading the movies: Twelve great films on video and how to teach them.* Urbana: NCTE.

———. (2004). *Great films and how to teach them.* Urbana: NCTE.

Crowley, S. (1989). *A teacher's introduction to deconstruction.* Urbana: NCTE.

Damon, M., & Affleck, B. (1997). *Good Will Hunting: A screenplay.* New York: Miramax Books.

Darabont, F. (1999). *The green mile: The screenplay.* New York: Scribner Paperback Fiction.

Davison, D., & Lee, R. (Producers). Agresti, A. (Director). (2006). *The Lake House.* [Motion Picture]. United States: Warner Bros. Pictures.

Firek, H. (2003). *10 easy ways to use technology in the English classroom.* Portsmouth: Heinemann.

Four aspects of visual literacy. Retrieved July 17, 2006, from http://www.siue.edu/~jandris/it590002/messaris1.html.

Golden, J. (2001). *Reading in the dark: Using film as a tool in the English classroom.* Urbana: NCTE.

———. (2006). *Reading in the reel world: Teaching documentaries and other non-fiction text.* Urbana: NCTE.

Goldsman, A. (2002). *The shooting script: A beautiful mind.* New York: Newmarket Press.

Grazer, B., and Howard, R. (Producers). Howard, R. (Director). (2001). *A beautiful mind.* [Motion Picture]. United States: Universal Pictures.

Hitchcock, A. (Producer). Hitchcock, A. (Director). (1960). *Psycho* [Motion Picture]. United States: Paramount Pictures.

Hobbs, R. (1996). *Know tv: Changing what, why and how you watch.* Curriculum and Video. Bethesda: Discovery Communications.

———. (2000). *Media literacy.* New York: Newsweek Education.

———. (2003). Understanding teachers' experiences with media literacy in the classroom. In B. Duncan and K. Tyner (Eds.). *Visions/Revisions: Moving forward with media education* (pp. 100–108). Madison: National Telemedia Council.

———. (2004). A review of school-based initiatives in media literacy education. *American Behavioral Scientist, 48*(1), 42–59.

———. (2005). The state of media literacy education. (Review of books by Buckingham, Goodman, and Potter.) *Journal of Communication 55,* 865–871.

Holden, J., & Schmit, J. S. (Eds.). (2002). *Inquiry and the literary text: Constructing discussions in the English classroom.* Urbana: NCTE.

International Visual Literacy Association. (2002). Retrieved November 10, 2006, from http://www.ivla.org/organization/whatis.htm.

Johnson, L. (1995). *Dangerous minds.* New York: St. Martin's Press.

Kaywell, J. (1997). *Adolescent literature as a complement to the classics* (Vol. 3). Norwood: Christopher-Gordon Publishers.

——— (2000) *Adolescent literature as a complement to the classics* (Vol. 4). Norwood: Christopher Gordon Publishers.

Kenny, R. (2001). *Teaching tv production in a digital world: Integrating media literacy (Student Workbook).* Lincoln: GPN.

Kist, W. (2005). *New literacies in action: Teaching and learning in multiple media.* New York: Teachers College Press.

Konrad, C., Maddalena, M., & Williamson, K. (Producers). Craven, W. (Director). (2000). *Scream 3* [Motion Picture]. United States: Miramax Films.

Lankshear, C., & Knobel, M. (2003). *New literacies: Changing knowledge and classroom learning.* Philadelphia: Open University Press.

Lehman, P., & Luhr, W. (1999). *Thinking about movies: Watching, questioning, enjoying.* Orlando: Harcourt Brace & Company.

Lightman, A. (1993). *Einstein's dreams.* New York: Warner Books.

McNulty, E. (1999). *Films and faith: Forty discussion guides.* Topeka: Viaticum Press.

Meeks, L., & Austin, C. (2003). *Literacy in the secondary English classroom: Strategies for teaching the way kids learn.* Boston: Allyn and Bacon.

Miller, s. (forthcoming). Demythologizing "real"ity tv: Critical implications for a new literacy. In D. Macedo and S. Steinberg (Eds.), *Handbook of media literacy*. New York: Peter Lang.

NCTE/IRA. (1996). *Standards for the English language arts*. Urbana: NCTE and Newark: IRA.

Norman, M., & Stoppard, T. (1998). *Shakespeare in love: A screenplay*. New York: Miramax Books.

Norris, L., & Johnson, S. (2002). *The methodology of movies: How to use film to promote critical literacy in the classroom*. Unpublished manuscript.

O'Driscoll, B. (2006, March 1–8). Image conscious: Teresa Foley wants you to consider the big picture. *Pittsburgh City Paper 09*, pp. 18–22.

O'Keefe, V. (1995). *Speaking to think, thinking to speak: The importance of talk in the learning process*. Portsmouth: Heinemann Boynton/Cook.

Platt, M., & Kidney, R. (Producers). Luketic, J. (Director). (2001). *Legally blonde* [Motion Picture]. United States: MGM Studios.

Smith, M. W., & Wilhelm, J. D. (2006). *Going with the flow: How to engage boys (and girls) in their literacy learning*. Portsmouth: Heinemann.

Steinberg, S., Parmar, P., & Richard, B. (2006). *Contemporary youth culture: An international encyclopedia* (Vol. 1) . Westport: Greenwood Press.

Tannen, D. (2001). *You just don't understand: Women and men in conversation*. New York: Harper Collins.

———. (2004). *He said, she said: Exploring the different ways men and women communicate* (Portable Professor Series). [CD]. New York: Barnes & Noble Books.

Teasley, A. B., & Wilder, A. (1997). *Reel conversations: Reading films with young adults*. Portsmouth: Heinemann.

Vandervelde, M. (2004). *Films and friends: Starting and maintaining a movie group*. New York: Thomas Dunne Books.

Vaux, S.A. (1999). *Finding meaning at the movies*. Nashville: Abingdon Press.

Wilhelm, J. D. (1997). *You gotta BE the book: Teaching engaged and reflective reading with adolescents*. New York: Teachers College Press.

———. (2004). *Reading is seeing: Learning to visualize scenes, character, ideas, and text worlds to improve comprehension and reflective reading*. New York: Scholastic, Inc.

Worsnop, C. (1999). *Screening images: Ideas for media education* (2nd ed.). Mississauga, Canada: Wright Communications.

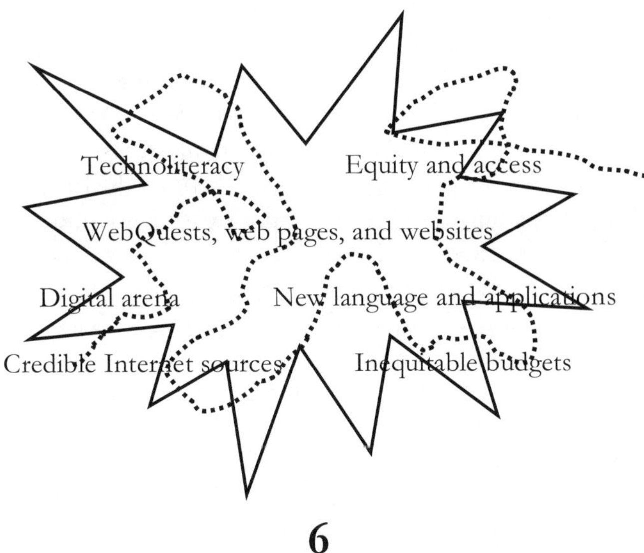

6

Can Technology (Re)load the Loaded Matrix?

> The goals for adolescents are quite complex: we want nothing less than to invite them to develop existing literacies in ways that will give them access to a portfolio of the competencies most necessary for them to be successful in our increasingly technological society.
>
> —Gee, 2000 in Moore & Hinchman, 2006, p. 113

Introduction

In this chapter we look at the importance of developing technology literacy or technoliteracy as a pedagogical tool in the English language arts classroom. We examine the underlying problems and successes with preparing preservice teachers to use technology in the schools including topics such as addressing issues about equity, teaching credible Internet searches, creating student web pages, and addressing inequitable budgets for equipment and services.

Loaded Matrix Chapter Context

Ethan came to our program with a strong interest in film and technology. In his school placement at Longview, he'd hoped to apply his background in technology to the junior English courses he was teaching, and he was pleased to learn that he could share one of the school's computer labs on his floor. He was also delighted to discover that his room was recently equipped with new Activboard technology (an interactive whiteboard, e.g., SMARTboard). Ethan was familiar with the whiteboard from his communications media course at the university, but like his cooperating teacher, he had not had extensive training with all of its features but was eager to learn. Most of his students came from impoverished neighborhoods, and some did not have access to computers at home. However, he was impressed by their repertoire of knowledge and understanding about popular culture that he hoped to bridge to the classroom environment as a connect to teach technoliteracy. He was concerned, though, about their resistance to learning about this when there were likely other sociocultural issues impacting them that were by far of much greater concern to their lives including students working more than twenty hours a week and teenage pregnancies. The following questions emerged as a guide to answer some of the concerns raised through the tensions facing Ethan in his teaching placement.

Focus questions for chapter 6:

1. **How do we cultivate, foster, and equip preservice teachers with technoliteracy skills?**
2. **How can preservice teachers build a technology-based bridge between students' discourse communities and school when they seem disengaged from learning?**
3. **How do preservice teachers apply and articulate university-based technology literacy learning that may be absent or invisible from a cooperating teacher's classroom?**

Issue #1: How Important Is Technology-Based Literacy?

Jeffrey Wilhelm wrote, "Technological facility is essential to literacy in the twenty-first century and yet few teachers truly use technology themselves or teach and assist students to learn how to use technologies for various literate purposes" (Wilhelm in Firek, 2003, p. vii). Today's preservice teachers are integrating more technology to accomplish secondary English goals than they did since Wilhelm's statement over three years ago, partly because they are becoming more and more comfortable with technology literacy themselves as an everyday necessity and also because program standards expect new teachers to integrate technology effectively in their certification evidence. Teacher training programs including our own require teacher candidates to submit electronic portfolios with artifacts that not only incorporate technology standards but also use them wisely and seamlessly with secondary English content area standards. The current National Educational Technology Standards (NETS) website states that "more than 90 percent of U.S. states adopted, adapted, or referenced the International Society for Technology Education's (ISTE) NETS in state department of education documents" (http://www.iste.org). Teacher candidates can access this site to learn more about how technology standards can work in conjunction with subject area standards. James Lerman's book *101 Best Websites for Secondary Teachers* (ISTE, 2005) provides further information on Internet Security Basics, Technology Integration sites, General Teacher Support, Career and College Exploration and Planning for students, and six disciplines including English (e.g., American Literature on the web, Media Literacy Clearinghouse, and Cyber English) and World Languages.

In order to prepare secondary English students with technoliteracy skills, we must first equip and prepare our preservice teachers with the technoliteracy knowledge and pedagogical skills they will need for their English language arts classrooms. Technoliteracy, as the intersection of technology and literacy, embodies a basic set of skills and language[1] needed to accomplish certain tasks relating to technology. This includes a techno-language, a sensitivity and disposition toward other users, and how to use the technology. As we build on students' funds of knowledge, the knowledge students bring with them from their communities of learning (Moll, Amanti, Neff, & Gonzalez, 1992) and their discourses, we can help enhance their literacy skills. Gee (1996) suggests that our discourses are more than our uses of language; they are the combinations of the "saying-writing-doing-being-believing-valuing," and ways of participating in a variety of social contexts. By bridging students' "d" discourses, primary discourse which originates with and within culture, family, friends, and language, to their "D" discourses, the secondary discourse that emerges from organizations (literacy communities) such as churches, political parties, gangs, schools, offices, jobs, professions, clubs, fraternities, athletic teams, cliques, hobby groups, and leagues (Gee, 1996), we can develop, along with our students (who no doubt, probably know more than we do about technology), innovative and relevant technoliteracy lessons.

In the Digital Arena

Earlier in this decade, Selfe and Hawisher (2004) conducted groundbreaking case-study research in technoliteracy and argued thus:

> Educators and policy makers have continued to base important local and national decisions on a minimal amount of information about how students acquire, or don't, the literacies of technology. Before we can hope to do a better, more informed job of

> making decisions about these literacies as they are taught in classrooms, homes, community centers, and workplaces across the United States, we need to learn much more about how various social, cultural, political, ideological, and economic factors have operated dynamically, in relation to each other, at various levels of influence, and over time, to shape the acquisition and development of digital literacies within peoples' lives. Equally important, we need to learn much more about how people, individually and collectively, have shaped the nature of technological literacy as it continues to be defined and practiced. (p. 3)

Their case-study research of twenty unique individuals and how personal computers changed their lives produced eight emerging themes about literacy and its relationship with technology (Selfe & Hawisher, 2004, pp. 212–234). In order to reach today's junior and senior high school students, preservice teachers will need to understand and apply these themes to their pedagogy, particularly that certain technoliteracy practices will come and go, depending upon their relevance in spacetime; socioeconomic factors, gender, and age can influence the acquisition or failure of students' technoliteracy skills and tools; and school is only one of what Selfe and Hawisher (2004) term "four primary gateways to digital literacy" (p. 223) with workplace, community, and home also playing vital roles in how students need, learn, and employ these new literacies. Families can pass on electronic literacy legacies from children to parents and parents to children and from younger to older or older to younger siblings (p. 229). Teachers can invite students to discuss how these different gateways teach them different technoliteracy skills and tasks and solve or pose specific problems. Schools have the ongoing responsibility to provide equitable computer access for students that is safe, inviting, and convenient, and teachers must provide differentiated instruction in the digital arena just as they do with other subject matter content for all ability levels. Students should feel that they can get technical support from the teacher when they need it, but they should also respect that the teacher can learn new techniques from and with them. And teachers must design meaningful lessons and units integrating technology with literacy as well as they integrate the more traditional reading, writing, speaking, and listening processes for authentic purposes.

In 2005, the Conference on English Education (CEE) convened to address the current state of affairs in English education and to create position statements that can guide future policy efforts in English teacher preparation. Specifically, the technology subcommittee noted that "newer technologies have altered the space in which the study of meaning-making and meaning-makers occur and these changes have important implications for teachers, learners, and communities" (Beliefs, 2005). The committee outlined how and what kinds of technoliteracy[2] skills teachers need for the classroom.

The committee made a call to include technology in preservice teaching methods classes and to prepare both preservice and inservice teachers to not only "meaning-making by using a variety of representational, interpretive, and communicative systems, but also to consider the synergistic relationships that exist between readers, writers, texts, contexts, and the situations in which texts, in their many forms, are written and read" (Beliefs, 2005). They further suggested that "it is essential for English educators to turn a critical eye toward the benefits and affordances; the limitations and liabilities of integrating these newer technologies into our teaching" (Beliefs, 2005). This means that English teachers must be open to writing or projects that include "sound, image, and video clips, and multiple modes of expression, such as music, artwork, poetry, and first person narratives of historical fiction, all providing different perspectives on the topic under study" (Beliefs, 2005) because

> multimedia texts that make use of technological innovations and integrate multimodal literacies provide a broader and more dynamic representation of ideas than afforded by the limitations of print; they also provide boundless, creative ways of connecting various forms of expression and, in turn, help to forge critical new understandings and meaning-making.

Issue #2: New Language and Applications

This new learning encompasses both a wide range of new language and applications and issues of equity and access to technology. Moore and Hinchman (2006) explain a "literacy framework" originally developed by Luke and Freebody: "[T]o become literate members of information societies, students must master at least three overlapping media of communication—oral (spoken language systems), written (print culture systems), and multimedia (linguistic and non-linguistic sound systems and visual representations of digital and electronic media)" (Moore & Hinchman, 2006, p. 114). They suggest that teachers adopt Luke and Freebody's "four resources model for literacy, a repertoire of practices students must master" including roles they define as Code Breaker, Meaning Maker, Text User, and Text Analyst (Luke & Freebody, 2000, in Moore & Hinchman, 2006, p. 115). This model "provides a way to help adolescents understand various aspects of literacy, what it can do for them, and how they can expand their own repertoire of practices to become better suited to their changing society" (p. 115).

Ethan, in collaboration with his cooperating teacher, introduced his eleventh-grade students to these four roles and combined oral, written, and multimedia forms of communication by inviting them to choose a partner and select a short multicultural tale to tell their classmates from ones he and his cooperating teacher thought would provide a variety of global perspectives. Student pairs were instructed to complete these goals—first, to dramatize the tale in some way, for example, by using sound effects and different voices for the characters and narrator and/or by using small props such as hats or stuffed animals Ethan brought to class in a cardboard box; and second, to help the rest of the class comprehend the story in one of three other ways: either by posting two key questions that they felt the story answered on the Activboard and explaining the answers to those questions, by drawing their representation of the story using computer software and projecting it on the Activboard, or by playing a short segment of a CD selection, approved by the teacher, they thought would be an appropriate background or parallel for this tale and explaining why. Ethan and his mentor teacher modeled one of the tales for the class by wearing clothing that represented their characters and by changing the pitch and tone of their voices from their usual classroom speaking voices. Ethan then showed the class a virtual representation of the tale he designed in Adobe Illustrator the night before, and he provided a brief explanation of how his graphics represented the main idea of the story as just one way of interpreting the tale. For the remainder of that class and the following two days, Ethan and his cooperating teacher worked with the student pairs on their presentations when they needed assistance but tried to give them space to come up with their own original ideas.

When the presentations were completed, Ethan reflected in his student teaching journal that students told him they enjoyed these lessons because they could choose their partners, their tales, and their comprehension activity. His reflections were similar to Kist's findings about the positive comments students made when teachers "infused … new literacies choices" (Kist, 2005, pp. 114–119). The experienced Calgary teachers Kist describes in his study advocate some "core beliefs" including "All text is equal," and "The teacher's job is to provide understanding in a variety of ways" (Kist, 2005, p. 111). Although Ethan and his cooperating teacher were moving in that direction by offering students with different learning styles and technology proficient ways to show and not just tell their tales to other classmates, the teachers Kist writes about allow students even more freedom to choose texts and formats for presenting their comprehension (Kist, 2005, p. 112–113). Even so, Ethan remarked that he was amazed at how attentive his students were to each other's presentations and that they came up with questions, drawings, and songs that he would have not considered, which were often surprisingly insightful understandings of the tales. Specific examples Ethan found memorable were one pair who selected the song "Circle of Life" from *The Lion King* to parallel the community of animals in the West African tale "Strength," and another team who designed two challenging multiple choice questions for the Indian tale "The Three Dolls" and conducted an Activote (each member of the class has a key pad about the size of a computer mouse where they can punch in their responses similar to the audience vote on *Who Wants to Be a Millionaire*?) to see how the whole class viewed the key points of the story before the team revealed their answers.[3]

Equity and Access

Like the literacy skills we teach and impart, when we bring technology into the classroom, we must also consider our purpose, the audience, and the skills the students will need and the relevance of such to their lives. For each of our students to have a fair and equal chance at school and employment, we must provide them all with the same starter set of tools. Even though inequities of access to technology abound outside of school and from one school to another, we can instill in each student the necessary knowledge and skill-sets that can be utilized in both school and the workforce. Unfortunately, not all schools have adequate access to hardware or software. Some students therefore graduate from public schools more prepared to meet the needs of a global workforce.

When preservice teachers develop a unit that requires use of technology, there are several things to keep in mind so as to not reinforce disparaging issues of inequity.

1. Assignments should not reinforce privileging gender, gender expression, sexual orientation, economic, social, ability, nationality, or linguistic backgrounds.
2. Access to the Internet and other forms of technology should be considered when assignments are designed so that every student has fair and equitable access.
3. Prior to being assigned a unit, students must be made aware of the legal and ethical issues of using technology such as plagiarism, deciphering credible sources, safe and fair use, and acceptable use policies (AUP).[4]
4. Teachers should help develop a student's sense of "netiquette," a sensitivity to users of different backgrounds.

⇒*Teaching Points*

∞Methods Courses

•Design a lesson that uses technology and that helps secondary students consider one or more issues relating to equity on gender, economic, social, gender expression, or linguistic backgrounds.
•Discuss how they would handle a situation in which one of their students plagiarized from the Internet.
•Create a list of what technologies are available to them at their university and school site. Compare and contrast the two.
•Do a critical analysis of the AUP at their school site and write a paper that analyzes its consideration of equity.
• In partners or threes practice writing a technology grant for the school site.
•Discuss what poor "netiquette" looks like.

⇒*Teaching Points*

∞**Secondary Classrooms**

•Teach about safe and fair use of technology through discussion and demonstrations.

•Teach about "netiquette" by drawing parallels between firstspace and virtual space.

•Ask students to consider how they would teach younger students about safe and fair use of technology and then pair up with another class.

•Rank the top ten worst things that could happen by using the Internet. As a class, decide on a master list and post it in the classroom.

•Search for information that seems to contradict common knowledge about gender, racial, linguistic, or social equity and deconstruct those findings. Provide answers to the questions: What were the differences? How did you come to that conclusion? What was the purpose of the posting? What was the most significant thing you learned?

•Ask students what would offend them if someone wrote to them using poor "netiquette."

•Invite students to design a lesson on something they know about using technology and ask them to teach it to their peers.

Additional Resources

Acceptable Use Policies and Internet Safety
http://www.4teachers.org/intech/AUP.shtml
To help parents assist their children with online safety

Center for Safe and Responsible Internet Use
http://responsiblenetizen.org/
A center that holds current rationales and policies for Internet use

Media Awareness Network
http://www.4teachers.org/intech/AUP.shtml
A watchdog network that addresses safe uses of technology and updates based on current issues

Superhighway Safety
http://safety.ngfl.gov.uk/schools/document.php3?D=d56
To help develop protocols for using the Internet at school

U.S. Department of Education
http://www.eduref.org/Resources/Educational_Technology/Computers/Internet/Internet_Safety.html
A clearinghouse of information for all kinds of Internet safety issues in schools

Credible Internet Searches

When we work with our preservice teachers, we must help them recognize and decipher between what material from the Internet is legitimate as almost anyone can post to the World Wide Web. In our methods courses, we must have conversations with students about pulling sources from the web. When designing assignments, here are some reminders:

1. Do not develop assignments that are dominated by web use. It is important that students do not substitute exclusive Internet use for the library. If an assignment requires sources, limit the number of web resources.

2. Ask students to complete an *evaluating sources* questionnaire per resource to determine if the resource seems viable.

- •What is the ethnicity(ies) of the author?
- •What is the gender(s) of the author?
- •Is the author credible? Find out something about the author, that is, other publications or profession.
- •Are voices of the disenfranchised represented?
- •How is gender(s) treated in the text?
- •Who is represented in the text? Who is left out?
- •Is the text current or dated?
- •Is the source valid? Is it factual? Do you have reason to doubt anything? Explain.
- •What kind of document from the Internet are you using? A journal? A personal web page? An encyclopedia reference?
- •Is the topic biased? If so, how?
- •Is the writing elevated or does it appear as a rant?
- •Who is cited in the bibliography? Are those references credible?
- •With what press are they aligned? What are the politics of that press?
- •How does the information seem relevant to the context of your research?

**If there is a ~, it is likely to come from a personal website and the content may or may not be relevant or cited by an expert.*

3. Consider access for any assignments you create. Often, asking students to work in teams helps to address this issue.

⇒***Teaching Points***

∞Methods Courses

•Locate two seemingly different kinds of Internet articles and then do an *evaluating sources* sheet for each. Compare and contrast the answers. Ask why they would or wouldn't use the sources.

•Create a list of what they think makes a resource credible. Discuss as a full class. Then create criteria for the list.
•Design a lesson to help secondary students determine credible Internet sources.

Once preservice teachers have a handle on determining credible sources, they can design lessons for their classroom students.

⇒*Teaching Points*
∞Secondary Courses
•Locate two seemingly different kinds of Internet articles and then do an *evaluating sources* sheet for each. Compare and contrast the answers. Ask students why they would or wouldn't use the sources.
•Create a list of what they think makes a resource credible. Discuss as a full class. Then create criteria for the list.
•Design a lesson to help other secondary students determine credible Internet sources.

WebQuests, Web Pages, and Websites
Hilve Firek (2003) explains that "The Internet presents its fair share of dangers, but it also offers English teachers resources that can help their students respond to and analyze literature, explore history, conduct research, share ideas, and write with a real purpose for a real audience" (p. 72). Today's teachers, no matter what their level of technological capability, can assist students in creating their own individual, student-team, or whole classroom community web pages and websites. WebQuests, like the detailed example provided by for an imaginary eighth grade on Anne Frank and the Holocaust in Firek's text (2003), carefully instruct teachers and students to navigate through credible, select Internet and multimedia resources in order to complete specific learning tasks. Firek also provides helpful links to free template programs and hosting sites for teachers to view other examples of student web projects and grading rubrics created by teachers and students (e.g., Project Poster, http://poster.4teachers.org/).

For educators who need more guidance in setting up web pages, Firek recommends several online activity sites including Quia.com and MySchoolOnline.com (p. 92). To form an electronic community, she advocates creating a whole-class website for students and their teachers: "in essence, your class website can be a virtual publishing center, a communications area, a homework zone, and an electronic library. Together, the Web provides opportunities for learning unlike any other" (p. 90).

Discovery Education has a complete website where teachers, students, and parents at all levels of technoliteracy proficiency can learn more about the

Internet and creating and maintaining web pages and sites (http://school.discovery.com/schrockguide/yp/iypabout.html). The Oracle Education Foundation, a nonprofit, advertising-free website, offers the international ThinkQuest competition (http://www.thinkquest.org/) where students between the ages of nine and nineteen, under the direction of a teacher mentor, form teams to create websites in a variety of educational areas; all student-generated web pages are placed in an archive on the site. For example, a team of four middle school students created a literary website with the theme chocolate. They researched the history of chocolate, candy trivia, created games, activities, a chocolate survey for viewers to submit their favorites, and designed learning materials for *Charlie and the Chocolate Factory*, *Chocolate Fever*, and *The Chocolate Touch* (http://library.thinkquest.org/J0110012/).

Firek (2003) suggests that we guide students in designing their own websites using the checklist she designed below based on Yahooligan's 4 As: Accessible, Accurate, Appropriate, and Appealing (p. 94).

Checklist for Developing Websites Based on Yahooligan's 4 As

Is the site *accessible*?

- Does it load quickly? (If not, cut down on the size or number of graphics).
- Can visitors find their way around easily? (If not, make navigation buttons or links more prominent).
- Do all the links work? (If not, replace them with new ones).
- Is a webspinner email address included? (If not, add one at the bottom of the opening screen).
- If users need plug-ins (e.g., Flash, QuickTime), are links to the download sites readily available?

Is the site *accurate*?

- Can visitors tell who is responsible for the information? (If not, be sure there is a statement identifying this site as student-generated).
- Can visitors easily identify the educational affiliation of the site? (If not, include a link to your school's main page).
- Are sources of information identified and cited properly? (If not, check an *MLA Style Manual* for help).

Is the site *appropriate*?

- Is the site appropriate for its intended audience? (If not, reconsider word choice and design).

Is the site *appealing*?

- Are layout and design pleasing? (If not, reconsider color and graphics).
- Is text on the screen easy to read? (If not, increase point size and switch to a sans serif font).

Issue #3: Inequitable Budgets for Equipment and Services

> The political, economic, and sociocultural influences operating upon the practice of the new literacies with the new technologies is one of the most important considerations in education....Since it is through communication that we exercise our political, economic, and social power, we risk contributing to the hegemonic perpetuation of rigid social/economic classes if we fail to demand equal access to newer technologies and adequately prepared teachers for all students. It is through adequate preservice preparation and ongoing professional development that teachers will expand their expertise in discussing issues of equity and diversity with their students.
>
> —Swenson, Young, McGrail, Rozema , & Whitin, 2006, pp. 365–366

The "Suggestions, Tools, and Guidelines for Assessing Technology in Elementary and Secondary Schools" website from the National Center for Education Statistics states that the annual public expenditure on K-12 education technology is currently $5 billion (http://nces.ed.gov/pubs2003/tech_schools/chapter2_2.asp#3); but the implementation and assessment of educational technology policies and plans varies widely from state to state and from school district to school district. Funding for technology continues to compete with other political school board agendas including sports, the band, the arts, the library, the school lunch program, and the sciences. Other factors besides money also affect how well schools are able to integrate technology into their curriculums. "Newer technologies and the literacies they engender carry costs. Not only do the hardware, software, and peripherals (and professional development) require monetary investments; the learning curves for students and faculty require what is often an even more precious commodity—time" (Swenson et al., 2006, p. 360). Teachers need both the funding and release time to attend educational technology forums, to conduct electronic and digital inquiries with colleagues, and to study and incorporate uses of technology to fit their teaching goals. School districts must communicate more both online and face to face about the commitments they are making to use technology to promote new literacies, why they are doing this, and what the tangible results have been. Bowen (2006) reported that in a six-month study conducted by Mann and Schafer in 1997, fifty-five New York school districts spent over $14 million on computer training and technology: "The study, one of the most exhaustive studies done to date, produced quantitative, qualatitive, and longitudinal data as well as anecdotal reports … 'that increased technology supports, facilitates, and encourages student achievement. The gains reach across schools and districts with different education policies and socio-demographic backgrounds'" (http://chiron.valdosta.edu/are/ebowenLitReview.pdf).

State-sponsored initiatives, such as Pennsylvania's *Classrooms for the Future*, a three-year $200 million grant program, include stipends for teachers in urban, suburban, and rural districts to become Technology Integrators and provides funding for operational materials and facilities, hardware, and technical assistance to create "technology-enriched instructional settings for English, math, science, and social studies classes" (http://www.pde.state.pa.us/ed_tech/cwp/view.asp?a=169&q=118849). The Education Reform Networks web page offers a link to equitable access of technology resources for all learners and provides information in five categories selected by educators in these fields:

1. *Technology resources*
   Access to learning technology resources (hardware, software, wiring, and connectivity)
2. *Quality content*
   Access to high quality digital content
3. *Culturally responsive content*
   Access to high quality, culturally relevant content
4. *Effective use*
   Educators skilled in using these resources effectively for teaching and learning
5. *Content creation*
   Opportunities for learners and educators to create their own content (http://digitalequity.edreform.net/).

Teacher educators should encourage preservice teachers to seek out both funding and release time opportunities to integrate technology in their classrooms, with a reminder that obtaining grants for using technology alone or more access to digital toolkits will not necessarily or automatically make students more technoliterate. Establishing classroom libraries (books, tapes, videos, and educational electronic and board games), providing access to public libraries, asking parents to donate books and educational electronic programs, shopping for bargain books and discounted electronic games, and book and computer recycling drives (Olson, 2007, p. 360) are other ways for new teachers to promote equity in literacy development in areas where they may not have the same quality and quantity of technology equipment and services as they had previously in another school or university environment.

Conclusion

Concluding with Ethan

During his days as a student teacher, Ethan was able to obtain access to a computer lab across the hall from his English classes on a semi-regular basis so that students who did not have computers at home or who had difficulty completing assignments outside of school could work on their assignments during class time and study halls or under his supervision at scheduled times before or after school. Longview's computer lab technician was also willing, when available, to help students with the technoliteracy projects Ethan assigned. Ethan included a mini-unit in his student teaching electronic portfolio he adapted from Firek's keypals project (Firek, 2003, p. 50) where he secured permission so his students could email the guidance counselor, nurse, or school psychologist to obtain information on issues they or their friends struggled with including drug abuse and teenage pregnancy, or questions they had about specific career pursuits or colleges they wanted to attend after graduation. They each wrote three turns of email messages to one of those school personnel to receive responses to their questions and then wrote written reflections on what they had learned from these correspondences. Ethan also assigned a multimedia project over the course of the semester similar to the one he had read about in Firek's book with a student self-reflection guide (Firek, 2003, p. 107). His students could choose from a range of popular culture topics they brainstormed on the Activboard and were excited about sharing with other members of the class including superhero comics, reality television, e-zines, and rock bands. Because he had eighty to ninety-minute blocked classes, Ethan was able to design hands-on activities in the lab and classroom with checklists due each week in order for all students to complete their inquiries, word processing, and PowerPoint presentations more successfully. On the advice of his cooperating teacher, Ethan also worked with his school's librarian, submitted the students' selected topics to him ahead of time so that he could access credible websites and hard-copy materials for the students before they arrived to conduct their research, and set aside specific days for his students to study information related to their projects from the library computers, book shelves, and periodical racks. His students were able to design their multimodal projects alone or with a partner, depending upon their interest in the same topics and how well or how frequently they were able to use technologies at school and at home. Ethan was able to match his lesson and unit plan artifacts with appropriate national, state, and International Society for Technology in Education (ISTE) standards he was required to include in his electronic teaching portfolio.

In order to bridge the divide between Ethan and his students' technoliteracy learning, our responsibilities as English educators included making Ethan and his preservice teacher peers aware of the following points before student teaching:

- Just as there are differences and similarities between a preservice teacher's understanding of reading, writing, speaking, and viewing and his/her students' understandings of those practices, there are *sociocultural and structural differences and similarities* between what the beginning teacher knows and prefers about integrating technology in those practices and what his/her students know and prefer; in order to connect with them, the new teacher's job is to take students beyond what they already know and to make uses of technology in literacy practices clear and relevant.

- Good teaching involves *how to apply the technoliteracy pedagogy* learned at the university, e.g., from reading texts such as Firek's [2003], from designing personal web pages, and from developing technological pedagogical content knowledge or TPCK as explained in Swenson et al., (2006) to different school settings, depending on factors including computer access for students both in school and at home, availability of hardware and software, and how the classroom is wired for different kinds of technology including SMARTboards and Internet access, and how much students already know.

- Students come with varying technoliteracy skills but won't use ones they already know or could learn in school *if they aren't motivated* by what they can do with them to communicate with different audiences including their peers, to function in a workplace, or to pursue their individual interests.

- The *budgets for electronic and digital equipment will vary greatly* from place to place; often financial support for prioritizing and advancing new technologies comes, "unfairly and characteristically, from the teacher's own pocket" (Swenson et al., 2006, p. 366).

- *Websites and centers for secondary school restructuring* such as the Center for Leadership in School Reform (www.clsr.org) and the Comprehensive School Reform Program (www.ecs.org) provide federal grants and support transformative education through ways technology can be used in schools (Moore & Hinchman, 2006, p. 200).

- More adept teachers *can pass on a legacy of knowledge and skills* of current technoliteracy practices and trends by tutoring, workshops, blogs, or in-service programs to other students, faculty, staff, and administration, but they should be fairly compensated for their time and must be supported by their schools so they will not feel burned out or used.

- Preservice teachers need to *work with technical support personnel and librarians* for assistance in providing adequate or better computer access to students and learn more about what new technologies are available for specific classes and goals.

Notes

1 Technoliteracy is a term that refers to the requisite skills and knowledge that embody technology-based learning.

2 See http://www.ncte.org/groups/cee/positions/122936.htm?source=gs for a starter set of technoliteracy language tools.

3 Ethan and his cooperating teacher selected multicultural stories from Holt, D., & Mooney, B. (Eds.). (1994). *Ready-to-tell tales.* Little Rock: August House, a required text in Ethan's university speech and communications methods course.

4 AUPs are a written contract between administrators, teachers, parents, and students to ensure that school computers are being used in safe, relevant and appropriate ways. An "AUP outlines the terms and conditions for Internet use by defining access privileges, rules of online behavior, and the consequences for violating those rules. The AUP can also be a helpful tool for teachers, offering guidance on how best to integrate the Internet into their classrooms" (Media, 2006). AUPs differ by schools and districts.

References

Beliefs about Technology and the Preparation of English Teachers. (2005). Conference on English Education Leadership and Policy Summit. Retrieved October 18, 2005, from the World Wide Web:http://www.ncte.org/groups/cee/positions/122936.htm?source=gs.

Bowen, E. R. (2006). *Student engagement and its relation to quality work design: A review of the literature.* Retrieved August 16, 2006, from http://chiron.valdosta.edu/are/ebowenLitReview.pdf.

Firek, H. (2003). *10 easy ways to use technology in the English classroom.* Portsmouth: Heinemann.

Gee, J. P. (1996). *Social linguistics and literacies: Ideology in discourse* (2nd ed.). New York: Falmer Press.

———. (2000). New people in new worlds. Networks, the new capitalism, and schools. In B. Cope & M. Kalnatzis (Eds.), *Multiliteracies: Literacy learning and the design of social futures* (pp. 43–68). New York: Routledge.

Holt, D., & Mooney, B. (Eds.). (1994). *Ready-to-tell tales.* Little Rock: August House.

Kist, W. (2005). *New literacies in action: Teaching and learning in multiple media.* New York: Teachers College Press.

Lerman, J. (2005). *101 best websites for secondary teachers.* Washington, DC: ISTE.

Media Awareness Network. (2006). *Acceptable Use Policies for Internet Use.* Retrieved May 22, 2006, from World Wide Web: http://www.media-awareness.ca/english/resources/special_initiatives/wa_resources/wa_teachers/backgrounders/acceptable_use.cfm.

Moll, L., Amanti, C., Neff, D., & Gonzalez, N. (1992). Funds of knowledge for teaching: Using a qualitative approach to connect homes and classrooms. *Theory Into Practice, 31,* 132–141.

Moore, D. W., & Hinchman, K. A. (2006). *Teaching adolescents who struggle with reading: Practical strategies.* Boston: Pearson Education, Inc.

Olson, C. B. (2007). *The reading/writing connection: Strategies for teaching and learning in the secondary classroom.* Boston: Pearson.

Selfe, C. L., & Hawisher, G. E. (2004). *Literate lives in the information age: Narratives of literacy from the United States.* Mahwah: Lawrence Erlbaum Associates.

Swenson, J., Young, C. A., McGrail, E., Rozema, R., & Whitin, P. (2006). Extending the conversation: New technologies, new literacies, and English education. *English Education, 38*(4), 351–69.

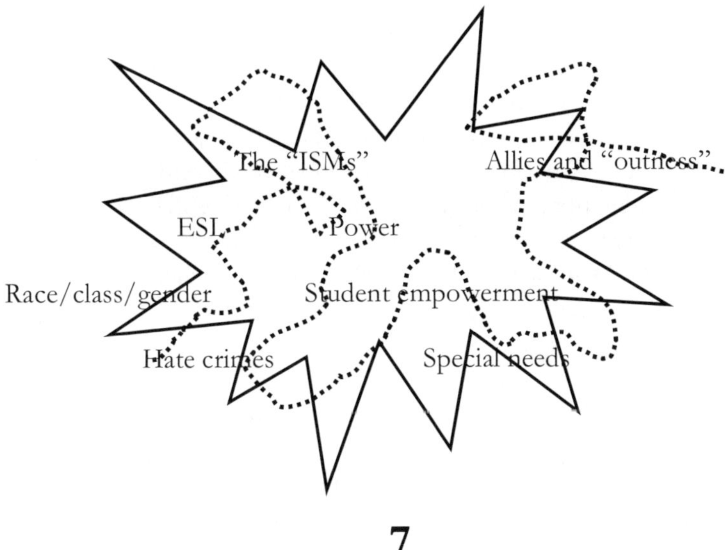

7

Social Justice and Sociocultural Issues as Part of the Loaded Matrix

This is a very important chapter for us. In it we unpack how social justice and sociocultural issues, which we believe are inseparable, are addressed by English education instructors and consider ways to support how preservice teachers understand and interpret them in the context of their classrooms. We reflect on this because both the university instructor as well as the preservice teacher inherently co-construct and inform student identity. Such issues will include but are not limited to the dynamics of power, students with special needs, English as a second language (ESL) learner, the "ISMs,"[1] and the intersections of race, class, and gender. We also reflect on some of the larger sociopolitical issues of being an "out"[2] educator or in being an "out" ally. The chapter concludes as we reconsider ways to help students become empowered in order to be proactive about these loaded issues.

Through this chapter, we continue our commitment to social justice by addressing in more detail some of the consequences of not addressing discrimination. Freire (1970) reminds us that "education, as the exercise of domination stimulates the credulity of students, with the ideological intent (often not perceived by educators) of indoctrinating them to adapt to the world of oppression" (p. 78). We do this work because our deepest fear is that a hate crime will be perpetrated against another and will render the victim(s) psychologically, spiritually, emotionally, physically impaired, or even dead. A hate crime is a crime committed against the victim who has been selected based on actual or perceived characteristics relating to: race, national origin, ethnicity, sex/gender, religion, sexual orientation, or disability and it hurts more than the individual; it instills fear in an entire community. As teacher educators we feel it is vital to our work that we take a stand against hate in all forms in teacher education and, as such, encourage our preservice teachers to incorporate a stance against prejudice and hate in their pedagogies.

Loaded Matrix Chapter Context

Beth was teaching at Hillcrest, which you may recall is situated in an ultraconservative community. The student body, which is fairly homogenous (white), was not the most welcoming. Beth brought her very open mind to Hillcrest but was encouraged by peers to be closeted about being bisexual for fear of ostracization. As an Asian-American teacher, we thought she would be readily welcomed by colleagues and students, since school climates seem to be more accepting and open, but this was not the case. To the contrary, Beth felt marginalized from the student body and her colleagues at the school site as she was passed over for helping put on the school play and the school-wide talent show despite her vast expertise in both. We offered her support and encouragement throughout her placement in the hopes that both she and her cooperating teacher, who she had an amiable rapport with, could help open up some of the students to diverse subjects that were obviously loaded for them. Beth's situation helped us consider three guiding questions.

Focus questions for chapter 7:

1. **How can preservice teachers' emerging understanding of pedagogy enhance their ability to address discrimination in all forms in classrooms and schools?**
2. **How do preservice teachers negotiate between their own beliefs and values and those imposed upon them by schools and individual districts?**
3. **How do preservice teachers apply and articulate university-based learning that is absent or invisible from a school?**

Rationale for Social Justice in the Loaded Matrix

Because teachers possess a tremendous amount of power over co-constructing and informing students' identities (Bhabha, 1994; Foucault, 1980, 1986; Freire & Macedo, 1987; Gilyard, 1999; Giroux, 1983; Gutierrez, Baquedano-Lopez, &

Tejeda, 1999; Hagood, 2002; Moje, 2002; Perez, 1998; Solorzano & Villalpando, 1998), they should be actively involved in their own "prejudice-free" development. Teachers should become aware of how their own biases and presuppositions of students based on family background, appearance, and discourse can disenfranchise and marginalize potential learners (McCarthey & Moje, 2002). While a wealth of factors besides school influence and co-construct a student's identity such as home, families, friends, institutional policy, popular culture, and social groups, the influence of schooling over a student is often a difficult negotiation for a student as he/she bumps up against the power of teacher as supreme authority (Apple, 2002; Giroux, 1983; Levinson, Foley, & Holland, 1996; McCarthey & Moje, 2002). Individual teachers and, in some cases, schools have sought ways to educate the disenfranchised while simultaneously helping to build students' self worth through validating home discourse and experience (Moll, Amanti, Neff, & Gonzalez, 1992; Perez, 1998). hooks (1994) describes a similar concept of increasing student self-worth in her ideology of an engaged pedagogy when she suggests "to teach in a manner that respects and cares for the souls of our students is essential if we are to provide the necessary conditions where learning can most deeply and intimately begin" (p. 13). Teachers have the ability to create wonderful and rich opportunities for learning through an infinite number of ways and yet have the power to destroy a student's sense of hope and squelch the desire to learn. On this, McCarthey and Moje (2002) attest that "identity matters because it, whatever it is, shapes or is an aspect of how humans make sense of the world and their experiences in it" (p. 228).

Beginning the Discussion on Social Justice—It Begins with You

Where and how should we begin the discussion on social justice issues in teacher education? We must begin by creating enough safety in our methods classes to address loaded issues; though, that can be especially difficult when such topics are perceived as taboo and have a long internalized history—even since childhood. Establishing and maintaining safety cannot be forced, and the instructor's stance needs to be clear and separate from the beliefs of the students. Foremost, there are six determinants that instructors must be willing to embody before they should even attempt to embrace social justice pedagogy.

First, teachers must be actively committed to doing their inner work prior to addressing loaded issues with students. This means that they are open, willing, and able to critically examine the prejudices they hold, reflect on how they have manifested and are willing to shift such perspectives. We do students and ourselves a grave disservice if we are teaching social justice without having begun to do our own inner work.

Second, the way teachers may use or misuse discourse has the power to affirm and marginalize students in their classes. Identities, according to Gee (2002), are dialogical and relational, constructed in relation to power (as through the discourse a professor uses), and in relationship to discourse. Teacher discourse has the ability to create various affirming and disaffirming social spaces in classrooms wherein the intersection and transaction of a mosaic of students' identities intersect. Within those various social spaces and through the way that a teacher models and uses discourse, and how a classroom reflects different identities (posters, texts, announcements), students' identities may stabilize or destabilize. Rich (1977) emphasizes that "until we can understand the assumptions in which we are drenched we cannot know ourselves" (pp. 18-19). Next, the instructor must be willing to somewhat disentangle from the reality that not all students will or are even able, let alone willing, to become social justice advocates. It is more important to present well-researched facts so preservice teachers will come to terms with a pedagogy that reflects a diverse range of beliefs that are oriented to meet all learners' needs. However, we must let go, like a benevolent parent, be supportive of students' growth, and encourage them toward a pedagogy that they can embody and which reflects their inner truths.

Fourth, once we've come to terms with our ability to disentangle from students' beliefs, we must also realize that to be a social justice teacher will no doubt create some form of backlash. Those of us who have taught social justice-based learning are likely to have experienced reproach through student evaluations, even colleagues, and from the political right—which has deemed social justice work to have extremely negative connotations because it is part of the liberal agenda.

Fifth, it is important that we approach teaching social justice not as we are trying to sell it, market it, or reify it (which in fact, contradicts social justice advocacy=equality for all); rather, we recognize that social justice work is a highly political stance and will invite controversy in some form, especially to the students who embrace it.

Last, we must be honest with our students about the controversy over being a social justice educator because they are likely to collide with individuals whose pedagogies malign from theirs and that such a stance will position them a particular way in their schools. If we are able to keep these issues in mind and are at peace with them, then we can proceed with how to establish safety in our methods courses.

When we align ourselves within social justice teaching, it is also important to be trained around how to handle and work with the diverse issues that have the potential to emerge in the classroom. Even when we are trained to teach about loaded issues, we can never be fully prepared to predict for the spacetime issues that might reveal themselves. Knowing this to be possible, we must be committed to our own praxis that can continue to help guide us to be as best prepared as we can, for what remains invisible but just beyond the horizon.

How can we best prepare ourselves to work with loaded issues? There is no one right way. University staffs can be trained a number of ways such as through local diversity training organizations, the Safe Zone Foundation,[3] or by inviting a national expert. It is more difficult to have diversity training for secondary school staff because it tends to require school board approval. I suggest that it is not enough to be trained but that we request support on how to facilitate loaded discussions in our classrooms. Once we are trained, it is important that there are ways to continue to discuss topics as they emerge. This might take the form of faculty reading circles, monthly faculty meetings, professional development, and attending conferences. We must practice as much as possible how to work with these loaded issues and often our best teachers are our colleagues sitting right next to us.

Establishing Safety for Social Justice Discussions

When I was in graduate school, Penny Pence, an instructor whom I hold deep reverence for, posed a question in one of my graduate courses and it has been on my mind for several years now. She asked, "How can you establish safety in your classrooms if you are constructing it? Does that counter the concept of safety?" I have wrestled with this for a long time because I have not been able to fully reconcile my own position without falling into a trap of contradictions. On one hand, I recognize that creating safety in a classroom context is vital prior to discussing loaded issues but that forcing students to become part of the discussion "saccharines" the authenticity of the discussion. How then do we create authentic safety in a classroom at either the university or the secondary level? I provide some suggestions.

Instructors at all levels might open up a discussion by exclaiming that in their classrooms all opinions are welcomed regardless of the student's stance, familial political affiliations, or religious backgrounds. Instructors should be cautious about taking a stance on an issue because they may either deliberately or inadvertently silence student output. They must allow ideas to emerge without imposing their own bias. In this way, students are more likely to talk and the instructor can then negotiate the flow of dialogue by posing open-ended questions. Although the instructor may disagree with a student's positionality that may seem prejudiced, we dishonor our work to social justice when we silence students who may have a view that is dissonant from others or even our own. We must work at developing our skills to negotiate the flow of dialogue and be willing to let students teach us about themselves even when we may perceive it as loaded. When dialogue becomes oppressive or when we perceive a threat has been made (chapter 3) and we feel we can no longer handle the issues at hand, that is when it is time to stop and reflect or to seek assistance.

Instructors can also model behavior that they hope to evoke from students. Acting with integrity on loaded issues and presenting well-researched facts may deepen a student's desire to recognize how no human should be maltreated. Developing assignments that encourage students to take a stance on loaded issues can also lead to an increased awareness of the importance of human equality.

More than ever before, social justice educators must rededicate themselves to the cause as even NCATE has removed social justice from their accrediting standards for teacher preparation as it has come under attack from the right for having loaded implications and political overtones. Even with setbacks such as these, over the past twelve years, practitioners and scholars in teaching and teacher education who connect their work to larger critical movements have begun to tie their work to a social justice agenda (Cochran-Smith & Zeichner, 2005). Although we have the research momentum and an expanding pool of social justice educators, we will inevitably face setbacks because of the larger social implications of what "social justice" means. We now turn to the issue of how to address specific loaded issues in teacher education while helping preservice teachers amass a cadre of tools for how they themselves can assist their students in working through some of the more incendiary issues in their lives. The areas that we will explore are intended to help facilitate the development of a preservice teacher's pedagogy so that they can empower their own students to become advocates and agents for social change.

Dynamics of Power

How can we help our students understand how the dynamics of power operate in their lives? As students become more conscious about the matrix of power that surrounds their lives, they can make choices about how to shift their own place within the dynamic. Power is the ability to influence others and to have access to decision-making opportunities to accomplish what one wants to have done. Power manifests itself visibly and invisibly through access to resources, work, institutions, physical security, housing, protection by the law, representation in government, and can be used to discriminate against people based on actual or perceived differences of ethnicity, gender, social class, sexuality, ability, national origin, religion, age, appearance, or weight (Miller, 2005b). Power is neither good nor bad; rather, how it manifests, begets its judgment. We can use power in ways that motivate people to create change for the better or we can use power for selfish reasons to hurt or impair others. For power, it is important to note the context of its manifestation, who is using it, and for what purpose or intent it is being used.

It is important to understand the context that power generally inhabits in the matrix. We live in a country dominated by white, Christian values and customs. As such, while schools have some independent reign over curriculum, students need particular social and academic skills to make it once they leave the school environment. Therefore, schools must also help socialize students to the expectations they will inevitably face whether it is in a job, a place of worship, or in higher education. Since we are all embedded within the matrix of hegemony, it is best to understand its expectations so we can prepare our students to navigate around and through some of the tribulations they will face.

The education system, which plays an active role in co-constructing student identities, is founded on principles and discourses based in hegemony—"white men (who) control Western structures of knowledge validation, their interests pervade the themes, paradigms, and epistemologies of traditional scholarship"(Collins, 2000, p. 251). These epistemologies shape "why we believe what we believe" and "point to the ways in which power relations shape who is believed and why" (Collins, 2000, p. 252). Hegemony as a powerful force may unapologetically distance students both covertly and overtly from graduating school with a healthy perspective of their own sociocultural power in the world by ignoring or invalidating their experience and/or home discourse (Gilyard, 1999). This kind of manifestation of power as prejudice experienced by students perpetuates divisive hierarchies in our country and in our schools. In particular, youth of color and students who are targeted or perceived as "different" are disenfranchised from the educational system and are victimized by these hierarchies. Students can be marginalized within the schooling experience when their discourses or inner or outer appearances are perceived as a mismatch against the dominant ones present in the schools. We cannot talk about discourses without speaking about identity because students' identities are formed by these school systems and the prejudices within (Gee, 1989). Gee (1989) refers to our discourses as "a socially accepted association among ways of using language, of thinking, and of acting that can be used to identify oneself as a member of a socially meaningful group or 'social network'" (p. 18), and which can grant us access to a particular group which has a particular identity (Gee 1989, 1996, 2002). When schools ignore "d" discourse as a viable source of scaffolding and bridge into institutional schooling, it reinforces this marginalization and the mismatch between home and school discourse becomes painfully teleological. Gee (1989) suggests that our core identities are formed by and within those discourses and each individual is on a trajectory through "discourse space" (p. 111), a space that opens up the possibility for acceptance into a social or affinity group. When a student feels invalidated or invisible at school, he/she is less likely to form healthy relationships and the dynamics of white power are strengthened.

Dominant culture speaks "Standard White English." Concomitantly, there is an unspoken etiquette that one needs to acquire cultural capital. In schools we can teach students to appreciate and honor the significance of their own language and also empower them to recognize the spaces where there may be a code of standard White conduct that may challenge them to assimilate. For instance, if a student expects to be hired for a job at a law firm, it is unlikely that he/she will earn an interview if the vitae submitted is full of grammatical and syntactical errors. Similarly, in a job interview, if a student spoke Ebonics or slang, it is unlikely that the law firm would hire the student. In other words, we can help our students recognize the hoops they must jump through if they want to have a particular kind of career while we must also encourage them to consider what is important to them in their futures. The invisible aspects of power have tremendous "power" over who we associate with, where we go, and even our careers.

Though some school districts attempt to address the negative aspects of power through prejudice-reduction, most educational systems fall prey to institutionalized prejudice. Institutionalized prejudice is the reproduction of white privilege as it is reinforced by government, universities, school systems, and the corporations that have absolute fiscal and social policy control over what goes on in schools (Apple, 2002). On this, hooks (1994) concurs that for the most part, institutions have perpetuated the notion of prejudice through the reproduction of white privilege.

Power can also manifest itself through privilege. Privilege refers to the choices, entitlements, and advantages granted based on membership in a culturally dominant group. Power can manifest itself through prejudice. Prejudice is the unconscious or conscious manifestation of dislike against another based on actual or perceived differences that can be, but does not necessarily have to be, legitimated by institutions. When we combine power + privilege + prejudice, it combusts into oppression. We have a moral and social responsibility to point this out to our preservice teachers so they recognize the extreme potential they have for diluting or manifesting dangerous possibilities in the classroom and society at large. We do have a responsibility to help interrupt the cycle inherited and unexamined by our ancestors.

We would be remiss if we did not recognize that we, as teacher educators, have great power over participating in and co-constructing our preservice teachers' identities. Through our curricular and pedagogical selections, we can make a huge impact. On the downside, we can also marginalize a preservice teacher whose beliefs we do not welcome or affirm. How do we work with preservice teachers whose values seem to be prejudicial and do we even have the right to interfere with their belief system? At what point do we interfere and at what point do we turn our backs?

It would be disingenuous to turn our backs on any of our students. We must be thoughtful about ways to recycle students' languages, help them reframe struggle into social activism, validate primary discourse, and help them make meaning of their own lives. We must put our best and most sincere effort forward and, like a benevolent parent, hope for the best outcome. Some of the ways in which we can begin to address this conundrum is to first be of the mindset to adopt the philosophy of "power with" our students and not "power over" them. Such a mindset can and will shift the underlying dynamics of power in the classroom and have the potential to impact how preservice teachers treat their own students. Next, we must adopt a discourse that reflects acceptance for all and welcomes all opinions. We must stand up for injustice in all forms and attend events where students recognize some form of injustice has transpired. Our curriculum and texts must be taught in ways that challenge the status quo, even if the text itself does not. Lastly, we must walk our talk. As previously stated, living social justice does not stop when the school day ends; it is who we are in all we do and embody, in our day-to-day lives.

What happens then if a student has a belief system that is biased or prejudicial? Do we interfere? The answer is yes. We do not have the right to tell students what to believe or what to think but we can ask a student to meet with us privately or with a colleague if what we see or read from them insinuates that they may oppress their own students. Of course this is subjective. We might ask them if there is something they need to talk about or if something is in the way of their learning or thinking. If all else fails and it does seem as if they are a liability to the teaching profession, we have a social and moral responsibility to counsel students out of our programs and help them consider an alternative profession.

⇒*Teaching Points*

∞Methods Courses

Assignments for Preservice Teachers—Furthering Inquiry for Social Action

•Reflect on power as it directly relates to students' lives. How do they use or misuse it? How do others use or misuse it? What are the reasons for that? Is there anything they want to change about the dynamics of power in your life? If so, identify them and make a chart that describes how they will each go about making change. For items they feel they cannot change, ask how they will address them?

•Design a lesson plan that will help their classroom students address issues of power.

•Annotate a list of books that they can put in their classroom or school library that center around the dynamics of power.

•Watch the news or a television show and log the number of times they observe how power manifests, through whom it manifests, and reflect on what are the larger social implications of its manifestation.

•What does it mean to be powerless? Identify individuals or groups who have less power than others. Consider the reasons for that.

•Identify a group in your local community that is affected by power dynamics but who seem to be attempting to shift such dynamics (such as with living wage or a group of color, fighting for equity at work). Research the reasons for this empirically and consider ways to support their efforts.

•Invite students to design lesson plans "with you" from time to time.

⇒*Teaching Points*

∞**Secondary Classrooms**

•Put up posters, announcements, and have classroom texts that reflect social equity.
•Design a lesson plan that will help your classroom students address issues of power.
•Ask students to reflect on power as it directly relates to their lives. How do they use or misuse it? How do others use or misuse it? What are the reasons for that? Is there anything they want to change about the dynamics of power in your life? If so, identify them and make a chart that describes how they will each go about making change. For items they feel they cannot change, ask how they will address them.
•Ask students to identify both positive and negative uses of power at school. Ask them to research the reasons for this empirically and consider ways to support their efforts.
•Ask students what does it mean to be powerless? Identify individuals and groups who have less power than others. Consider the reasons for that.
•Invite students to design lesson plans "with you" from time to time.
•Ask students to watch the news or a television show and log the number of times they observe how power manifests, through whom it manifests, and reflect on what are the larger social implications of its manifestation.

Students with Special Needs

Students with special needs have always been marginalized from mainstream schooling, even if they are mainstreamed. Before this discussion begins, we want to challenge the use of the word disabled that is often associated with students who have special needs. Instead, we propose the word "otherly-abled" as an affirming term that means that the individual does whatever task is at hand different than someone who is able-bodied—one whose body is not impaired by any physical problems. What does it mean to be a student with special needs? A student who has special needs can range from a physical issue to one that is psychological, to one that is emotional, academic, neurological, or even gifted.

Some special needs students are in self-contained classrooms whereas others may be mainstreamed for some or part of their schooling. We are often not privy to the put-downs incurred by these students nor do we necessarily even address them in our classes. It is vital to the well-being of every student that we discuss the impacts of taunting and bullying against all people and that we help our students take a stand against perpetration of violence in whatever form against students with special needs.

Some of the ways in which we can begin to address special needs from within the loaded matrix is by locating it within our patterns of discourse and by being inclusive with our language in our preservice classrooms. We can begin by working through our own biases and prejudices about students with special needs—even though we may not be aware we carry them. We must also be conscientious about designing lessons that will include all students' abilities and not inadvertently marginalize an "otherly-abled" student. When we talk about social justice with our preservice teachers, we must address all students who face discrimination and highlight particularly vulnerable populations. Unless all students are supported, vulnerable populations of students will continue to be pushed into the margins of school.

⇒*Teaching Points*
∞**Methods Courses**
Activities for Preservice Teachers—Furthering Inquiry for Social Action
•Ask students to recall their own experiences with students who have special needs when they were in school. How were they treated? Was anything positive done for them? Was there a relationship between the classroom teacher and the special needs educator? Were they teased or treated poorly? Did their own classroom teacher try to integrate the students with special needs into the classroom?
•Design a lesson plan around an issue or topic related to a special need for classroom students.
•Annotate a book list on topics related to special needs and find books to stock your classroom or school library.
•Choose a topic related to special needs and research ways to encourage your classroom students to support the student who has special needs.
•Discuss ways that will not draw undue attention to the student who has special needs.

⇒*Teaching Points*
∞**Secondary Classrooms**
•Make sure that lesson plans are inclusive or that modifications are subtle and do not single out the students with special needs.
•Be inclusive with language.
•Stock classroom or school library with texts that students can read about students who have special needs.
•If the special needs student has an assisted support, be sure that the support helps everyone so that the student is not singled out.
•Never draw undue attention to the student who has special needs.

English as a Second Language

Students who come to our public school classrooms may speak a language that we do not understand. Sometimes, we may not even have support staff in our schools who speak a student's first language. Imagine how frightening it would be to be in a sea of people and unable to communicate through the same language. Sometimes teachers are guilty of marginalizing these learners because they lack the tools to communicate with these learners or teach literacy in ways that benefit them. ESL learners can deeply reward and enhance our classrooms and bring with them a wealth of knowledge and clues about literacies different from our own. By building bridges between our first and second language learners we deepen and enrich everyone's experience as we also broaden our understanding of diversity. This section addresses some of the issues of prejudice that may impact students whose second language is English and provides insights about how to empower them in the schooling process.

By ESL, we refer to the teaching of English to nonnatives. An ESL designation assumes: learner's L1 (L1 is first or native language) is not English; learner is in school environment; the "majority" language is English; and English is the dominant language. ESL learners are a vulnerable population in schools because not only do they struggle to find a place as an outside community but may stand out because of their physical, behavioral, oral, or lexical differences. It is all the more important that we draw attention to this in teacher education so that our preservice teachers have the tools to model inclusivity in their classrooms. Therefore we can prepare our preservice teachers on how to consider fostering and maintaining a classroom space that is sensitive to the needs of our friends whose second language is English.

In methods, we can help our preservice teachers by working through their own biases, presuppositions, and prejudices about ESL learners. We might ask them what are their beliefs about ESL learners and how that might affect their teaching. It may not be obvious to them because "Standard White English" is so entrenched in American society that it has a longstanding history of being privileged as the "correct" way to speak and think. As we bump up against prejudice, though, we can redirect them to consider ways that they can include all students in lessons. In fact, unless we point this out, preservice teachers are likely to inadvertently perpetuate and privilege dominant ideologies. We can also help our preservice teachers consider how their own discourse patterns may inadvertently silence ESL learners. For instance, we need to help them understand differences in discourse patterns and how they are linked socioculturally. If they speak very fast they may silence students who are just starting to grasp newer language patterns and as such might need to slow down. If they expect students to always respond, they may not receive the feedback they anticipated. They may also have to be more deliberate about enunciating their words. Additionally, studies reveal that ESL learners benefit from visual or pictorial images and so any lesson should be accompanied by as much visual or logographic aids as possible (Ariza, Morales-Jones, Yahya, & Zainuddin, 2002). We must also help our preservice teachers develop competence in understanding how literacy is viewed by other cultures. This means inviting a discussion about how sociocultural issues impact learning and discuss ways that their lessons bridge to students' cultures. All of these points can help preservice teachers develop a pedagogy that honors equity and which does not privilege one language over another. Lastly, we can teach preservice teachers about different student learning styles and encourage them to vary the way they teach material. Gardner's (1983) work on the Multiple Intelligences is a wonderful approach to consider ways to diversify teaching and it can help students learn through many mediums. As such, we enrich students' abilities to look at the world in expansive ways.

We can introduce sociocultural theory as a meaningful way to work with all students, especially those from non-English speaking backgrounds. From a sociocultural perspective of literacy, students read, write, think, and construct meaning from printed and nonprinted texts within a sociocultural context (Erickson, 1984; Gee, 1992: Snow, 1983). This theory of learning considers and seeks to understand the cultural context within which children have grown and developed. It theorizes how children interpret who they are in relation to others, and how children have learned to process, interpret, and encode their world. Sociocultural theory is derived from Vygotsky (1978), whose views emphasize the social interactive world where learning and literacy emerge: "human learning presupposes a specific [sic] social nature and a process by which children grow into the intellectual life of those around them" (as in Perez, 1998, p. 88). The skills, concepts, and ways of thinking that an individual develops reflect the uses and approaches that permeate the community or social group of which the person is a member. Likewise Rogoff (1990) and Baker (1994) each suggest that the cultural practices and ways of understanding them depend on the social conditions and culture in which they are learned. Similarities occur in different linguistic environments and the processes children exhibit appear to be developmentally ordered (Perez, 1998). Culture contains different linguistic environments.

ESL Literacy

It will be difficult to have a well-stocked repertoire of materials that can meet the needs of all learners, but there are some basics that our preservice teachers can be prepared to use with any student. In our methods courses we can give our students book lists of young adult literature that reflect different cultures and ways of being in the world. Such lists are relatively easy to locate and some can be found on my website under books for teens: www.chss.iup.edu/sjmiller. We can also study sociocultural contexts of literacy together with young adult books or other texts so that we can possibly understand student differences better. When teaching writing, we can assist preservice teachers to recognize and be aware of different discourse patterns and encourage them to develop assignments that bridge home discourse in writing alongside "standard English" writing. For the more accelerated ESL learner and, in fact, for all classroom students, it might be interesting to teach students about how hegemony and dominant culture govern our capital job force and help them see and understand that dominant society has "white standards" into which they are expected to assimilate. Instructors can teach their methods students about the power and reasons for "code switching" between primary "d" and secondary "D" discourse. As such, students will begin to recognize what assimilation means, why, how, and when they are pressured to do so, while the teacher can also encourage the student to retain and value his/her "d" discourse. We must remind them about the importance of maintaining cultural identity.

Second Language Assessment

We cannot stop here, for we also need assessment practices that align with our teaching of ESL learners. We do our students a great disservice if we use homogenous assessments. Since ESL learners are likely to struggle somewhat with the language barrier, we cannot penalize them for their defects or even be of a mindset that they are making errors. Assessment should be heuristic, fluid, and holistic and should focus on how students are improving with skill and comprehension. We need to encourage them in ways that they will want to continue to learn the second language and feel mastery over newly acquired skills. It has been suggested that grading practices should include a function illustrating the student's beginning state of knowledge and skill (Bartholamae, 1980; Gee, 1992). In fact, Bartholomae (1980) in his seminal work on "writing error" promotes the notion that what is often perceived as error by a teacher is, in fact, not an error, but a by-product of cultural schemata or simply a miscue. According to schemata theorists, knowledge is stored in schematic structures or schemata, which are organized representations of one's background experiences. Cultural schemata are ways that show how students are affected by their cultures and provide a way to interpret meaning (Au, 1998; Pritchard, 1990). Seeing student work as "error-based" may in fact shut down and undermine the student as he/she comes to terms with a new culture and language. Here are some tips on how to create equitable and liberatory grading assessments.

Assignments and Liberatory Assessment for ESL Learners

- Balance recommendations with commendations on all assignment feedback.
- Consider cultural schemata when evaluating assignments.
- Always remember that what a student does or doesn't do is not error but rather is a developmental stage of the learner.
- Give anecdotes as much as possible and look at skill and comprehension improvement over time.
- Focus on one main idea of growth at a time.
- Isolate skills when there seems to be a gap and work one-on-one with the student to help improve his/her skills and comprehension and evaluate improvement.

• Individualize assignments as much as possible and develop an individualized learning chart for the student—when possible develop assessments with the students.
• Invite students to offer feedback on what and how they are growing in their new language skills and ask them what they want to continue to become more adept at.

Benefits to ESL Learners

As students begin to feel empowered with their new language skills, they are likely to feel more at ease in school and with their assignments. As they grow more in their new identity and feel more comfortable on new turf, they are likely to feel better about themselves and in relationship to the matrix that encompasses them. When we graduate students from our schools and into the world at large with tools that embody liberatory teaching, not only do students systemically make a difference in the world, but also what they offer others becomes a trajectory for future global practices about language, culture, and human agency.

⇒***Teaching Points***

∞Methods Courses

Activities for Preservice Teachers—Furthering Inquiry for Social Action

•Observe how an elementary teacher approaches teaching ESL learners. Take notes, notice the artifacts, texts, use of language, student positioning, and any issues you see. What works well? What needs improvement? What did you learn?
•Unpack institutional barriers that affect ESL learners. How does a nearby school district address the needs of linguistically and culturally diverse learners?
•Research and make class presentations about laws, past and present, that impact ESL learning.
•Develop a lesson plan that challenges students to "code-switch" between "d" and "D" discourses and which pushes students to also consider the larger implications of such an assignment.
•Annotate a book list of at least fifteen different cultures and identify the reading level.
•Compile a list that will help to remind each student of ways that they are entrenched in dominant culture and write a solution that will help them step out of it each time they fall back into those ways of being.
•Help students recognize the benefits of a dialogical relationship between assessment and assignment development.

⇒Teaching Points

∞Secondary Classrooms

Activities for Secondary Students

•Openly address students to consider ways they feel oppressed at school based on their actual or perceived differences. Discuss how they can respond to such oppression.

•Ask students to tell you about themselves in an informal questionnaire that has questions such as Describe your family's customs; Describe your culture; What does your family like to do together? What are your favorite books, authors, TV shows, songs, musicians, actors, or films? What do you like to write about? What can you teach me about your past and present home? Tell me about your favorite subjects; Do you like to use the Internet?

•Ask students to identify a social problem relating to a language barrier in the United States or abroad and research reasons for the problem. Present findings to the class.

•Ask students to write poetry about their concerns, their lives, their hopes, and their dreams.

•Have students "code-switch" between "d" and "D" discourses on their poems or an essay and ask them to consider the larger implications of such an assignment.

•Create a word wall of common American phrases and pair them with phrases that mean close to the same thing of the ESL learner.

•Invite students' suggestions for readings and writing assignments of films.

•Look for positive images of ESL learners and research how the individual assimilated into the United States. Include childhood, schooling, jobs, etc.

•Invite in guest speakers who are second language learners who hold different positions in the community (workers, athletes, poets, musicians, dancers), and ask them to speak about their experiences.

•Involve parents as much as possible by inviting them in to make presentations, to offer input, to help.

•Set up a mentoring system in class so that students can go to certain people for specific needs.

The "ISMs"

Most of us and even our students have some basic awareness about the "ISMs"—"words that become 'nouned' and are laden with pejorative connotations based on actual or perceived differences" (Miller, 2005b, p. 88). We find it all the more important then to build upon the "ISMs" and look for ways to disrupt their systemicness and insipidness in schools. Our preservice teachers must be prepared to recognize and identify the presence of "ISMs" and then disrupt them from fortifying. This section addresses how to support preservice teachers as "ISMs" manifest in their classrooms.

The common "ISMs" we see present in universities and schools are:

- •Able-bodiedism, based on physical abilities
- •Ageism, based on age
- •Anti-Semitism, based on a person's being Jewish or from a Semitic country
- •Classism, based on social class
- •Heterosexism, based on the belief that everyone should be heterosexual
- •Lookism, based on appearance
- •Racism, based on a person's race, ethnicity, or national origin
- •Religionism, based on religion
- •Sexism, based on gender
- •Sizism, based on weight or height. (GLSEN, 2001)

I illustrate the insipidness of the "ISMs" through three *true,* brief examples. Recently, I heard a teacher flippantly say to her class, "I saw a TV show last night that had a *fat* person in it." The use of reckless discourse can oppress a student who may be weight challenged (an example of sizism). Perhaps unbeknownst to that teacher, the student identity may destabilize and begin to isolate, shut down, and create a social space to survive because of the imprudent use of language that was not deliberately used to oppress and silence the student. In a second example, a teacher I once worked with said, "The *fags* go in one group." The student who most likely already felt marginalized because of his/her actual or perceived sexual orientation, both inside and outside of the classroom space, may destabilize and begin to gravitate toward a space in the classroom where he/she may grow withdrawn, cease to do schoolwork, and even become suicidal (an example of heterosexism). Third, a preservice student teacher I observed said to me, "I can't believe how many *Mexicans* are in the school now." Though her use of the word Mexican was seemingly benign, the context in which she used the sentence wasn't (an example of racism). Her tone insinuated that the school was falling apart and the Mexican students played a contributing factor to the breakdown of the school. Had a student overheard her, he/she may begin to create social spaces to avoid her and likewise shut down, withdraw, and oppress the self.

In the first situation, the intent behind the teacher's use of language was innocent. In the second situation, the intent behind the teacher's language was deliberate and meant to exclude particular identities. In the third situation, the intent behind the teacher's language was naïve and careless. What all three scenarios share in common, though, is that they illustrate the danger inherent in using derogatory words carelessly. Because of who was using the words (teachers) the words carried great power and had the potential to oppress students.

How do we help preservice teachers understand and recognize the impact of prejudice on students? We can begin with a discussion about the consequences on the student. For students who are pounded daily at school with any form of oppression whether it is verbal, psychological, physical, or mental, it adversely impacts a student's well-being and ability to function at potential. Students who have poor coping skills and are not able to buffer themselves from taunts or who may lack a support system may internalize the oppression[4] and hurt themselves. By teaching preservice teachers about the "ISMs" they can be more conscientious about their own uses of terms that may inadvertently oppress students and undermine learning. We can contextualize the "ISMs" within the matrix and teach preservice teachers about how a cycle of violence begins with myths or misinformation, stereotypes, or a biased history. The cycle continues as myths are validated and reinforced by institutions, culture, media, family, religion, and friends and then become socialized into the cycle. With enough repetition, the misinformation and myths become truth and anything that differs is perceived as abnormal. The cycle concludes with a behavior that can be prejudiced, or oppressive, or even a hate crime (Miller, 2005b). Teachers need to be taught to interrupt the cycle anywhere they can and help their own students rethink their attitudes and beliefs.

Related to the "ISMs," the following list of terms or phrases have the potential to upset or shut down students. It is important to look at and create such a list yearly, even though it may be offensive because often times our own students use and know terms which are derogatory but with which we are unfamiliar. In fact our students have much to teach us about the pejorative terms that seem to emerge every day.

Able-bodiedism
Gimp
Freak
Disabled
Retard
Broken

Ageism
You're too young
You're too old
You just don't understand
Teens can't do that
S/he won't remember

Anti_Semitism
Cheap
Sheister
Christ-Killer
Smarty-pants
Kyke

Racism
Spic
Wetback
Fork
Nigger
Raghead
Diaperhead
Pig
Chink
"Don't Jew-me"
Tonto
Chinaman
Rice patty
Beaner
Redskins
Dothead
Gringo
Granola
Quickie Mart

Sizism
Fat
Obese
Whale
Large marge
Tubby
Stick
Anorexic
Twig

Heterosexism
Dyke
Lesbo
Faggot
Home-breaker
Pedophile
Carpet-muncher
"Hole in one"
Limp wrist

Classism
White trash
Beggar
Stuck-up
Baby mama

Sexism
Slut
Pimp
Ho
Stud
Hoochie

Racism	**Heterosexism**
Soap	Queer
Wangster	Jota

Once we compile such a list, and as we add to it, we must commit to never using these words in our classes in a pejorative way. We must commit to stand up when these words are spoken by our students in pejorative ways and interrupt the cycle of prejudice. Eventually, students will challenge each other to such a duel. We do not advocate posting these words in a classroom as they can easily be misconstrued. Writing them onto butcher paper that can be stored for later use might be the most effective way to approach this.

Preservice teachers can select texts and develop assignments that challenge their students to become agents of social change by standing up for others who face adversity. They may select texts where individuals have been oppressed or faced discrimination in some form (see chapter 3 book lists and critical literacy section later in this chapter). We should encourage them to challenge their classroom students on how they use and perpetuate the "ISMs" through discourse and behavior and invite them to speak and act differently. We can frame this for secondary students by looking more at the root issues and causes. We can invite our preservice teachers to discuss with their students the different social movements in the history of the United States and look at how their legacies live on through socialization and inherited value. Such movements can include but by no means are limited to: women's rights, civil rights, Gay, Lesbian, Bisexual, Transgender, Queer (GLBTQ) rights, immigrant rights, children with special needs rights, Native American rights, Asian American rights, bilingual rights, ways that immigrants are perceived post 9/11, and the new culture wars (Spring, 2001). While more people have rights than ever before, that does not mean that we don't still have much work to do, nor does it indicate that there won't be a recycling of prejudice. In fact, the spacetime of values has regressed into rewriting prejudice into the Constitution as evidenced recently with the threat of amending it for purposes of defending heterosexual marriage and marginalizing gay marriage. We still have work to do, and in our efforts to maintain a momentum for social change, we cannot afford to stop or become comfortable with the changes we now have, for the legacy of oppression still lives in the minds of many and is deeply entrenched into the fabric of American society.

⇒Teaching Points

∞Methods Courses and Secondary Classes

Assignments for Preservice Teachers—Furthering Inquiry for Social Action

•Brainstorm other "ISMs" with students and write them on the board.

•Ask students to identify the "ISMs" that are apparent in the university or school. Create a chart that ranks them from most to least pervasive. Are they departmental? Are they on billboards? Memos? Walls? Bathrooms? Desks?
•What terms do students see or hear on campus or at school that perpetuate the "ISMs?" Brainstorm ways to change such language.
•Observe "ISMs" in day-to-day life and record them.
•Have students reflect on how they have been oppressed by an "ISM" and ask how that felt? When did it stop? What did you do?
•Start an anti-"ISM" campaign on campus or at school.
•Design a lesson plan that can teach classroom students about the "ISMs."
•Come out in support to stop "ISMing" in class.
•By watching the news, a TV series, comedy show, listening to music, etc., research how the media perpetuates the "ISMs."
•Ask students to write a letter to the person against whom they committed an "ISM." What did they do? To whom did they do it? How did that person feel? If they had a chance to tell that person something, what would it be?

The Intersections of Race, Class, and Gender

Recently, there have been discussions at NCTE about reflecting on the significance of "Race, Class, Gender" in teacher education. The commission with the Conference on English Education states its position on this that while these topics are important to address, teacher education needs to target the skills, behaviors, and attitudes needed for teachers to teach children from linguistically and culturally diverse backgrounds. The commission chair, DeBlase (2005), writes:

> The challenge before our Commission is to develop and uncover models of teaching that are flexible enough to capture and reflect the ways these elements function together; to determine how we in English education see ourselves and others; and to delineate the opportunities for transformation, constructive growth, and change in our profession. (p. 248)

This section reviews the intersection of race, class, and gender and the significance of addressing our beliefs about them in methods classes. It is important not only to address their intersections because of their loaded natures but because much of the divisive hierarchies of power are centered on them.

When we begin to address race, class, and gender, we need to foster an atmosphere of trust, respect, and challenge through a seminar format (Bolgatz, 2005). As much as possible, instructors should attempt to normalize the discussion around these issues so that when they surface, they are no longer loaded. Instructors can ask students to reflect on their own positions through questions, inviting questions and discussion, by discussing personal experiences, and by drawing from current happenings in society and the media. Instructors should be well informed by drawing on different points of view and be able to articulate and support a rationale on each of these areas. Each of these areas is complex, and the instructor should be well informed and thorough when attempting to illicit responses from students.

As we unpack these issues with our preservice teachers, we have to recognize that there may be some pain in owning some of the prejudicial beliefs that our students hold. As such, we must prepare ourselves for what may be unleashed and support and encourage them through any difficulty. We cannot take any of this personally and each of us must use our own unique style of teaching to address the loaded issues that we ask our students to consider. If the challenge feels too daunting, then it is best to refrain from unleashing what you, personally, do not feel ready to handle. Perhaps co-teaching a methods class that addresses loaded content or shadowing a colleague may initially be a way to begin.

In our methods courses, it is vital that we begin to help our preservice teachers unpack their beliefs and presuppositions around race, class, and gender so they do not inadvertently marginalize students, which can undermine learning opportunities. Depending on rapport with our classes, we can begin with a warm-up activity by asking them to respond aloud to describe a teacher they looked up to and reflect on the attributes that contributed to that teacher. We can then pair that by asking the complement question to respond aloud and describe a teacher they did not like and reflect on the attributes that contributed to that teacher. From here, we can begin to make sense of what those teachers' beliefs and attitudes were about humanity and even focus in on the skill set the teacher embodied that contributed to how she/he taught.

Next, we can ask preservice students to respond in writing to questions such as:

•What are your beliefs about race?
•What are your beliefs about social class?
•What are your beliefs about gender?

We can ask them to look carefully at their answers, or pair up with someone who may help them reflect and highlight which of those beliefs have the potential to be oppressive to classroom students. Once this stage is completed, they can reflect on the potentially oppressive beliefs in a dialogical journal and the instructor can begin to look at the loaded content along with the preservice teacher. We are by no means insisting that preservice teachers shift beliefs but we are providing the critical thinking opportunities that may help unpack some of the underlying prejudices about which they may not be conscious. As a follow up, we can then ask, how do such beliefs shape their teacher identities? If they are pleased with their answers, then we affirm that, and if they are still struggling, we continue to guide them to a space where they become more at ease with their inchoate teaching identities. In bringing this piece to a close, we might ask our preservice teachers to reflect on the kinds of teachers they want to be and ask them to consider why being that kind of teacher is significant to them. As preservice teachers gain confidence in who they want to be as teachers, affirming their identities becomes a fundamental part of their confidence in the classroom (Miller, 2005a).

In our methods courses, we can invite discussions that look at race, class, and gender through nonbinary lenses. To teach in a way that perpetuates the status quo reinforces dominant cultures and ideologies. However, introducing preservice teachers to consider nonbinary understandings on these topics challenges the status quo and has the potential to be disseminated across spacetime and into new contexts altogether. For instance, as preservice teachers negotiate their teacher identities, we can pose questions that encourage thinking outside of the box. We can inquire:

- Describe where and how you first developed your concept of your own ethnic or cultural identity.
- Describe where and how you first developed your concept of your own gender identity.
- Describe where and how you first developed your concept of your social class. What were you told?
- Why did you believe that to be true? Who told you?
- How were those beliefs socialized?
- At what age did you begin to challenge what you learned about yourself? What made you reconsider those beliefs?
- Was there ever a time where you thought your answers did not fit the images society had ingrained into you? How did you respond?

As preservice teachers start to see a link from present to past, they can begin to consider strategies to expand the ways in which they bring up such loaded issues with their classroom students. Once preservice teachers have a concrete, visceral understanding of where their beliefs come from, we can contextualize it within a historical framework of oppression in the United States. When all this is done and said, we can explain that the problem is not race, class, and gender, but rather how they can manifest into racism, classism, and sexism.

Racism

Racism "is a system involving cultural messages and institutional policies and practices as well as the beliefs and actions of individuals. In the context of the United States, this system clearly operates to the advantage of Whites and to the disadvantage of people of color" (Tatum, 2003, p. 7). We can educate preservice teachers to understand that whites benefit from racism albeit many do so unconsciously. We can work with all of our students to help them recognize the advantages that some have acquired and how the system continues to benefit some of them. We can ask them provocative questions such as:

•How does your skin color benefit you in society?
•What do you take for granted?
•Have you ever been denied access somewhere because of your skin color?
•What do you worry about at the end of the day (see McIntosh, 2002, for further ideas on questions)?

As whites are still the dominant identity in the United States, if they do not examine how they benefit from their racial identity, then their racial privilege goes unacknowledged. A problem herein is that for so long whites have systemically benefited from the system that it has become synonymous with their coexistence and there may be an unconscious sense to not challenge a system from which one benefits. What can we do then to challenge our white students and help them recognize the benefits they have acquired because of their ethnicity?

Although we are beginning some of these discussions in methods classrooms and for some students it is their first time ever looking at racial privilege, Tatum (2003) suggests that these discussions should begin in preschool. At an early age, we can build a critical consciousness around racial issues so that when we are faced with them, we have a sense of how to conduct ourselves. First, we can begin by explaining that because whiteness has gone unnamed and unexamined for so long, it has become normalized. Because of its normalized "invisibility," "it has fostered an illusion that those who succeed do so because of their superior intelligence, their hard work, or their drive, rather than, at least in part, their privilege" (Rothenberg, 2002, p. 2). Although one certainly cannot change their skin color, they can select and choose how they behave in relation to it. While some can't help to benefit from the system, they can learn how to shift their attitudes toward it. Rothenberg (2002) reminds that "the first step toward dismantling the system of privilege that operates in this society is to name it and second is for those of us who can to use our privileges to speak out against the system of privilege as a whole" (p. 4).

Next, we can teach our preservice teachers how whites, like other ethnicities, have been "raced." We do not often think that whites have been "raced" in the ways that other ethnicities have been. To the contrary, whites have been "raced" to believe that they are superior and more intelligent than others (Rothenberg, 2002). Because these attributes are so embedded in white identity, whites have indeed been "raced" to believe in certain qualities that encumber white identity. It is important to have an ethnic identity because our ethnicities and cultures provide us with a sense of belonging, ritual, language, worldview, family, music, foods, and values. But unless we unpack some of the elitist values that are also associated with white identity, whites are likely to perpetuate a sense of entitlement that continues to perpetuate racism. So while an individual may not be blatantly racist, particular habits that uphold and sustain institutionalized dominant culture can be so, if left unexamined. White power will sustain itself unless it is named, but to name it threatens the very foundation upon which society was established.

Third, we have a moral responsibility to point out to our preservice teachers the consequences of not examining whiteness. Wildman and Davis (2002) say that "failure to acknowledge privilege, to make it visible in legal doctrine, creates a serious gap in legal reasoning, rendering us unable to address issues of systemic unfairness" (p. 89). Along the same lines, the invisibility of unexamined whiteness strengthens it and the "the power it creates and maintains. The invisible cannot be combated, and as a result privilege is allowed to perpetuate, regenerate, and re-create itself" (p. 89). Silence sustains its power. Consequently, we raise a society bereft and ignorant of how privilege manifests and how it fosters a perpetual spacetime of oppression. We need to assist preservice teachers to be conscious of racist attitudes and beliefs so that they do not pass down a legacy of oppression. This means that we encourage them not to participate in either active or passive racism. This means that when a racist joke is made we do not laugh, or when we see someone unfairly discriminated against because of skin color, we stand up to stop the treatment, or when we see biased curriculum and unfair hiring practices, we speak out. This is how we interrupt the cycle. We live in a melting pot society of multiple identities that are forming and being reconstituted every second and in order for systemic change to occur, we each have to do our part.

Classism

Classism is the systemic oppression of individuals that privileges and economically disadvantages one social class over the other, generally the wealthy over the less wealthy. Generally stemming from institutional policies and social values, in the context of the United States, this system operates to the advantage of the wealthy and to the disadvantage of the poor. It is important that we develop a social consciousness with our preservice teachers around class issues because they are likely to be teaching students from disparate backgrounds in which some have advantages that others don't. It would be very easy to marginalize students from a particular social class by requiring them to have access to materials which may be far outside of their means.

We can begin to educate our preservice teachers on class issues by unpacking what they bring with them to methods. We can ask them to reflect on how they benefit or are disadvantaged from class privilege. We can ask them to reflect on what advantages they had while growing up. For instance, we can survey them with questions such as:

- How many books were in your home while growing up?
- Did your family take vacations?
- Did your family have a second home?
- Did you have your own computer or other kinds of technology?
- Did your family belong to a club?
- Did your family eat at expensive restaurants?
- What kinds of car did your family own?

While other factors may certainly impact these answers, it is important to understand how social class grants individuals access to particular spaces and material items that may place them at an advantage over their peers. On the other hand, we might also further inquire when preservice teachers' responses were negative to these questions, to follow up with:

- How does it make you feel to see how some people are born with particular entitlements?
- What does it mean to you how social class advantages some while it disadvantages others?
- Describe what you take for granted?
- What spaces do you not have access to because of your social class?

Granted, tension may ensue from these responses, and we must attempt to clear the air on these issues within ourselves before we can try to teach about them to our secondary students.

Once we've unpacked preservice beliefs around social class, we can navigate it toward helping them consider ways to be proactive about social class in their teaching. We must help them understand that when they design lessons, anything they ask students to produce or even read, each student must have equal access to the required material so that we are not reinforcing a class hierarchy. For instance, when teaching a novel, poem, or short story, each student should have free or equal access to materials. This means making sure the school or local library has class sets of materials. We should not make our students spend money on texts that they may not be able to afford. Similarly, if we want to take students on field trips, we should be able to provide each student with a ticket somewhere or else write grants for them to attend. We should never require students to spend their own money on events or activities but, instead, should provide opportunities for in-school fundraisers. We also cannot force our students to type papers at home when they may lack funds to have computers. Students should always be provided with school-time for typing assignments and having access to technology for which they may otherwise not have access to. Lastly, it is important to keep in mind that some of our students are working to support their families. As a consequence they may be overly tired, underprepared with their assignments, and may even be hungry. Each of these things may place them at a disadvantage to their peers who do not face the same issues. Therefore, we need to develop in ourselves an empathy and a sensitivity to be thoughtful about how we respond to the changing realities faced by our youth without lowering our expectations for achievement. We fail our students and do them a disservice if we do not try to meet youth where they are in their lives. This does not mean we throw expectations out the window or become authoritarians, but it does mean focusing on how to bridge schooling to students' lives. As preservice teachers come to terms with interrupting the cycle of prejudice, ultimately they help shift dynamics of power in society.

Sexism

Sexism is the systemic oppression of individuals that privileges one gender, generally men over women. Generally stemming from a history of institutional policies and social values defined by men, this system operates to the advantage of the men, and more often white men, and to the disadvantage of women. Like racism and classism, it is vital that we develop a social consciousness with our preservice teachers around gender bias issues so as not to perpetuate oppressive gender-based hierarchies that are deeply entrenched in society. As we deepen preservice teachers' awareness about gender oppression, we ultimately shift gender dynamics in dominant culture. We can do this by introducing the history of rights of women, men, queers, and transgender individuals in the United States. While most people have a basic background in women's and men's rights, it is important to introduce the transgender movement in this spacetime.

The transgender movement seeks to have equal protection for transgender people that prohibits discrimination based on "gender identity or expression" and ensures that all transgender and gender nonconforming people are protected by law. This includes jobs, housing, health care, hate crimes legislation, legislative language, antidiscrimination bills, foster care and adoption, marriage, bathrooms, changing birth certificates to reflect the chosen gender, students in school, and being visible in the mainstream eye (discussed in more detail in the *Allies and "Outness"* section).[5] This also means claiming words and pronouns that speak to their experiences. Common pronouns that many transgender people embrace are "zhe," "hir," and "per" that correlate to he, her, and person. Such as "zhe is going to the bathroom" or "what is hir name?" or "who is that per?" Such ownership over the pronoun draws visibility to the movement and places it within the context of different spaces.

Once we provide a historical context of gender rights for our students, we can begin to unpack preservice teachers' beliefs about gender and look at their existing attitudes. For instance, we can ask them how their gender has ever advantaged or disadvantaged them in jobs, school, sports teams, family dynamics, marriage/partnership, while shopping, waiting in line for service, going to a mechanic or doctor, or with police officers. We can ask them how they felt based on how they were responded to and how they, in turn, responded. We can ask them what they take for granted about their gender. Once beliefs and attitudes are unpacked we can shift toward helping them consider ways to prevent perpetuation of gender bias in their own classrooms.

We have a social and moral responsibility to develop gender-inclusive language along with our preservice teachers. This means that we remind them that they must be careful about speaking in ways that privilege one gender over the other and which must include our transgender students who do not fall into any of the gender categories. This means that we ask our students how they want to be referred to, what pronouns we should use, what name they want to be called, and if there is anything that we should be made aware of about their gender identity. Some students may be hesitant to disclose until they feel safe enough, but unless teachers demonstrate through discourse and behavior that they are an ally, students are likely to assume that they cannot open up. Along similar lines, we must also be concerned about fostering competitions in classrooms albeit they may appear fun; they reinforce power dynamics and binary roles and beliefs about gender. This means eliminating activities and categories of boys versus girls. It means that we are sensitive with our language all the time and we are deliberate in our actions when designing lessons so we do not marginalize nor reinforce sexism on any level.

When we work with our preservice teachers on supporting them to develop lesson plans around sexism, we can discuss mainstream generalizations about gender roles as a means of tackling some of the gender bias. For instance, we can inquire about the roles the students played in their homes while growing up and about their parents' beliefs and attitudes about household chores and roles. We can bring this into modern society and ask them how the media perpetuates or challenges gender roles. We can ask them about how they intend to either conform or challenge these roles in their own lives. No doubt, some students will be resistant to challenging what for so long has been normalized as oppressive to one gender, but through dialogue and a historical examination of women's, men's, and transgender rights, preservice teachers can come to a more informed decision about their beliefs that will inform their developing pedagogies.

In closing this section, we remind the instructors that there is no one simple way to challenge individual belief systems nor to necessarily ensure that preservice teachers will opt to apply some of the issues related to social justice teaching. At best, we can hope that preservice teachers teach in a way that embodies their belief system and that it is not oppressive to their students. Preservice teachers will learn how oppressions intersect and play out soon enough as they are teaching in their own classrooms, and if the values of the school in which they teach are a mismatch to their own, then they may make necessary adjustments or leave the school altogether. Just because a teacher struggles in one school, it doesn't mean he/she will not thrive in another (Miller, 2005a). Working with preservice teachers and helping them develop a deeper social consciousness about how oppression can manifest in their classroom is vital to the well-being and survival of their classroom students.

⇒*Teaching Points*

∞Methods and Secondary Courses

Questions for Preservice Teachers and Classroom Students—Furthering Inquiry for Social Action

•Describe how you experience your culture in relation to dominant society.

•Describe how you experience your gender in relation to dominant society.

•Describe how you have experienced your social class in relation to dominant society.

•What do you think race means? How do race, ethnicity, and culture differ?

•What are your beliefs around gender? Is it socially constructed?

•How does social class affect one's ability to have access to certain social spaces?

•Are there other intersections of issues or ideas that you feel need to be addressed together? If so, describe them.

⇒*Teaching Points*

∞Methods Courses

Assignments for Preservice Teachers—Furthering Inquiry for Social Action

•Design a lesson plan that addresses the intersections of race, class, and gender. Be sure to address how individuals can be oppressed because of their race, class, or gender.

•Research the different historical origins of race as either a social construct challenge or as essentially determined. Write a position statement on what you believe.

•Research the different ways gender is viewed from biological, environmental, social, and religious standpoints. Write a position statement on what you believe.

•Research how social class manifests in day-to-day life. Create a list of where and how people are discriminated against or affirmed based on their social standing. Consider other reasons other than social class that they may either be discriminated against or affirmed.

•Annotate a list of books, poems, and short stories that address race, class, and gender. Describe the grade level that it is best suited for.

•Annotate a list of books, poems, and short stories presenting nonbinary views of race, class, and gender and describe the grade level that it is best suited for.

•Look for examples on how the media perpetuates or challenges oppressive stereotypes based on race, class, and gender.
•Research the hiring practices in your place of employment or place of internship. Who is protected? Who is left out? Does anything seem particularly discriminatory? If you don't work, choose a local company and research its hiring policy.

⇒*Teaching Points*
∞Secondary Courses
•Develop a vocabulary around loaded issues such as prejudice, oppression, power, privilege, gender, class, and race.
•Discuss how to address oppressive issues school wide. How can students help to shift the climate of the school?
•Consider ways to create social networks in other classes that focus around issues relating to social justice.
•Report on topics of oppression observed in school and in the local community.
•Watch a film that has prejudicial overtones and deconstruct oppressive language and images present in the film as a class.
•Listen to music that has prejudicial overtones and deconstruct oppressive language and images present in the lyrics as a class.
•Keep a log of oppressive language students hear and write it down for later sharing.
•Look for examples in the media on how it perpetuates or challenges oppressive stereotypes based on race, class, and gender.
•In your place of employment or place of internship, research the hiring practices. Who is protected? Who is left out? Does anything seem particularly discriminatory? If you don't currently have a job, choose a local company and research its hiring policy.

Allies and "Outness"

When we address loaded issues, we cannot do it alone. It is important that within our matrix we develop a support system of individuals who also have the tools to address incendiary issues. This may not always be easy, but we can attempt to foster a network of relationships with people who will speak out on behalf of loaded issues. This network contains all of the people whom we interact with daily and includes but is not limited to our families, friends, colleagues outside our departments, our doctors, dentists, coaches, parents of students, administrators, and politicians. To be an ally means to speak "out" for those individuals who may not be able to, or for those who have less access to decision makers, or those who have been silenced into submission. It also means to do whatever it takes until every person has been spoken for and gains equal rights. Where do we begin when even some of our classroom instructors and secondary teachers are vulnerable to losing their jobs because of the ever-present pervasiveness of discrimination based on sexual orientation?

While the current Federal Human Rights Act does not protect GLBTQ educators from unfair hiring or firing practices, there are individual states and cities that have "Employment Non-discrimination Acts."[6] The Congress is currently considering the Employment Non-Discrimination Act (ENDA), which would extend employment protections to GLBTQ individuals, but the law has little chance of passage under the current Congress. Currently, in thirty-four states GLBT employees are not protected from being fired or hired based on their sexual orientation and in forty-four states they are not protected based on their gender identity. Seven "state courts, commissions or agencies have interpreted the existing state law to include some protection against transgender individuals in Connecticut, Florida, Hawaii, Illinois, Massachusetts, New Jersey and New York" (Human, 2006). According to a report from the National Gay and Lesbian Task Force (2006):

> As of April 2004, 14 states and the District of Columbia prohibit discrimination based on sexual orientation in both the public and private sectors. An additional 11 states have an executive order, administrative order, or regulation that prohibits discrimination against public employees based on sexual orientation. At the municipal level, 285 cities, counties, or government organizations provided some level of protection against employment discrimination based on sexual orientation. Of those, 152 extend protections to employment in the private sector as well.
>
> Public sector employees have laws protecting them from discrimination based on "gender identity and/or expression" in six states and the District of Columbia. Of these six, Minnesota, Rhode Island, New Mexico, California, and the District of Columbia extend protection to private sector employees. At the local level, 52 cities and nine counties in the U.S. have nondiscrimination laws that cover both sexual orientation and gender identity.

In our very own state of Pennsylvania, we do not have an Employment Non-Discrimination Law but there is an executive order that protects state employees from discrimination based on gender identity and expression. It is important to understand that an "executive order" is a unilateral decision made by the current governor only, and is therefore null and void as soon as the governor leaves office. Additionally in Pennsylvania, the law does not address school issues relating to sexual orientation or gender identity. This means teachers, faculty, and students have no state protection based on sexual orientation or gender identity but individual cities in Pennsylvania do. While Pennsylvania has no safe schools laws, "the regulations of the State Board of Education state that access to educational programs shall be provided without discrimination on the basis of a student's sexual orientation (among other factors). *State Bd. of Ed. Regs. §4.4(c)"* (Human, 2006).

Patrick (1994) conducted a study that examined the effect of tenure, state laws, inclusive contracts, and local ordinances on the openness of public identities of gay teachers. He found that most of the participants were not "out" because of fear of professional, social, and physical retaliation. Statistically speaking, the national average number of teachers per public school is 23.4, and it is likely that 2–3 of those educators are GLBT (Harbeck, 1984). At the university level, it is likely that there are several GLBT instructors per department who generally have more protection contractually than their secondary school colleagues. For secondary schools, while this statistic can provide disastrous consequences if the school has a large GLBTQ student body and no teachers who are either willing or able to be an ally or "out" in fear of retribution, at the university level, there is generally a larger acceptance of difference and open-mindedness.

Why else then is it so difficult to be an ally or to be "out," and more importantly, why is it important to be an ally or be "out" in school? First, there are loaded politics involved in coming out at school. One cannot simply look at sexual orientation or gender expression in isolation as other factors confound treatment such as race, age, ability, national origin, and religion (Rasmussen, 2004). Second, some people who ally themselves as advocates for GLBTQ individuals may be labeled as such and fear public retaliation for their alliances. Third, not all individuals will have job protection if they come out. We are not advocating that someone come out *per se* as the choice is highly personal, but that we find it necessary to draw attention to the issue so preservice teachers who are GLBT are informed about possible redress if they choose to come "out."

On the other hand there are some viable reasons to come out. In secondary schools and at the university level, students who are GLBTQ and their allies need emotional, psychological, and physical safety. An ally or an "out" teacher/instructor can provide that source of comfort. Similarly, if a teacher/instructor is an ally or "out" it may lessen the frequency of harassment, alienation, and hate in the school or university setting. Having an ally or being "out" can also mean the difference between life and death for some students who may not have the support they need at home or who are away from their families for the first time. Some schools have formed gay/straight alliances (GSA) for these very reasons. Unless someone in a school speaks on behalf of GLBTQ students and their allies, it may be assumed that they are deviant and unwelcome. Likewise, unless we come out on behalf of GLBTQ students and their allies, we may inadvertently undermine learning when we do not speak out and may silence or shut down students by not speaking up. When we do speak out we may boost self-esteem and provide life-changing opportunities for students.

It is important that we speak about the importance of being an ally in our methods courses. We can explain to our preservice teachers the possible redress of coming out and we can also explain the significance of coming out. As an ally, we can help them to make a stand against oppression and prejudice in all forms and address concerns they may have early on. We can help them consider the benefits of being an ally and the significance of that in both their own as well as their students' lives. To be an ally and to be either "out as an ally" or "out of the closet" takes tremendous courage and an act of selflessness. We want our student teachers to be doing what is best for not only them but for the students' lives they will impact. Being "out" begets responsibility and it is imperative that preservice teachers recognize the role they will embody once they come out of the proverbial closet.

⇒*Teaching Points*
∞Methods Courses and Secondary Classes
Questions to Consider
•What does being an ally look like to you?
•How can you best support a GLBTQ student who is being oppressed?
•What kind of support will you need to continue in your effort as an ally?
•How can you support others who want to become allies?
•What type of ally work exists at your school or university site?
•How can you do ally work in your community?
•What would a network of allies look like? How can you train and educate people to be allies?

Techniques That Empower

Teaching takes on and is embodied by many different shapes and forms. We are of the belief that teaching should seek to connect literacy to real life and give students tools to act on and change the world in which they live. Teaching should help fill in gaps of knowledge and the world, people, texts, and the nuances that we cannot account for. There are four ways that highlight how teacher educators can help empower preservice teachers to work with some of these more loaded issues: (a) through self-reflection, (b) recontextualization of the word power, (c) developing a liberatory pedagogy, and (d) appropriation of critical literacy perspectives into classrooms.

First, teachers who do not examine themselves critically disservice the students they are teaching. In order to liberate and validate students when we teach, we must first closely look into our own souls at the prejudices we carry with us into the world. hooks (1994) says, "teachers must be actively committed to a process of self-actualization that promotes their own well-being, if they are to teach in a manner that empowers students" (p. 15). However in America, hooks pleads, "it is even more rare to hear anyone suggest that teachers have any responsibility to be self-actualized individuals" (p. 16). She suggests that teaching should work toward increasing student self-worth by embodying an engaged and liberatory pedagogy. She suggests that teachers "teach in a manner that respects and cares for the souls of our students [, which] is essential if we are to provide the necessary condition where learning can most deeply and intimately begin" (p. 13). We reemphasize that we must do our own inner work first.

Second, according to Freire, power is a generative term that generates discussions about social and political realities. Appropriating from Guinier and Torres (2002) the concept of "power with," it comes from and means the "psychological and social power gained through collective resistance and struggle through the creation of an alternative set of narratives. It is relational and interactive"(p. 141). When we see ourselves as partners in learning "with" our students, we open up the space for learning for everyone while we also begin to shift dynamics of power in society that have perpetuated hegemony and status quo values.

Third, I draw from Freire's (1970) humanistic-centered, liberatory pedagogy that has great potential to benefit teachers when they choose to merge it with their cadre of teaching pedagogies. A liberatory pedagogy seeks to educate students to act on and transform their worlds through acts of cognition first, and action, second. He suggests that when we adopt a liberatory pedagogy, two distinct changes will occur: "when the oppressed unveil the world of oppression and through the praxis commit themselves to its transformation," and "in which the reality of oppression has already been transformed, this pedagogy ceases to belong to the oppressed and becomes a pedagogy of all the people in the process of permanent liberation" (p. 54). In so doing, we help free the oppressed from the oppressor, which then activates the oppressed to become agents capable of acting on and transforming their worlds; thus, we emancipate the oppressed. Although our students are not oppressed per se, they certainly are embedded within a matrix that sustains a hegemonic power and which reinforces particular social values and morals. A liberatory pedagogy prepares them to think critically about their worlds and gives them the tools to be informed citizens so that when they need to act, they know how.

Lastly, critical literacy offers a pedagogy, praxis, and practice of liberatory education that is consonant with Freire's notion of liberatory education and which provide tools that can help develop critical thinking skills. Comber and Simpson (2001) suggest that the agenda of critical literacy is such that it "examines the relationships between language practices, power relations and identities" (p. 271). They suggest that teachers must respond to the changing times amidst "conflicting and changing cultural practices" when selecting texts so as to help students make meaning of the world in which they live (p. 277). They also concur "that race, ethnicity, language, poverty, location and gender impact students' educational success and the ways in which they participate in the authorized discursive practices available in educational institutions" (pp. 275–276). Since each of these larger issues is situated within larger bodies of discourse and impact a student's identity development and success in school, teachers must truly strive to assist students in developing an identity that retains the self as the co-construction of self bumps up against the construct of self within institutions. However, this tension between the retention of an authentic self and the vulnerability of the self to social, political, cultural, and historical factors provides teachers with a tremendous agenda.

Lewinson, et al. (2002) suggest that the field of critical literacy is defined by "disrupting the commonplace, interrogating multiple view points, focusing on sociopolitical issues and taking action and promoting social justice" through texts (p. 3). Therefore, critical literacy can be a vehicle through which identity is negotiated as texts bump up against the self. Since critical literacy is "political practice influenced by social, cultural and historical factors"(Barton & Hamilton, 2000; Street, 1995 as in Hagood, 2002, p. 249) and is "committed foremost to the 'alleviation of human suffering and [to] the formation of a more just world through the critique of existing social and political problems and the posing of alternatives'"(Hagood, 2002, p. 249), texts taught through a poststructuralist lens can be a way to help youth negotiate and affirm their identities as they make meaning of the world in which they live. A poststructuralist reading of texts can be a powerful way to assist youth in holding onto their authentic selves while it teaches them to interact with the world so they may act on it in a fashion that does not perpetuate hegemony or the status quo. Youth, with an affirmed authentic self, can seek to transform the world through a subjective self that does not ascribe to the construction that the school system seeks to impose upon them. Consequently, the world/environment becomes vulnerable to a new subjectivity as it transacts with authentic selves, free of construction.

Hagood (2002) contends that critical literacy should assist students in developing an understanding of how texts "produce particular formations of self" (p. 248). Texts are situated within certain social and cultural groups. By all intensive purposes, texts are imbued by larger sociopolitical issues of power that are associated in cultural and social groups. Texts reflect the changes in society, such as in how power may change within particular ethnicities, classes, and/or social patterns. In other words, as perceptions of ethnicities change and as they may each gain access to positions of power and authority, texts reflect those changes. Our identities are impacted by their transactions with those texts and when the texts shift along with the changes in society, so too do our identities shift. This means that from a poststructuralist perspective identities are constantly in flux.

Activating Critical Literacy

I teach through four specific models of literacy, which often intersect at any one given point: reading comprehension, literary analysis, cultural heritage, and engagement and experience. In the reading comprehension model, I strive to help students become better readers of all kinds of texts. Through literary analysis, we develop a vocabulary of literary terms (diction, syntax, point of view, figurative language, theme, allusion, archetypes) and practice ways of applying them to our writings by highlighting specific components of each in our readings. Through a cultural heritage perspective, we look at human behavior, larger sociopolitical issues, and how individuals affect and are affected by one another. Lastly, through engagement and experience, we read for our own purposes and begin to develop or extend our own love for reading. I cannot assure that this happens, so I try to choose texts which best reflect my students' cultures and values for that particular class or select texts about areas in which we need to enhance our understanding of humanity. When selecting texts, I ask myself what voices do I need to have echoed back to my students? The answer often resides in the class itself. As I come to know my students through the dialogic (Freire, 1970) and understand their issues and home lives, I become more informed so I can select authors who echo to them their own stories. I often teach authors of color and select authors who have been marginalized by dominant society. I also deliberately select texts that have characters or story lines that point to prejudice and that elucidate deeper sociopolitical issues.

When I teach preservice teachers about critical literacy, from day one students interrogate hegemony and how hegemony exists as a means that reinforces dominant culture's power over others. We reflect on our own ethnicities and the power dynamic inherent within each of those ethnicities and compare that to dominant culture. We do this by looking at past and present laws so that we are well informed prior to critically reading texts. This process enables my students and me to develop a common framework that we can use as a basis to create a classroom that activates critical literacy. We also spend time looking at different forms of prejudice and their manifestations. I illustrate this with a unit I developed in teaching the novel.

Daily, students digest and peel back layers of the text through class discussion, in-depth text analysis, student teaching (appendix A), daily check-ins,[7] vocabulary building (appendix B), an essay, and lastly, a social action project (appendix C—I have attached several ideas for other social action projects here). I treat texts with great reverence and by modeling my love and passion for reading, my students often inherit a deep sense and commitment to interrogating reading through their own lenses. Together, we interrogate deeper sociopolitical issues as they intersect with the readings. What I have seen students learn from studying each novel, short story, and poem this way is a new and more critical way of transacting with their own experience through the text (Rosenblatt, 1978). As individuals, we each make meaning of the text in our lives, and often, we make meaning as a community; I illustrate this by teaching *Native Son* by Richard Wright.

Teaching *Native Son* and Disrupting the Commonplace

When I teach *Native Son*, students must complete the following tasks: write a final paper (questions form out of our dialogic), take a vocabulary check-in (vocabulary comes from the words they select from the text that they don't already know), students teach a portion from the text any way they want, highlight and complete marginalia within the text itself (students highlight the how and why an author conveys meaning through a key that is created in the front of their texts: allusion, diction, figurative language, archetypes, syntax, point of view, theme, imagery and symbolism), and generally the most exciting aspect for them is to complete a social action project.

Interrogating Multiple Viewpoints and Sociopolitical Issues

On the first day of the new unit, I provide a brief background of the author, time period, and major social and economic issues during which the book was centered. For *Native Son*, I discuss communism, the abolition of slavery and its legacy, and the personal politics of Richard Wright and of his subsequent alienation by other Black protest writers. This segues into self-selecting partners who will team-teach a portion of the book. I break down the book into readings by chapters or page numbers, and the students choose their groupings. I find this works best because students tend to soar when they can select partners rather than be pre-assigned partners. Students will make the time to meet outside of class and will teach the class in whatever way they want about their portion of the text as per rubric requirements. Over the years I have seen the most fascinating student teachings: *Jerry Springer* shows, AA meetings, *Jeopardy* games, sidewalk chalk, collages, human trivial pursuit, sling shots, and *Survivor* shows. Students decide how they want to teach a section of the book, and in so doing, they gain power over their own experience and can make meaning of the text in whatever way they need to.

Most students have never been taught this way nor felt ownership over their classroom experience; and it tends to work positively for them. After a given student teaching, we always have discussion on that reading and make meaning of the text as it transacts with our lives. Students develop their own questions from the reading and bring them in for discussion in a dialogic setting. I tend to facilitate the dialogue passively, quietly taking notes and occasionally jumping in, but for the most part, I want them to challenge each other and discuss multiple perspectives. This is a modified form of Socratic Seminar. I do not force students to participate in seminar, although each student must sit in the circle. I do not want to perpetuate nor invalidate a student's home discourse that may be to remain silent. So for those students, especially Native Americans and often times Hispanic females, although they are encouraged to speak, it is not required; instead I invite them to talk if they so choose. Additional requirements for each day of the readings are to bring in three vocabulary words defined (that I collect and assemble into their vocabulary building and test), and to be prepared for a check-in over the night's reading. Check-ins often include a reflection on the marginalia they were to complete the night before and often serve as a check that they read. Students write a final paper on the text and through their writing have an opportunity to express themselves and even take action and promote social justice. Questions for the essay derive out of classroom experience and almost always point to deeper social issues.

Taking Action and Promoting Social Justice

Usually I create social action projects, and students have choices for which project they want to tackle. Sometimes students initiate their own projects with prior consent. The point of a social action project is that it becomes a concrete experience for students to have an aesthetic, lived through transaction (Rosenblatt, 1978) with the text. Years after students read a book they generally forget names and even plots, but a lived through experience is always embedded in the human psyche and becomes a way for people to reapply, reactivate, and activate a memory into a new context. For *Native Son*, they were to participate in a cooking show and show prejudice through cooking any of the "ISMs" which exist throughout the text: racism, sexism, lookism, heterosexism, classism. Their task is to create a recipe for the book and "cook" in front of the class a solution that would both symbolically and allegorically explain and attempt to heal any of the "ISMs" found present throughout the text. Oftentimes, we follow up on the project with a "what comes now" question. We ask ourselves what do we do with these new insights and how do we transform our own experience into social justice. This brings us to close each and every unit.

Summation on Critical Literacy

Bomer and Bomer (1999) articulate that "curriculum [is] a metaphor for the lives we want to live and the people we want to be," and I take this to mean that what we teach is a foreshadow of what is to come and a flashback to what has already happened. Teachers must choose texts that are relevant to their students' lives and that encourage an interrogation of larger sociopolitical issues. Teachers are instruments of social change and creators of agents, that is, students, who become ambassadors for social change. Agency is "a personal narrative in which the self is a protagonist who confronts and solves problems, with associated motives and affect"(Dozier, Johnston, and Rogers, 2005, p. 12). We must choose curriculum wisely, we must teach with the intention to create a better world, we must implant the seeds of knowledge and the understanding of oppression in our students. Students are the future; they are my investment of what is and can happen in the future. We feel a social responsibility to our friends, family, local and national communities, and to the world to help students recognize that they are participants in society and carry with them as citizens of the United States democratic ideals and principles and therein lies a personal responsibility to step up and create the change they want to see in the world if and when they see that change is necessary to their own and others' survival. We must teach and show students how *Native Son*, *To Kill a Mockingbird*, *Song of Solomon*, *Night*, and *House on Mango Street* transact with their lives and we must foster a classroom environment that enables them to ferret through texts and peel back the deeply important layers.

I retain hope for the teaching profession that teachers will actively engage in self-examination and look at how their own presuppositions of students based on discourse, appearance, and family background may marginalize and interrupt the normal process of schooling. Since prejudice perpetuates divisive hierarchies in our country and in our schools, we should be relentless in our pursuit to understand the self so we can graduate students with healthy stabilized identities and honest perspectives of all people, wherein the dialectic can be utilized in ways that foster power with another, and not power over. In conclusion, hooks (1994) states, "professors who embrace the challenge of self-actualization will be better able to create pedagogical practices that engage students, providing them with ways of knowing that enhance their capacity to live fully and deeply" (p. 22). All teachers should strive to liberate and empower youth by modeling a prejudice-free discourse, and in so doing, we liberate others and ourselves from oppressive structures. According to Scout in *To Kill a Mockingbird*, True Democracy means equal rights for all, special rights for none, and I hope in our quest for social justice, we continue to honor such prophetic wisdom. Shannon (2002) affirms this with, "the ability to name the world through critique and hope brings us some power in and over our lives. We do not defeat capitalism, patriarchy or social structures single-handedly, but we can contest the interpretations of the world that are handed to us" (p. 206).

Concluding with Beth

Beth, as mentioned at the onset of the chapter, faced lookism, heterosexism, and racism at Hillcrest. In methods, she brought her story forward and shared how she had experienced oppression during her teaching placement. When Beth said she's been overlooked to help with the school play, we gave her reassurance that the school had a strong drama program and that she shouldn't take it personally. That would have been fine, but when she approached the drama teacher to offer her help, the drama teacher told her that he had plenty of support. Later the same week, a memo went out asking for volunteers to help with the school play. Beside herself in anguish, she brought this episode to methods and shared what had transpired. We assured her that there were many reasons for what could have happened such as: bad timing, there were already many volunteers, or that the drama teacher was in a bad mood that day. Even though we offered her assurance, she continued to feel that the reason she was not asked to help was because of how she was perceived by others in school. Even she kept her sexual orientation quiet because she did not feel safe or welcomed; she could not hide her ethnicity, however.

On our advice Beth spoke with her cooperating teacher, with whom she had an amiable rapport. Her cooperating teacher laid out some painful truths to Beth about the people at Hillcrest. Beth learned that the school was in a close-knit community that was leery and generally unwelcoming of outsiders. Since there was little diversity, the students learned about difference from reading and films and not experientially. Many of the students would stay in the community after graduation and support local business, and as such, there was little need for exposure to difference. Her cooperating teacher told her that the school had a history of individuals who had traditional values about teaching and were quite resistant to new reforms. All of the teachers in the school were white, mostly heterosexual, married, and protective of maintaining a profile of excellence. None of these reasons necessitate prejudice; however, in this the case it was made evident to Beth at Hillcrest. Faculty and the community were extremely threatened by outsiders, and Beth represented everything they feared. Fortunately, Beth's cooperating teacher encouraged her to create lessons that reflected diversity, and to teach students about issues outside of their own cultures. Her cooperating teacher was of the mindset that students needed exposure to situations that did not mirror their own, and in fact, she had taken quite a bit of flack from others for her teaching values and pedagogy.

We illustrate Beth's pain because it speaks to the need to address difficult issues in methods courses where we can create a heterotopia so that preservice teachers will have skill sets to help them cope with some of the invisible and visible dynamics in the matrix that are constantly impacting them. The frustration and marginalization can be demoralizing, and some preservice teachers may quit teaching when they experience that which they are so committed to changing. Social justice teaching is not easy especially when others are not of the same mindset. Nonetheless, we must support our preservice teachers' development about maintaining their self-esteem, embodying their multiple identities, and teaching with confidence in spite of the adversity they may encounter at their school sites. Although the placement was not easy for Beth, she told us that in the end it was important for her to see how much more work still needs to be done in the quest for social justice. The tensions she experienced in her placement strengthened and fortified her own commitment to teaching for social change.

Appendix A

Richard Wright's *Native Son*

Name:
Date:

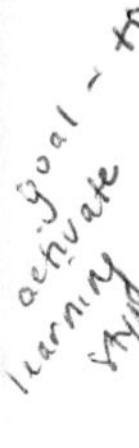

Expectations for teaching and facilitating the class:
You are expected to teach the class for no more than 30 minutes. You MUST develop a method for teaching your chapter and for engaging ALL the students and myself. Remember, have fun with this—this is your opportunity to shine in front of your peers.

Suggestions:
1. debate
2. role play
3. dramatization
4. open-ended questions
5. talk show
6. art/music/dance

Grading as follows:
Preparation(10) ___
Organization(10) ___
Audience engagement(10) ___
Eye contact(10) ___
Oration(10) ___
Acts appropriately(10) ___
Stays on task(10) ___
Redirects class on task(10) ___
Handles problems as they arise(10) ___
Teaches material in chapter(10) ___
Describes the archetypes(10) ___
Identify and then address how Wright uses individuals as symbols to enhance meaning or thematic content(10)___(i.e., what do certain people represent)
Discusses stylistic concepts—choose only 3 (i.e., point of view, syntax, figurative language, diction, tone)(30) ___
Identifies and ties in a theme of text, that is, assimilation, racism, classism, feminism, sexism, internalized oppression, human need, human motives, individual vs. society (any appropriate theme)(25) ___
Discusses allusion(10) ___
Teaches a new perspective(10) ___
Everyone in group participates(20) ___
Originality(10) ___
Cleans up(15) ___

Total(250) __
Comments:

Appendix B
Class:
Date:

Native Son Vocabulary Total(56)______

PART 1 (2 pts each)
Directions: Define the following words in complete sentences. Then use the word in a sentence and underline the word.

1. indignation—
Sentence—

2. clandestine—
Sentence—

3. galvanize—
Sentence—

4. pensive—
Sentence—

5. indelible—
Sentence

PART 2 (2 pts each)
Use the following words to write a paragraph. Underline the word in the sentence. Proper sentence structure and grammar count! The paragraph should make sense: ruse, evade, adulation, belligerently, union.

PART 3 (2 pts each)
Draw a picture that best represents the word—be sure to write a caption to explain the picture. Choose only 3.
a. guffawed

b. fatigue

c. comrade

d. translucent

PART 4(2 pts each)
unscramble and DEFINE the following words
1. dygid-

2. yrlus-

PART 5 (2 pts each)
Match the antonym for the following words: galvanize, depressed, to respect another, changeable, candid.
1. deference—

2. irrevocable-—
3. exuberant—
4. mollifying—
5. looming—

PART 6 (2 pts each)
Define the following words briefly:
1. capitalist—
2. prophesy-—
3. indelible—
4. laden—
5. seething—

PART 7 (2 pts each)

List one of your vocab words for NS not used on this test and define it.
1. ________________-

PART 8 (2 pts)
Come to me for a "pop" definition—you have no idea what I may ask!

Appendix C

Names of students:
Due Date:

Native Son, Final Project

Task: There are several "ISMs" which exist throughout this text: racism, sexism, lookism, hetero-sexism, classism—many of these "ISMs" polarize bigger from fitting into the status quo. Your task is to create a recipe for the book and "cook" in front of the class a solution that will both symbolically and allegorically explain and attempt to heal any of the "ISMs" you found present throughout the text. These cooking shows will be completed in groups of 5 students.

Rubric:
handing me this rubric(10) ___
explains the thesis(20) ___
"ISM" is first identified(10) ___
each element of food is explained to have deeper meaning(25) ___
the "cooking process"(15) ___
the final product(15) ___
the share of the final project(15—must be edible) ___
explanation of solution (i.e., the final product)(25) ___
hand out something tangible to take away from activity—-a reminder of problem and solution(20) ___

each member participates(20) ___

Total(160) ___
Comments:

Other Suggestions for Social Action Projects
Each of these projects can be modified to fit the course and the needs of the students. I have not included the specifics of each rubric as it is important that they are created based on your own particular agenda. Please contact me for detailed rubrics.

Dostoevsky's *Crime and Punishment*

How to commit the prefect crime and get away with it.

Your final project for *Crime and Punishment* is to think about, plan, act, and rationalize the perfect crime. The following rules apply:

Do not:

1. commit a crime that is punishable by the law tagging, stealing, defacement/destruction of property
2. commit a crime that can or has the potential to cause injury to others or to yourself
3. be insensitive toward any living being or creature (these are punishable by me!!)

Do:

1. write out the crime(25 pts) ___
2. write a plan for how you would commit the crime(25pts) ___
3. act out the crime and write about it(50 pts) ___
4. write a rationale for your crime (research may be necessary here—you may have to study some philosophies)(25 pts) ___
5. write how you felt about yourself after you committed the crime; would you do it again? Why or why not?(25 PTS) ___

Total (150 pts): ___

*A crime may consist of something you do which contradicts your value system. You may say something to another you would not normally say; you may act in a way that is out of character for you. If you do something out of the "ordinary" be sure to explain it to the person after you've done it. You do not want to create enemies for committing your crime.

Shakespeare's *Hamlet*

Good vs Evil

Are people born evil or do they learn evil from their lives? Your job is to discover the answer to this conundrum.

Your task: You must think of a way in which to test whether evil is innate or learned. Though a test of three samples may not prove conclusively, it will throw light on the shadow of the potential and propensity in "all" of us to create evil. You might consider labeling something you own with your phone number and name and leave it somewhere purposefully in order to test whether or not it is returned to you. You may also think of another "appropriate way" to put evil on trial.

Joseph Conrad's *Heart of Darkness*

Task: Within most of us, the potential to live out our darkness and our light coexist. Sometimes, they each act on their own; at other times, they feed into one another, and in the worst-case scenario, our dark can submerge our light. Your task is to create a project that reflects the light and the dark inside your heart and display this as a collage, a mixed media project, a mobile, or any other form of expression you choose (so long as you consult with me). To figure out what reflects darkness and light, ask yourselves, (for dark) what angers me? What hurts? What do I do that causes self-injury? (for light) What makes me happy? What brings me fulfillment? What do I do well in the world?

Morrison's *Song of Solomon*

Inhumanity against Humankind

For your final project you are to propose a thesis and prove it. The method for how you accomplish it is entirely up to your discretion. However, I do not want you to under any circumstance put yourself in any physical or moral danger!

You must propose a thesis which proves that there is some form of inhumanity against humankind in your community. In other words, where does racism, classism, ageism, or injustice exist in ____? This may take the form of an interview (recorded on tape or video), a written up survey, photographs, art or any other method you deem as appropriate. You may want to visit a store where migrant workers work, visit a fast food restaurant, visit a prison, visit the hospital, an abortion clinic, visit a court hearing, watch the news, and further investigate a crime against humanity.

Anderson's *Speak*

Combating/transforming prejudice project

Task: Reflect on your school environment. You are to develop an action plan for your school environment. This is a plan and you actually have to do the action. Should this work out well, you have the potential to actually transform your school community. This activity may be done with as many peers as you would choose (even the entire class).

Walker's, *Color Purple*

Task: There are several "ISMs" which exist throughout this text: racism, sexism, lookism, heterosexism, classism—many of these "ISMS" polarize Celie and other characters from fitting into the status quo. Your task is to create a recipe for the book and "cook" in front of the class a solution that will both symbolically and allegorically explain and attempt to heal any of the "ISMs" you found present throughout the text. These cooking shows will be completed in groups of 5 students.

Camus's *The Stranger*

Task: Define a thesis and then "re-create" Mersault into a she. Choose any scene you'd like and dramatize the scene from how a female Mersault might think and behave. Show what this world would be like, what people would think, how they would behave differently—who would/would not be accepted; essentially how would society's perception of Mersault be different if he were a she? This is a group project.

Any book

For your final project, you are to try something you've never done before and report back to the class. In other words, I want you to face an "ISM" you have and then think of a way in which you can somehow either heal the "ISM" or attempt to at least try to understand why you feel what you feel. For example, if you feel racist toward Anglos, I want you to think of a way to face your "ISM," for example, talk to a person you feel uncomfortable talking to and try to push through your feelings. This project will be presented orally— prepare note cards and turn them in for each part below.

Rubric:
a. Identify and state your prejudice or "ISM" (25) ___
b. Describe your face to face with that prejudice(20) ___
c. Rationalize why you have your prejudice(15) ___
d. Explain how your confrontation did or did not change your prejudice(25) ___
e. Describe how you could teach others about how to not be prejudiced toward this particular "ISM."(15) ___

Total(100) ___

Notes

1 "ISMs" are "words that become "nouned" and are laden with pejorative connotations based on actual or perceived differences" (Miller, 2005b, p. 88).

2 "Out" means either being open about one's sexuality or gender expression or being open about supporting one's sexuality or gender expression. Either way it is used sometimes warrants negative attention.

3 Safe Zone is a nationally recognized training program for universities on issues related to homophobia and prejudice reduction through building allies with heterosexuals. For more information go to: http://www.lgbtcampus.org/faq/safe_zone.html.

4 Internalized oppression is the consequence of believing the distorted messages about one's group (Tatum, 2003, p. 6).

5 For more information on transgender rights and current laws go to: the *ACLU* www.aclu.org/getequal/trans.html, the *Human Rights Campaign* http://www.hrc.org/index.html, the *Transgender Law and Policy Institute* http://www.transgenderlaw.org/, the *National Gay and Lesbian Task Force* (NGLTF) http://www.thetaskforce.org/ourprojects/tcrp/, and http://www.mappingourrights.org for current rulings on discrimination by state.

6 For more information on the "Employment Non-discrimination Acts" go to www.aclu.org or http://www.hrc.org/index.html.

7 I do not use the word quiz as it tends to reinforce a fear in most students. While a quiz is monological, a check-in infers reciprocity.

References

Apple, M. (2002). *Official knowledge*. New York: Routledge.

Ariza, E., Morales-Jones, C., Yahya, N., & Zainuddin, H. (2002). *Why tesol?* Dubuque: Kendall/Hunt.

Au, K. H. (1998). Social constructivism and the school literacy learning of students of diverse backgrounds. *Journal of Literary Research, 30*(2), 297–319.

Baker, L. (1994). Children's emergent literacy experiences in the sociocultural contexts of home and school. *A Newsletter of the National Reading Research Center*, 4–5.

Bartholomae, D. (1980). The study of error. *The Journal of the Conference on College Composition and Communication, 31*(3), 253-269.

Barton, D., & Hamilton, M. (2000). Literacy practices. In D. Barton, M. Hamilton, & R. Ivanic (Eds.), *Situated literacies: Reading and writing in context* (pp. 7–15). New York: Routledge.

Bhabha, H. A. (1994). *The location of culture.* New York: Routledge.

Bolgatz, J. (2005). *Talking race in the classroom.* New York: Teachers College Press.

Bomer, R., & Bomer, K. (1999). *Reading and writing for social action.* Portsmouth: Heinemann.

Cochran-Smith, M., & Zeichner, K. M. (Eds.). (2005). *Studying teacher education: The report of the AERA panel on research and teacher education.* Mahwah: Lawrence Erlbaum Associates.

Collins, P. H. (2000). *Black feminist thought.* New York: Routledge.

Comber, B., & Simpson, A. (2001). *Negotiating critical literacies in the classroom.* Mahwah: Lawrence Erlbaum Associates.

DeBlase, G. (2005). The place of gender, race, and class in constructing teaching lives. *English Education, 37*(3), 248–250.

Dozier, C., Johnston, P., Rogers, R. (2005). *Critical literacy/critical teaching: Tools for preparing responsive teachers.* New York: Teachers College Press.

Erickson, F. (1984). School, literacy, reasoning, and civility; An anthropologist's perspective. *Review of Educational Research,* 54, 525–544.

Foucault, M. (1980). *Power-knowledge: Selected interviews and other writings, 1972–1977.* New York: Pantheon Books.

———. (1986). Of other spaces (J. Miskowiec, Trans.). *Diacritics, 16*(1), 22–27.

Freire, P. (1970). *Pedagogy of the oppressed.* New York: Continuum Publishing.

Freire, P., & Macedo, D. (1987). *Literacy: Reading the word and the world.* Westport: Bergin & Garvey.

Gardner, H. (1983). *Multiple intelligences.* New York: Basic Books.

Gee, J. P. (1989). Literacy, discourse, and linguistics: An introduction. *Journal of Education, 171*(4), 5–25.

———. (1990). *Social linguistics and literacies: Ideology in discourses.* New York: Routledge/Falmer Press.

———. (1996). *Social linguistics and literacies: Ideology in discourses* (2nd ed.). New York: Falmer Press.

———. (1992). Socio-cultural approaches to literacy. *Annual Review of Applied Linguistics, 12,* 31–48.

———. (2002). Identity as an analytic lens for research in education. *Review of Research in Education, 25*: 99–125.

Gilyard, K. (1999). *Race, rhetoric, and composition.* Portsmouth: Boynton/Cook.

Giroux, H. (1983). Theory and resistance in education: A pedagogy for the opposition. In C. A. Torres & T. R. Mitchell (Eds.), *Sociology of education* (pp.143–153). Albany: State University Press.

GLSEN Terms. (2001). *An Anti-Homophobia, Prejudice-Reduction Curriculum* [Nonpublished document]. Santa Fe: GLSEN/Santa Fe Rape Crisis Center.

Guinier, L., & Torres, G. (2002). *The miner's canary.* Cambridge: Harvard University Press.

Gutierrez, K. (2002). Studying cultural practices in urban learning communities. *Human Development, 45* (4): 312–321.

Gutierrez, K., Asato, J., Pacheco, M., Moll, L., Olson, K., Horng, E., Ruiz, R., Garcia, E., Gutierez, K., Baquedano-Lopez, P., & Asato, J. (2001). English for the children: The new literacy of the old world order. *Bilingual Review Journal, 24* (1 & 2), 87–112.

Gutierrez, K., Baquedano-Lopez, P., & Tejeda, C. (1999). Rethinking diversity: Hybridity and hybrid language practices in the third space. *Mind, Culture, and Activity: An International Journal, 6*(4), 286–303.

Hagood, M. (2002). Critical literacy for whom? *Reading Research and Instruction, 41*, 247–266.

Harbeck, K. (1984). *The homosexual educator: Past history/future prospects.* Paper presented at the Annual Meeting of the American Educational Research Association. San Francisco: California.

hooks, b. (1994). *Teaching to transgress.* New York: Routledge.

Human Rights Campaign. Retrieved June 20, 2006 from http://www.hrc.org/Template.cfm?Section=Employment_Non-Discrimination_Act.

Levinson, B. A., Foley, D. E., & Holland, D. (Eds.). (1996). *The cultural production of the educated person.* Albany: State University of New York.

Lewinson, M., Flint, A.S., & Van Sluys, K. (2002). Taking on critical literacy: The journey of newcomers and novices. *Language Arts, 79*(5), 382–392.

McCarthey, S., & Moje, E. (2002). Identity matters. *Reading Research Quarterly,* 37(2): 228–238.

McIntosh, P. (2002). White privilege: Unpacking the invisible knapsack. In P. Rothenberg (Ed.), *White Privilege* (pp. 97–101). New York: Worth Publishers.

Miller, S. (2005a). *Geographically 'meaned' preservice secondary language arts student teacher identities. Ann Arbor,* Umi Dissertation Publishing, www.lib.umi.com/dissertations/fullcit/3177097.

———. (2005b). Shattering images of violence in young adult literature: Strategies for the classroom. *English Journal, 94*(5), 87–93.

Moje, E. (2002). Reframing adolescent literacy research for new times: Studying youth as a resource. *Reading Research and Instruction, 41*, 211–227.

Moll, L., Amanti, C., Neff, D., & Gonzalez, N. (1992). Funds of knowledge for teaching: Using a qualitative approach to connect homes and classrooms. *Theory Into Practice,* 31, 132–141.

National Gay and Lesbian Task Force. Retrieved June 20, 2006 from http://www.thetaskforce.org/theissues/issue.cfm?issueID=18.

Patrick, J. T. (1994). *Tenure, civil rights, inclusive contracts, and fear: Legal protection and the lives of self-identified lesbian, gay male, and bisexual public school teachers.* Paper presented at the meeting of the Northeastern Educational Research Association. New York.

Perez, B. (1998). *Sociocultural contexts of language and literacy.* Mahwah: Lawrence Erlbaum Associates.

Pritchard, R. (1990). The effects of cultural schemata on reading processing strategies. *Reading Research Quarterly, 25*(4), 273–293.

Rasmussen, M. L. (2004). The problem of coming out. *Theory Into Practice, 43*(2), 144–150.

Rich, A. (1977). *On lies, secrets, and silence.* New York: W.W. Norton.

Rogoff, B. (1990). *Apprenticeship in thinking.* New York: Oxford University Press.

Rosenblatt, L. (1978). *The reader, the text and the poem.* Carbondale: Southern Illinois Press.

Rothenberg, P. S. (Ed.). (1995). *Race, class, and gender in the United States* (2nd ed.). New York: St. Martin's Press.

———. (Ed.). (2002). *White privilege.* New York: Worth Publishers.

Shannon, P. (2002). Critical literacy in everyday life. *Language Arts, 79*(5), 415–424.

Snow, C. E. (1983). Literacy and language: Relationships during the preschool years. *Harvard Educational Review, 53,* 165–189.

Solorzano, D. G., & Villalpando, O. (1998). Critical race theory and the experience of students of color in higher education. In C. A. Torres & T. R. Mitchell (Eds.), *Sociology of education* (pp. 211–224). Albany: State University Press.

Spring, J. (2001). *The American school 1642--2000.* Boston: McGraw Hill.

Street, B.V. (1995). *Social literacies: Critical approaches to literacy in development, ethnography, and education.* London: Longman.

Tatum, B. D. (2003). *Why are all the black kids sitting together in the cafeteria?* New York: Basic Books.

Vygotsky, L. S. (1978). *Mind and society.* Cambridge: Harvard University Press.

Wildman, S., & Davis, A. (2002). Making systems of privilege visible. In P. Rothenberg (Ed.), *White Privilege* (pp. 89–95). New York: Worth Publishers.

Wright, R. (1940). *Native son.* New York: Harper Perennial.

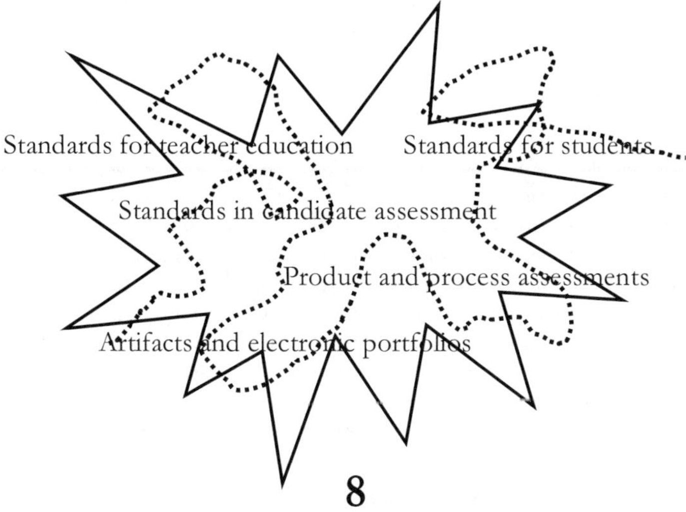

8

Applying the Standards to the Loaded Matrix

Introduction

This chapter invites and instructs readers to consider standards and how they apply to the topics previously discussed in the text. We offer an overview of the standards affecting the English language arts and discuss working documents including journals, videotapes, lesson and unit plans, and electronic portfolios.

Loaded Matrix Chapter Context

This chapter began with an email I received from Acazia during her student teaching. Acazia asked whether she could just put the Pennsylvania state standards on her lesson plans instead of listing all of the National Council of Teachers of English (NCTE), International New Teacher Assessment and Support Consortium (INTASC), International Society for Technology in Education (ISTE), and English education competencies she had learned about and used in meeting various requirements in her university English education courses, professional education sequence, and clinical experiences that she was required to take in order to be state certified. Acazia's cooperating teacher told her that the state standards were the only standards his principal required on the lesson plans faculty members submitted at Doverville Middle School, so Acazia wondered whether she had to list every standard she had learned in her university experiences on every lesson during her student teaching. Would including the state standards alone be enough evidence that she was teaching students what needed to be taught in her seventh-grade language arts classes? How should preservice English teachers learn about standards, know what standards are most important, when to use which ones, and why any of them matter?

Focus questions for chapter 8:

1. **What does the current research in English education tell us about standards?**
2. **Does the heavy emphasis on state standards, national standards, and university expectations for teacher certification serve to support or to confuse preservice teachers as to what might be worthy goals for the classroom?**
3. **How do university educators help preservice teachers to create meaningful and practical teaching artifacts and not just apply standards because they are required?**

Issue #1: The Role of Standards in Teacher Education Programs

There is no doubt that standards affect both teacher educators and preservice teachers as they shuttle between the university space and the school space. When we discuss the standards with preservice teachers, it is important to begin by explaining that there are standards for teaching and standards for teacher education programs, and that there are different kinds of standards in both arenas. Standards may not seem to be a loaded issue for experienced teachers because we trust that hundreds of other dedicated experienced teachers with other committed professionals spend years perfecting and developing standards to promote quality teacher education and student learning. We know that this occurs because we have served, along with dozens of colleagues, for many years on both national and state teams and commissions and have debated the meanings, implications, and effectiveness of standards in teacher preparation and in the secondary English classroom. However, it is in fact these commission recommendations and debates about standards that teacher candidates are not yet privy to or don't yet have a voice about in the university space that we feel should be scaffolded into teacher preparation, since currently standards do play such a large role in the teaching life.

Standards for both teacher preparation and student achievement, then, can be loaded issues for teacher candidates because they are required to submit and to adhere to various standards in order to complete their accreditation, often without permitting time for them to critique the standards, without discussions about whether they believe the standards are sound and appropriate, and without informing them about the debates departments and commissions are often split over in their political alignment on whether standards serve or fail teacher education programs and the students we teach (Honawar, 2006; Newman & Hanauer, 2005).[1] It is our duty as teacher educators not only to address standards in the university and school spacetimes but also to allow for preservice teachers to consider the ideological underpinnings of the various standards they use or are required to meet as they become certified teachers. Today's teacher candidates will be those who serve the commissions on what to do with standards in the future, and so we cannot have them following standards without forming opinions about them as well.

Educators currently have a dizzying array of standards to contend with from local, state, national, and international agencies. Both teacher educators and the preservice teachers they instruct must be fully aware of the different national, state, and university standards, what they represent, and how they apply at various stages of a teacher preparation program as well as in the schools. Preservice teachers are not only introduced to and must meet or exceed several standards for their performance as teachers in the university experience, which extends into the school experience if they expect to become certified and employed, they are also introduced to and must demonstrate their knowledge and capabilities of integrating standards for student performance in both university courses and field experiences. Teacher educators have the responsibility to provide the necessary information about existing standards to preservice teachers which not only includes access to various kinds of standards but a discussion of their value, their political implications, and the arguments that surround them.

Standards for Teacher Education

As teacher educators and student teacher supervisors, we identify certain standards for our candidates' licensure and certification, for example, as in chapter 4, we evaluate how well preservice teachers in our state are able to create a classroom environment according to the Pennsylvania Department of Education Standards. Accreditation agencies and the standards they set such as NCTE/NCATE and National Council for Accreditation of Teacher Education/Teaching English to Speakers of Other Languages (NCATE/TESOL) have come under fire as educators become more and more concerned about the quality of teacher preparation and as voluntary reviews of teacher preparation programs are now state-mandated (Newman & Hanauer, 2005). Some teacher education programs are regularly required to complete and pass two or more different kinds of accreditations at the national specialty program area (SPA), and state levels, and each agency requires evidence organized in a specific way (reports, aggregated data, on-site visits) that matches a different set of standards. Newman and Hanauer state that "the TESOL/NCATE Standards fail because of their prescriptivism, instrumentalism, and impracticality" (Newman & Hanauer, 2005, p. 762). They denounce what they consider to be an industrial or factory model and advocate "a new, more professional model of teacher education accreditation" that upholds "peer accreditation control … [and] some basic academic principles: democracy, flexibility, self-definition, and respect based not on conformity but on rigor and creativity" (Newman & Hanauer, 2005, p. 763).

Likewise, a recent *Education Week* article called attention to a 140-page report from Arthur E. Levine, past president and professor of education at Teachers College, Columbia University, claiming that most teachers are "in low-quality programs that do not sufficiently prepare them for the classroom" with a "recommendation to improve quality control through a complete redesign of the system used to accredit teacher programs" and more attention placed on "professional development through classroom practice and student achievement as the primary measure of teacher education program success" (Honawar, 2006). In that same article, NCATE's President Wise countered Levine's report stating that "the nine criteria used by [Levine's] report to evaluate education schools bear a strong resemblance to NCATE standards," even though Wise agreed with Levine about his report's recommendations and "said his group [NCATE] has been working assiduously over the past decade to move those goals forward" (Honawar, 2006). Nonetheless, some universities are pulling their teacher education programs out of NCATE and are opting for other accreditors such as the Teacher Education Accreditation Council (TEAC) or aligning with the National Board for Professional Teaching Standards (NBPTS). Informing preservice teachers about these debates empowers them to have a better insight into the kinds of criteria comprising teacher education programs and how teacher educators differ in their opinions about teacher training.

Standards for Students

While the debates about accreditation standards for teacher education programs continue, as instructors of methods courses and guides during clinical experiences, we also require candidates to incorporate standards for students into their secondary English artifacts such as lesson plans, unit plans, and electronic portfolios; for example, preservice teachers might incorporate three of our learned society's or specialty program area's standards (NCTE/IRA, 1996) into a forty-minute lesson plan. But are we instructing them to understand why they chose those standards and how those standards fit in accomplishing their goals?

As Farstrup and Myers describe in the Introduction to *Standards for the English Language Arts*, creating standards requires two processes, "defining them and translating them into practice in classrooms" (NCTE/IRA, 1996, p. viii). According to the standards document, "defining standards is worthwhile because it invites further reflection and conversation about the fundamental goals of public schooling" (p. 1). The 1996 English Language Arts Standards Project took four years to complete and involved thousands of K-12 teachers and hundreds of researchers, parents, administrators, and political leaders and analysts; the 1996 project members agreed that in the English language arts,

> Standards are needed to prepare students for the literacy requirements of the future as well as the present … [they] can articulate a shared vision of what the nation's teachers, literacy researchers, teacher educators, parents, and others expect students to attain … and what we can do to ensure that this vision is realized; and [they] are necessary to promote high educational expectations for all students and to bridge the documented disparities that exist in educational opportunities … [and] to ensure that all students become informed citizens and participate fully in society. (NCTE/IRA, 1996, p. 4)

This document further points out that the English Language Arts Standards are to assist teachers as guidelines, not meant to stifle creativity, and "are not meant to be seen as prescriptions for particular curricula or instructional approaches" (NCTE/IRA, 1996, p. 2). In methods courses we encourage inchoate teachers to study issues surrounding the standards, for example, the role of grammar in the secondary classroom through an examination of NCTE/IRA standard nine and the study of texts like *Grammar Alive! A Guide for Teachers* (2003) to allow them to discover for themselves where they stand on the continuum from the dominant culture of a "correct" way to speak and write and the focus on error to understanding the languages of a culturally inclusive classroom (Haussamen, 2003, pp. xii–xiii). When preservice teachers, through shared written reflections and class discussions, respond to texts and teaching demonstrations in ways that support or question the standards, they realize that their peers and instructors do not all have the same views and that conceptually and in practice, teaching styles and opinions about best practices can differ considerably. They begin to realize that there is a continuum or range of ways they and their peers may be interpreting any one standard and that they do not all stand in the same place.

Teacher educators and peers in the university classroom can also provide observations of contradictions in a preservice teacher's selection of standards matched to student goals and what the preservice teacher actually does in practice to achieve those goals. For example, if a teacher candidate writes in a teaching demonstration lesson plan that she engages students in the social construction of knowledge but spends the better part of a forty-minute lesson standing in the front of the room talking to the class, there is an obvious misreading of the standard that she will need to address. This deep process is necessary and sometimes even earth-shattering as beginning teachers rethink and reconsider positions they hold about teaching and learning prior to entering an English education program based on the ways they were taught, what they imagine teaching/learning to be, and during their time at the university from observations of their professors, peers, and experienced mentors teaching on school sites. What Milner and Milner (2003) describe in their argument on "correct English" as "dangers at each extreme: relativism—the loss of standards—and dogmatism—the rigidity of standards" (Milner & Milner, 2003, p. 57), we believe also applies to teaching preservice teachers about standards in general. It is essential for teacher candidates to be able to articulate their positions on teaching all the language arts thoughtfully and intelligently and to recognize that they may shift and alter their opinions as they integrate theory and practice over time and space.

As sj emphasizes throughout chapter 3 concerning the precarious position of the preservice teacher in relation to NCLB and standardized testing, preservice teachers can easily become pawns who blindly accept and follow imposed standards, or they can learn to think for themselves. Teacher educators must do more than just expose preservice teachers to different kinds of standards and require them in lesson plans, actions that signal that we condone reducing teaching to a random selection of numbers and letters. In order to empower new teachers, we have to challenge them about what they believe are the stated and implied expectations of standards that others have produced and how these will impact the students they teach.

The claim in the *Guidelines for the Preparation of Teachers of English Language Arts* (1996) is that "as the development of standards for English language arts teachers continues, those in the profession will need to stay abreast of the latest findings, contribute ideas whenever possible, and utilize the best suggestions in order to enhance English language arts teaching" (p. 36). The *Guidelines* provides a listing of the NCTE/IRA, INTASC, NASDTEC, NBPTS, and ETS Standards and a table correlating these five sets of standards with the *Guidelines'* four underlying principles of diversity, content knowledge, pedagogical knowledge, and opportunity (NCTE, 1996, p. 37). Since the *Guidelines* have undergone a revision every ten years for the last eighty-five years, it appears that a general consensus of what English teachers should be able to do and need to know is important for teacher preparation programs (NCTE, 1996, p. 1). The next set of *Guidelines* should be published just about the time or slightly before this book goes to press. This means that preservice teachers who are graduating from our program next year will be governed by a new and different set of guidelines than teachers who graduated from our program this year. Teacher educators must make preservice teachers aware that guidelines shift and change in spacetime as do other standards frameworks and that they need to be prepared and understand that these movements will occur throughout their teaching careers and will influence their content and pedagogical knowledge, attitudes, and abilities in both subtle and profound ways.

Standards in English Education Programs and Candidate Assessment

The special issue of *English Education* from NCTE's 2005 Conference on English Education (CEE) includes the program assessment strand working group's discussion of the history of English language arts teacher preparation and the responses to their key question on the effectiveness of English education programs and how they might be most thoughtfully assessed (Koziol, Stallworth, & Tompkins et al., 2006, pp. 370–383). In that article, the committee acknowledges, "formal, legal responsibility for determining what an individual needs to know and be able to do in order to teach in a public school resides in the states" (p. 371). The team offers a framework of six recommendations or "Belief Statements," notably that program assessments "should include evidence that the program provides experiences consistent with NCTE Guidelines and Standards" (p. 375), although the committee reveals that NCTE has no formal relationship with the states in determining certification requirements (p. 371) and raises concerns about the current *Guidelines* "showing a research basis for the recommendations made" (p. 373). They also advocate that field placements should act as a bridge between what candidates learn in university spacetime and the workplace they will eventually "inhabit as practitioners" (p. 376). The commission calls for a "combination of product-based and process-based summative assessments [which] would also allow programs to document candidates' integration of content knowledge, current theories, and culturally relevant pedagogical practice" (p. 381). They note examples of the kinds of traditional product assessments that are currently in place and suggest additional process assessments to provide a clearer picture of candidates' performances as they move through their program toward certification:

Product Assessments

- Portfolios
- Tests
- Assignments
- Lesson Plans
- Student Teaching Evaluations

Process Assessments

- Videotapes of Teaching
- Peer Observations
- Students' Feedback on Teacher Candidates' Performance
- Reflective Journals
- Context-dependent Implemented Lesson Plans. (p. 381)

As preservice teachers learn about different standards in their methods courses and field experiences and consider how those standards will impact them and students they teach, they can create both product and process artifacts in their portfolios like the ones suggested by our CEE colleagues above to meet or exceed those standards without losing sight that the artifacts they design must also concur with their developing teaching philosophies and repertoires. Similar to other teacher preparation programs, our candidates are required to submit an electronic portfolio that meets specific criteria at each of three steps of the teacher certification process; but we can make a difference in supporting attentive candidates who are not just moving through the program by assisting them in making conscientious choices that directly relate to student learning and achievement. English education programs that include a variety of both product and process assessments aid both teacher educators and the candidates they instruct in achieving a better understanding of preservice teachers' knowledge, abilities, and attitudes and how these three transform and expand between the university and school spacetimes.

Issue #2: How Do We Instruct Preservice Teachers about the Standards? English education programs are responsible for introducing teacher candidates to a wide array of standards that link pedagogical and subject area topics including classroom management, technology, social justice, and discipline-specific epistemology. Our framework for secondary English teacher education combines specific English language arts outcomes that coincide with NCTE/NCATE Standards and Guidelines (2003) and more general teaching principles and outcomes based on the work of Danielson (1996) that center around the four domains of Planning and Preparation, Classroom Environment, Instruction, and Professional Responsibilities aligned to the INTASC Standards. To view these documents, readers can go to http://www.coe.iup.edu/teach%5Fed/. Candidates in our eight-semester undergraduate program follow a three-step process that includes preparing working, showcase, and electronic portfolios that reflect their development through course work, two thirty-five hour clinical experiences, and fifteen weeks of student teaching.

⇒*Teaching Points*

∞**Methods Courses**

The denotative and connotative meanings of the standards should be emphasized and discussed all along an English education candidate's program of study—in education classes, English content-area courses, English education methods courses, and in field experiences. But in order not to mystify and overwhelm inchoate teachers with different standard sets and what they represent, and so that teacher candidates can consider and practice standards that emphasize different areas such as technology, subject matter, pedagogy, and state specific requirements, certain standards may best match specific times and assignments in a teacher education program. As each set of standards is introduced, it can be used to create and debate specific artifacts and should be revisited and reemphasized in subsequent courses as the teacher candidate continues to construct her/his teacher identity. Speaking and writing about how these standards intersect, connect, overlap, and assert power and authority will provide new teachers with discernment for how they use these standards in creating process and product assessments, how they incorporate standards in their teaching, and how they talk about if and why standards should matter to their students. In these courses and field experiences, we can provide the following links to the standards for preservice teachers, discuss with them what they mean, and how they might be implemented more meaningfully in the secondary classroom:

- NETS-T or ISTE Standards

http://cnets.iste.org/ncate/pdf/NETST_INTASC_S.pdf
These technology standards are often introduced in the first education course in which students learn to create an electronic or digital portfolio that will build with artifacts they design and match to various other standard sets throughout their program of study. Teacher candidates may discuss how these standards can protect and guide them and their students as they use the Internet and incorporate technological tools to enhance their practice.

- NCTE Standards

http://www.ncte.org/about/over/standards/110846.htm
Our SPA or learned society's standards may be introduced and reemphasized in all English education methods courses including the teaching of reading, writing, speech, and communications. They are most often used in the discussion and creation of lesson plans, unit plans, assessments, goal statements, journals, position papers, teaching philosophies, projects, and video critiques.

- INTASC Standards

http://www.coe.ilstu.edu/ncate/intascprinciples.htm
These generic pedagogical standards are frequently introduced in the seminars accompanying the first and/or second clinical experiences. Seminar discussions about how these more general standards apply to teaching observations and discipline-specific practices may be beneficial to teacher candidates preparing for student teaching and preparing professional portfolios.

- Pennsylvania State Standards

http://www.pastatestandards.org/

These K-12 reading, writing, and speaking standards are required in our state's public schools; all public schools must post these discipline-specific standards in their classrooms and include them in lesson plans. They are introduced in the methods course prior to student teaching and required on lesson and unit plans during student teaching. Discussions around how appropriate these standards are at different grade levels and questioning biases about what students are expected to know and do prove useful in the methods course before and during student teaching.

- English Education Standards

http://www.coe.iup.edu/teach_ed/Forms/Comps20040301/Englishcomp.pdf

These program assessment standards are introduced in the first clinical experience course and revisited in the second clinical experience, final methods course, and student teaching experience. Teacher candidates are evaluated on these standards both in clinical experiences and in student teaching. They connect directly to the NCTE/IRA standards.

- National Board for Professional Teaching Standards

http://www.nbpts.org/

In the methods course before student teaching or during student teaching, teacher candidates should be informed that, as they gain more experience in the classroom, they may want to consider becoming National Board certified with recognition as accomplished teachers. Preservice teachers may be interested in their specific qualifications and researching different states' rewards and honors for teachers who become National Board certified.

- NCATE Standards

http://www.ncate.org/public/unitStandardsRubrics.asp?ch=4

Six standards and conceptual framework for teacher education program accreditation for some colleges and universities. Discussions in the methods course before student teaching of these standards and the Teacher Education Accreditation Council Standards (TEAC, http://www.teac.org/) inform preservice teachers about competing teacher education accreditation programs, their similarities and differences.

- NCTE/NCATE Program Standards

http://www.ncte.org/library/files/Programs/Teacher_Prep/RevisionApprovedStandards904.pdf

An explanation of the program and candidate assessment standards for initial preparation of English language arts teachers in grades seven to twelve. Preservice teachers in the second clinical experience or methods course before student teaching may review these standards as a way of better comprehending their certification program and the specific knowledge, skills, and dispositions these agencies believe graduates should acquire in order to teach adolescents. The CEE Leadership and Policy Summit group noted in their *English Education* article that "NCATE reports that 178 programs in English teacher preparation are currently identified as having achieved status as 'nationally recognized,' the term used to note that a program has passed its review by NCTE" (Koziol et al., 2006, p. 372).

⇒*More Teaching Points*

Here are some suggestions, correlated to the current NCTE/NCATE program standards (in parentheses below), for what teacher educators can do to better prepare preservice teachers with the knowledge, skills, and dispositions they will need in the secondary English classroom:

1. Engage prospective English teachers in articulating sound instructional theories and practices and help them understand the implications of these theories and practices in their developing teaching philosophies and repertoires. (NCTE 2.0 Attitudes for English Language Arts [ELA]).

2. Provide opportunities for preservice English teachers to teach English/language arts in both live and simulated situations, to receive constructive feedback from peers and mentor teachers, and to promote confidence in them that they will be providing their students with appropriate, challenging, well-grounded, and enjoyable experiences. (NCTE 4.0 ELA Candidate Pedagogy).

3. Read, write about, and discuss current teaching theories and practices with preservice English teachers (see list of suggested texts below) to prepare for student teaching and careers in English education. (NCTE 3.0 Knowledge of ELA).

4. Provide preservice English teachers with "real world" resources including novice teachers, experienced teachers, and students, as well as possibly librarians, parents, staff, and administrative personnel who can enlighten them on a variety of topics such as curriculum, classroom management, certification, job interviews, assessment, technology, extracurricular activities, teaching and learning styles, and current issues that affect teachers, students, families, and communities. (NCTE 4.0 ELA Candidate Pedagogy).

5. To the extent that is possible, ensure that graduates leave the university program with a clear and solid understanding of critical literacy practices

beneficial to classroom and academic settings as well as the ability to demonstrate those practices themselves. (NCTE 1.0 Structure of the Basic Program).

In different methods courses before student teaching, teacher educators might also provide sample websites with lesson plans with standards incorporated for preservice teachers to critique and discuss how the standards were used by experienced teachers and if they match their suggested teaching goals. Preservice teachers should also create their own lesson plans with an explanation of how the standards they selected meet their goals for students and then discuss those lesson plans with their peers and instructor before and after they teach the lesson. Some examples are listed below:

For reading—
http://www.pastatestandards.org/curriculum/reading/high/poetry.htm

For writing—peer editing
http://www.pastatestandards.org/curriculum/writing/grade8/peeredit.htm

For technology—oral report rubric
http://www.pastatestandards.org/curriculum/technology/high/aoral.htm

For reading, writing, speaking, listening—
http://www.pastatestandards.org/curriculum/reading/grade12/annfrank.htm

For a unit plan on survival grade 7—
http://www.pastatestandards.org/curriculum/reading/grade7/survival.htm

Multicultural/diversity—
http://cwx.prenhall.com/bookbind/pubbooks/gollnick/chapter9/deluxe.html
http://www.eastern.edu/publications/emme/

Issue #3: Developing a Professional Portfolio

According to Campbell, Cignetti, Melenyzer, Nettles, and Wyman at California University of Pennsylvania, "the portfolio may be used by a university program as a way to keep students and faculty focused on goals or standards valued by the program" (Campbell et al., 2007, p. 8). A portfolio is defined as "an organized, goal-driven documentation of your professional growth and teaching competence" (Campbell et al., 2007, p. 24). Preservice teachers can build teaching portfolios not only to meet the requirements for teacher certification but also to create a set of self-selected, meaningful, and useful artifacts for employment in the public schools. Campbell and her colleagues agree that

"Portfolios are being recognized as tools for supporting teacher evaluation, rewarding outstanding practice, issuing permanent certification and license, awarding advancements, and certifying accomplished practitioners" (p. 84). They remind us that although portfolios currently abound in teacher education, "A well-developed professional portfolio, organized around standards, is the perfect vehicle for documenting growing competence as a teacher" (p. ix). Their text walks preservice teachers through creating both hard copy and electronic portfolios matching candidate-created artifacts to the INTASC Standards.

Our English education students are introduced to the portfolio text during their second clinical experience course and before they submit an electronic portfolio at step two of their teaching certification. Campbell's text provides examples of fifty-two artifact possibilities including peer critiques, journals, rubrics, and volunteer experience descriptions preservice teachers can design for their portfolios (pp. 89–102); the authors also provide a detailed explanation of each of the INTASC Standards, how preservice teachers can write rationales for including each artifact in their portfolios, and how the artifact fits the standard. Preservice teachers are also instructed in this text on how they might display and discuss their artifacts during a teaching job interview. When our preservice teachers are ready to submit their electronic portfolios at each of the three steps in the university certification process, we as their mentors and instructors complete a checklist that matches our requirements to candidates' electronic CD portfolios. Students in our program produce portfolios that receive ratings of "Exemplary" or "Met With Distinction" or "Adequate or Met" or "Emerging or Met with Weakness" or "Not Met," depending upon both the quality of their artifacts and the number of artifacts necessary to achieve that rating.

Sample Documents
⇒Teaching Points
∞Methods Courses

Preservice teachers are instructed to prepare the following documents or artifacts, connect them to the INTASC, NCTE, or National Board Standards in working portfolios (drafts they can revise) and showcase portfolios (three or more final draft artifacts they submit for a grade), and share them with their peers in the methods course prior to student teaching. These documents often appear in the electronic portfolio preservice teachers build for teacher certification and employment opportunities.

- *Classroom set-up*: Design a classroom diagram (see http://teacher.scholastic.com/tools/class_setup/ to do this electronically), create a mini-bulletin board, and develop a classroom management plan. Use the required and/or optional methods texts as references in your explanations (see the list of required and suggested readings below).

- *Unit plan*: Prepare a unit plan with a brief written explanation and calendar for the unit. Use the required and/or optional course texts as a reference. Considerations should be made for thematic, culturally responsive, and/or cross-disciplinary pedagogy.
- *Lesson plans* (e.g., twenty- and forty-minute): Design and lead a twenty-minute lesson or engaging activity demonstrating your knowledge of teaching a diverse student population. You will receive both peer and instructor commentary. Design, prepare, and write a forty-minute lesson plan that you could use if asked to teach a demonstration lesson for a prospective teaching position. This lesson must include the use of media and any other course readings helpful to the lesson design. You will receive peer and instructor commentary. Your lessons must demonstrate a clear understanding of rationale, objectives, procedures, engagement, adaptations, and assessment. Each lesson plan must include at least one NCTE Standard, one INTASC Standard, and one Pennsylvania State Standard that you feel is appropriate to the rationale and objectives of the lesson and at least one English education outcome with performance indicators.
- *A test and a project with rubrics for each*: Prepare a test and a project both with scoring/grading rubrics. The test and project can coincide with any teaching experience you have in this course. Use the required and/or optional texts as a reference in creating your test and project.
- *Tutorial activity*: Tutor at least one student for at least one hour; the hour can be divided into more than one meeting for shorter periods of time (For example, could conduct three separate twenty-minute writing conferences with a university or secondary student.). Include a tutorial record (dates and times you met), your procedures, and what you learned about your teacher-self and the student in a one-on-one situation.
- *Student group activity*: Design, teach, and write up specific activities assigned to a group of students. Write a brief explanation of the activities including your lesson plan and discovery paper (no more than five pages) on what you learned from this experience. Of particular interest might be how this experience compared to your individual tutorial and what you learned about your teacher-self in a group dynamic.
- *Email activity*: Email another teacher (student teacher, co-operating teacher, colleague, mentor, or supervisor) at least three times successfully and keep a record of your correspondences (both what you and your partner wrote and the dates). Then, in a short paper (no more

than two pages), explain how this electronic experience helped you to become a better teacher.

- *Responses to four core questions*:

1. Explain how reading the texts for this course has directly influenced your development as a secondary English teacher.
2. Which assignments/activities were most beneficial to you and why? Least beneficial and why?
3. What did you learn *from* teaching and *about* teaching in this course?
4. What questions do you still have about English education? Where might you go for answers to these questions besides our class?

- *Teaching philosophy:* Write a clear teaching philosophy.
- *Professional leadership*: Attend at least two professional activities this semester such as NCTE/IUP affiliate meetings to evidence leadership and interest in the profession (or provide a reasonable equivalent such as participating in a local, state, or national conference).

Further Reading to Assist Preservice Teachers in Methods Courses and Preparing Artifacts for Teaching Portfolios:

Alsup, J., & Bush, J. (2003). *But will it work for REAL students?* Urbana: NCTE.

Antinarella, J., & Salbu, K. (2003). *Tried and true: Lessons, strategies and activities for teaching secondary English.* Portsmouth: Heinemann.

Brandvik, M. L. (2002). *English teacher's survival guide.* New York: John Wiley & Sons.

Burke, J. (2003). *The English teacher's companion: A complete guide to classroom, curriculum, and the profess-ion.* (2nd ed.). Portsmouth: Heinemann.

Emmer, E., Evertson, C., & Worsham, M. (2006). *Classroom management for middle and high school teachers* (7th ed.). Boston: Allyn & Bacon.

Golub, J. N. (2000). *Making learning happen: Strategies for an interactive classroom.* Portsmouth: Boynton/Cook/Heinemann.

Haussamen, B., with Benjamin, A., Kolln, M., & Wheeler, R. S. & members of NCTE's Assembly for the Teaching of English Grammar. (2003). *Grammar alive! A guide for teachers.* Urbana: NCTE.

King-Shaver, B., & Hunter, A. (2003). *Differentiated instruction in the English classroom.* Portsmouth: Heinemann.

Maxwell, R. J., & Meiser, M. J. (2001). *Teaching English in middle and secondary schools* (3rd ed.). Upper Saddle River: Merrill/Prentice Hall.

Milner, J. O., & Milner, L. F. M. (2002). *Bridging English* (3rd ed.). Upper Saddle River: Prentice Hall.

Mitchell, D., & Christenbury, L. (2000). *Both art and craft: Teaching ideas that spark learning.* Urbana: NCTE.

Noden, H. (1999). *Image grammar: Using grammatical structures to teach writing.* Portsmouth: Heinemann.

Olson, C. B. (2007). *The reading/writing connection* (2nd ed.). Boston: Pearson/Allyn & Bacon.

Smith, M. W., & Wilhelm, J. D. (2006). *Going with the flow: How to engage boys (and girls) in their literacy learning.* Portsmouth: Heinemann.

Strickland, K., & Strickland, J. (2002). *Engaged in learning: Teaching English* (6-12). Portsmouth: Heinemann.

Teasley, A., & Wilder, A. (1997). *Reel conversations.* Portsmouth: Heinemann.

Digital Portfolios and Mentoring

Besides working one-to-one with students in methods courses in the planning and preparation of artifacts for their portfolios, universities may provide a Portfolio Assistance Center on campus where teacher candidates with a range of technological capabilities receive hands-on training to design and compile an electronic portfolio from the documents they create in their course work. NCTE affiliates on campuses may also assist newer undergraduates entering the English education program by having candidates who are further along mentor them through areas where they have questions including Praxis test preparation, understanding standards, and learning how to create web pages for their portfolios.

One example of a digital portfolio website designed by teacher candidate Jamie during her student teaching and demonstrating how she matched her artifacts to the standards can be found at http://iteachenglish.org/index.html.[2] Below are two sample artifacts of how Jamie met INTASC Standard 7 in her electronic portfolio. Jamie includes a rationale for each of her artifacts. Also note how Jamie incorporates the state standards into Artifact #2, her poetry unit plan (in bold on her chart below).

INTASC Standard #7

The teacher plans instruction based upon knowledge of subject matter, students, the community, and curriculum goals.

Artifact #1:
The Rome of Shakespeare: *Julius Caesar*
A Unit Plan for Grade Eleven English

This unit focuses on William Shakespeare's famous historical tragedy, *Julius Caesar*. I believe that many students struggle with complex texts, such as *Julius Caesar*, because they frequently have difficulty connecting to literature that is centuries old. Research and my personal experiences as a teacher and learner have shown me that students are more likely to comprehend literature when they are able to engage in meaningful activities and to make connections with the reading. As such, I have developed a cross-curricular unit that enables students to grasp the unit in context by combining a series of pre-reading activities, reading journals, media and film literacy, directed self-assessment, and discussion/seminars.

This unit will help to guide students with different needs through one of Shakespeare's greatest historic tragedies, *Julius Caesar*, by starting with a series of pre-reading activities to build context. Next, the teacher will model reading strategies, and then encourage students to work collaboratively and individually to strengthen reading comprehension. Each activity the student completes will build within a special portfolio. The unit also possesses built-in, periodic review and self-assessment, as well as film to reinforce major concepts while bringing the play alive. The lesson will culminate with portfolio collections, a final paper, and an exam that helps students to synthesize ideas while practicing Pennsylvania System of School Assessment (PSSA) skills. (Jamie includes a unit plan overview calendar and her detailed unit plan on her website at http://iteachenglish.org/index.html.)

Artifact #2: O, Poetry!

I love poetry and love to share that passion with as many people as possible. Unfortunately, many students—and even adults—seem to think that poetry is dull, sappy, or difficult to understand. Even before I decided to teach, I wished that I could explain to others that poetry doesn't have to be any of these things! In fact, poetry infiltrates all aspects of our lives, whether we realize it or not. For instance, most people listen to music on the way to or from school or work. If the music has lyrics, it can be considered poetry.

As I designed this unit, I learned a number of things about myself as well as my students. First, I have not always loved poetry. When I was younger, I would pretend to read poems, but not necessarily understand what I was reading. As I grew up a bit, I came to understand that poetry often had much deeper meaning and felt that I could not grasp it. During my middle school years, I fell in love with music. I won't even pretend to have any musical ability whatsoever, but have always felt that I could somehow relate to the "emo" (emotion-centered) strains of the bands I loved! Regardless, I was shocked when my tenth-grade English teacher casually mentioned that she knew for a fact that I not only liked poems, but that I could understand them—I listened to them every day and could even recite several from memory! My teacher taught me a valuable lesson which has truly enabled me to grow professionally—that as long as learners can make connections to their lives, they will be much more likely to become impassioned by the subject matter in their classes.

The beginning of my poetry unit will review fundamental concepts of poetry—for instance, the "history" of poetry and its presence in contemporary society; the latter portion of the unit will discuss certain types of poetry. Throughout the unit, students will work on writing their own persona poem, a relatively easy poem that's a blast to make and share! (See figure 8.1).

TEACHER: Jamie M. Lee *XXX School District* SUBMITTED: ________
CLASS/SUBJECT: English 8 **SECONDARY (7–12)** FOR WEEK OF: ________

Week 2

180 DAY PLAN	**DAY**	**M**	**DAY**	**Tu**	**DAY**	**W**	**DAY**	**Thu**	**DAY**	**Fri**
NUMBER/ DATE	10	9-15	11	9-16	12	9-17	13	9-18	14	9-19
TOPIC	**Poetry Overview**		**Persona Poem**		**Persona Poem**		**Persona Poem**		**Persona Poem Presentation**	
OBJECTIVE(S) By the end of the lesson, each student will be able to	Students will develop a fundamental knowledge of poetry, including the history and purpose of poems.		Focus will be placed on the basics of a persona poem.		Focus will be placed on students spending class time working on their persona poems.		Focus will be placed on students finishing their persona poems, if necessary, and presenting them to the class.		Focus will be placed on students presenting their persona poem to the class.	
APPLICABLE PA STANDARDS	**1.3.8 B, C, F; 1.6.8 B, D, E**		**1.3.8 B, C, F; 1.4.8 A**		**1.4.8 A; 1.5.8 A, B, C, D**		**1.4.8 A; 1.5.8 A, B, C, D**		**1.6.8 A, D, E**	
PROCEDURES and TECHNIQUES To reach objectives	A PowerPoint presentation developed by the instructor will be shown. Handouts will		Students will be guided through the basics of a persona poem with		Students should have all materials from the previous day.		Students should have their poems with them. If needed,		Students should have all materials to present their poem.	

	accompany the presentation, and students will be encouraged to take notes. Group discussion before and after the presentation will also help the students to develop a sound understanding of poetry.	overheads, and be given accompanying handouts. Students will then select graveyard photos that interest them in a large group setting. Rubrics will be distributed and explained so that students are aware of what will be expected of them.	Students will continue to work on their persona poems. Overhead slides will be left up for students to refer to.	time will be given so that students may finish up their persona poems.	
MATERIALS / RESOURCES (Describe relevance to objectives)	Instructor's Computer Handouts	Overhead projector Photographs Handouts	Overhead projector Handouts	Photographs, if needed. Individual props may be used if the students desire.	Photographs, if needed. Individual props may be used if the students desire.
STUDENT ACTION During this class, students will be expected to	Students will follow the presentation, taking notes. Questions and group discussion will be encouraged.	Students will follow the presentation and take notes. Time permitting, students will begin work on their persona poems individually.	Students will continue to work on their persona poems.	Students will spend time polishing up their poems, if necessary. Students will then present their poem to the class verbally.	Students will present their poem verbally to the class.
HOW AND WHEN WILL OBJECTIVE(S) BE EVALUATED	Observation of effort and cooperative learning during group discussion.	Observation of effort will be evaluated.	Observation of effort and research and preparation as related to final review and cooperative learning.	Observation of effort and participation will be evaluated.	Observation of effort and participation will be evaluated.
HOMEWORK ASSIGNMENT	Students should look for old mementos/ photographs to bring in.	Students should reflect on what they learned, and work at home on their persona poem.	Students are to continue working on their persona poem at home.	Students should reflect on today's presentations, and prepare for their own the following day.	Students should reflect on all presentations.

ADDITIONAL NOTES:	Students will be guided during discussion to recognize poetry in contemporary society (in the form of songs, commercial jingles, billboards, etc.).	I will be staying after school to allow students access to equipment and materials, if necessary.	Students are encouraged to discuss their thoughts on this project with other students and myself.	I will be staying after school to aid students with presentation skills.	All students should have presented by the end of class. Grades for this assignment will be completed over the weekend so that students receive feedback at the start of class on Monday.

Developing a portfolio throughout a program of study allows preservice teachers to practice combining and embedding standards into several different kinds of artifacts they will use in the classroom with their students. As Jamie's artifacts illustrate, by the time preservice teachers enter student teaching, they should have a relatively sophisticated understanding of the general principles of standards like INTASC and how they provide the frame for instruction, where more specific state standards fill in the picture of the knowledge and skills necessary for students to reach the specific goals of the lesson or unit.

Other Process Assessments and Their Value

Reflective Journal

The following is an example of student teacher Kristen's reflective journal entry after her second week at a rural school site where she was team-teaching tenth grade with her cooperating teacher, Jane. In this entry, Kristen discovered something new about what she had previously thought about teaching writing standards from observing her cooperating teacher:

> On Friday, during the 10th grade Honors class, I had the opportunity to witness what educators call a "teaching moment." Although the plan was for the students to write a politically correct fairy tale, during the brief prewriting discussion, the subject of gay marriage came up. Several of the students, very conservative in nature, responded very negatively to this. The more liberal students attempted to challenge these responses. Very quickly the students had engaged themselves in a full debate. However, it became evident that the more conservative students had difficulty separating the idea of religion from the idea of a civil union between two people of the same sex. As each side spoke, Jane challenged them to think critically about the reasons they believe as they do. She tried to get them to look beyond their personal, emotional responses to the logic behind them. They did not get to writing their fairy tales.
>
> After discussing this with Jane after class, I discovered that when these students get into such heated debates, she sometimes lets them have a discussion on that topic. The students do

not often get to discuss or debate issues in an unbiased way. They do not always get to form or express their ideas in other classes.

After thinking about this problem for a while, I came to see that this class worked only slightly differently than the way in which I wanted my own lesson to go. English teachers in Pennsylvania must teach in a way that addresses the Dept. of Education standards. However, the more time I spend in a high school classroom, the more I believe that our over-riding goal as teachers should be to teach students to think critically and for themselves. The students did not get to practice writing short fiction today. They did, however, get to practice their critical thinking skills. They did get a chance to think for themselves and express their thoughts without fear of ridicule. Even though Jane did not get to follow her plan, this was far from wasted time for these kids.

Kristen comes to the revelation that rather than focusing on the standard written into the lesson plan for the day, it is more important to engage students in thinking for themselves. Just as important is that she sees that through her cooperating teacher's modeling of teaching and encouraging critical thinking, she has permission, no less the duty, to teach this way, the way she intuitively thought she should be teaching. This kind of process assessment is helpful for both preservice teachers and their mentors from the university and the school site so they can converse about these "teaching moments" and practices that are relevant to students' lives. Teacher educators and cooperating teachers can enlighten candidates like Kristen that through reflective journaling, they are attending to many professional standards as well, both for students and for themselves. After talking with Kristen about her journal entry, she recognized that she and her students were actually meeting the following standards:

- NCTE/IRA Standard 12, "Students use spoken, written, and visual language to accomplish their own purposes (e.g., for learning, enjoyment, persuasion, and the exchange of information)" (http://www.ncte.org/about/over/standards/ 110846.htm).
- Pennsylvania Department of Education, English content standard I.E.:
  - contributing to and participating in small and large group discussions and individual and group presentations,
  - speaking appropriately in formal situations,
  - listening to others for different purposes such as interviewing, extracting information, summarizing, and reflecting (http://www.teaching.state.pa.us/teaching/cwp/view.asp?A=135&Q =93761).
- INTASC Standard 9, "The teacher is a reflective practitioner who continually evaluates the effects of his or her choices and actions on others (students, parents, and other professionals in the learning community) and who actively seeks opportunity to grow professionally" (Campbell et al., 2007, p. 54).

Demonstration Lessons, Videotapes, and Observations

⇒Teaching Points

∞Methods Courses

Often preservice teachers are asked to teach practice or demonstration lessons to their peers during their program; in my methods class the semester before student teaching, teacher candidates teach two lessons to the whole class and the second lesson is videotaped. As a teaching tool, videotapes of lessons can be beneficial for preservice teachers, their peers, and their instructors in studying teaching styles of both new and experienced teachers and in oral and written reflections of what was done well and what could be changed if the preservice teacher teaches the lesson again. Student teachers are advised to videotape lessons during their clinical experiences in the schools and discuss them with their cooperating teachers and supervisors to gain a more in-depth insight into the goals of the lesson and how the novice works to accomplish them. Some teacher candidates are also incorporating short videotapes of their teaching into their electronic portfolios and taking them to job interviews. When we discuss lesson preparation, we focus on these questions:

1. Why do I want to teach this lesson?
2. What students do I have in mind for this lesson?
3. What rationale, goals, and objectives do I have? What do I really expect to accomplish?
4. What materials and procedures will I need to do this? How will I have to set up the room?
5. How much time will be teacher talk/thinking versus student talk/thinking?
6. What alternative plans do I have if the lesson is too short? Too long? Too advanced? Too easy?
7. What would my plan be before and after this lesson? Is it part of a larger unit?
8. Does this lesson integrate teaching methods that allow for different teaching/learning styles?
9. How will I use my voice, proximity to students, gestures, eye contact?
10. How will I give directions, monitor students, check for understanding, assess the lesson?
11. Is there a beginning, a middle, and an end to this lesson (does it have separate parts)?
12. What successes do I anticipate and what concerns or problems do I think might arise? How will I handle these?
13. What questions would observers be likely to ask me about this lesson? What would I want them to observe?
14. What other questions should we add to this list?

Another process assessment that can assist the preservice teacher is for all members of the class and the instructor to provide feedback to the lesson and for the candidate to read and reflect on that feedback, checking for patterns of both supportive and corrective feedback from the group. Instructors can use a simple form (see figure 8.2) where the preservice teacher suggests what s/he might want the participants to observe such as wait time, pacing, eye contact, meeting certain standards, questioning strategies, vocal quality, classroom management, or any number of other teaching practices that the candidate may ask the class to observe. In shorter lessons, preservice teachers can ask for one to three behaviors they may want us to observe. At the end of the lesson, the preservice teacher receives the comments from everyone and writes a reflective response on what s/he learned from teaching the lesson and the feedback s/he received.

Dr. Norris Lesson Feedback Form Lesson # _____

Name ________________________________ Date ________________

Responder's Name ____________________________________

What would you like us to observe?

Supportive Feedback:

Corrective Feedback:

Figure 8.2 Lesson feedback form.

Encouraging peer observations during methods courses develops habits in preservice teachers of obtaining regular feedback on their teaching. During student teaching, teacher candidates should receive daily oral and/or written feedback and at least one formal observation per week from the cooperating teacher, and they should obtain feedback from their students on their performance at several intervals in the student teaching experience, perhaps, after each unit or project. Receiving student feedback can be as easy as providing an index card for them to jot down what they liked about the unit or project, what they learned from it, and what suggestions they would have to make it better next time.

Prior to student teaching, it is also helpful to invite a student teacher and his/her cooperating teacher to the methods class to examine actual lesson plans and discuss how and why standards are integrated. Figure 8.3 is an abbreviated version of one of student teacher Dana's lesson plans for her seventh-grade class incorporating the Pennsylvania State Standards. When Dana came to our methods class, she explained how each of the required state standards she chose for this lesson fit her objectives for the inner-city students she was teaching, and she answered questions our teacher candidates posed about connections she made between the standards, her rationale, and her goals.

Rationale
Understanding the context and time period in which a novel is set are keys to a student's understanding of and connection to the plot and characters in a novel. This lesson will assist the students with the background they need to begin reading *The Watsons Go to Birmingham*.

Objectives

- Students will complete a free writing journal entry about what they know and want to learn about civil rights.
- By viewing a PowerPoint presentation about the Civil Rights Movement and the Birmingham Church bombing, students can discuss the context and time period (1963) in which *The Watsons Go to Birmingham* is set.
- Students will create a news article about the bombing by working in collaborative groups.

Standards
PA State Standards:
1.1 Learning to Read Independently
1.3 Reading, Analyzing and Interpreting Literature
1.4 Types of Writing
1.5 Quality of Writing
1.6 Speaking and Listening

Assessment Students will be given daily points for their completed journal entry and a writing grade for their newspaper article based on a rubric I will explain to students ahead of time.

Figure 8.3 Abbreviated lesson plan for seventh-grade class incorporating the Pennsylvania State Standards.

Conclusion

Concluding with Acazia

As I considered the response to Acazia's email about which standards she needed to include in her student teaching lesson plans, I thought about how she was trained to incorporate standards into her artifacts, by scaffolding different sets of standards and having her decide where she stood on the issues surrounding them at different points in her program of study, and by having her examine what other preservice and experienced teachers said and did in relation to the standards required of them in their teaching and teacher preparation. Burke reminds us that "Effective instruction requires a purpose and meaningful context that establishes not only *what* but *why* students must learn the assigned materials. Rationales such as 'To meet the standards' or 'To pass the test' lack meaning and do not motivate" (Burke, 2003, p. 258). As she was writing her lesson plans, I don't think Acazia initially asked, "Which standards am I teaching to today?" Rather, she was taught to ask, "What am I teaching and why am I teaching this today?" In order to support our preservice teachers, if we instruct them to ask the latter questions first while we introduce and debate standards carefully and deliberately throughout a program, and if we provide models of how other teachers consider standards to promote student achievement, they will be able to apply the appropriate standards that they believe answer those questions.

University teacher training programs may be focusing too much on imposing standards and not enough on asking preservice teachers to think about how standards influence or deter them to teach meaningfully, thoughtfully, and responsibly. The real goal of using standards is that through them we are able to better discern and confirm why we are teaching what we are teaching to specific students in a specific classroom setting. The introduction to the Pennsylvania State Standards recognizes that "Although the standards are not a curriculum or a prescribed series of activities, school entities will use them to develop a local school curriculum that will meet local students' needs" (http://www.pde.state.pa.us/stateboard_ed/cwp/view.asp?A=3&Q=76716).

Acazia experienced a disconnect between what the university required in terms of applying different sets of standards on her lesson plans for methods courses and what her cooperating teacher did each week when he provided lesson plans to his principal with only the state standards included. I answered that Acazia could just use the Pennsylvania standards if that is what her cooperating teacher and the school where she was student teaching required because I had seen Acazia's previous documents from her working and showcase portfolios in the methods course and knew that she had already selected specific NCTE, INTASC, and ISTE Standards to match her teaching artifacts effectively. The electronic portfolios she submitted as part of the process for teacher certification during her two clinical experiences before her student teaching experience demonstrated her understanding of standards and how they applied to her teaching and to students' learning. I trusted that she could now begin to responsibly select any of the standards she had been taught in her university program to match her secondary English teaching goals in the schools.

In closing this chapter, I refer to what Kathleen and James Strickland wrote to teachers and for teachers about student evaluations, achievement, and accountability in their earlier work on assessment. I find that what they concluded almost ten years ago about how teachers should evaluate their student parallels and must also apply to how we as teacher educators consider standards in educating and evaluating teacher candidates today:

> Assessment and evaluation that are authentic should make us more accountable. Like naturalistic researchers, our job is to look for evidence from a variety of sources, piece it together to make sense of what is happening, and use this information to support our decisions for the sake of student learning. We are the professionals and we are responsible for making this happen—for all kids, in all schools. That is the promise and the hope of education. (Strickland & Strickland, 1998, p. 211)

Notes

1 Whether or not the National Council for Accreditation of Teacher Education (NCATE) accreditation and standards should be linked to the specialty program areas (SPAs) such as NCTE, whether these reviews are legitimate models of professional teacher education accreditation, and whether they should or should not be mandatory continue to be loaded issues. NCATE accreditation has been the topic of many English education programs' ongoing and often heated conversations; however, mandatory NCATE accreditation across education disciplines university-wide at some institutions is required by their states.

2 My gratitude goes to new teachers Jamie Lee, Kristen Burden, and Dana Yarrison-Hill who gave me permission to use their artifacts and to so many dedicated cooperating teachers including Jane Mastro, Roxanne Rouse, and Dan Macel I have worked with over the years who help others become better teachers of English language arts for their students. Thanks also to my colleague Nancy Hayward for her advice on issues in this chapter.

References

Burke, J. (2003). *The English teacher's companion: A complete guide to classroom, curriculum, and the profession* (2nd ed.). Portsmouth: Heinemann.

Campbell, D. M., Cignetti, P. B., Melenyzer, B. J., Nettles, D. H., & Wyman, Jr., R. M. (2007). *How to develop a professional portfolio: A manual for teachers* (4th ed.). Boston: Pearson.

Danielson, C. (1996). *Enhancing professional practice: A framework for teaching.* Alexandria: ASCD.

Haussamen, B., with Benjamin, A., Kolln, M., and Wheeler, R. S., and members of NCTE's Assembly for the Teaching of English Grammar. (2003). *Grammar alive! A guide for teachers.* Urbana: NCTE.

Honawar, V. (2006). Prominent teacher-educator assails field, suggests new accrediting body in report. *Education Week.* Retrieved on September 20, 2006, from http://www.edweek.org/ew/articles/2006/09/20/04teachprep.h26.html?levelId=10000&rale2.

Koziol, S., Stallworth, B. J., & Tompkins, R. H. with Bickmore, S., Harden-Luster, L., Ketter, J., Marshall, J., & Philion, T. (2006). Candidate and program assessment in English education: A framework for discussion and debate. *English Education, 38*(4), 370–383.

Milner, J. O., & Milner, L. F. M. (2003). *Bridging English* (3rd ed.). Upper Saddle River: Merrill/Prentice Hall.

NCTE. (1996). *Guidelines for the preparation of teachers of English language arts.* Urbana: NCTE.

______. (2003). *NCTE/NCATE program standards for initial preparation of secondary English language arts, grades 7–12.* Retrieved on September 3, 2006, from http://www.ncte.org/library/files/Programs/Teacher_Prep/RevisionApprovedSatndards904.pdf.

NCTE/IRA. (1996). *Standards for the English language arts.* Urbana: NCTE and Newark: IRA.

Newman, M., & Hanauer, D. (2005). The NCATE/TESOL teacher education standards: A critical review. The forum. *TESOL Quarterly, 39*(4), 753–764.

Strickland, K., & Strickland, J. (1998). *Reflections on assessment: Its purposes, methods and effects on learning.* Portsmouth: Boynton/Cook.

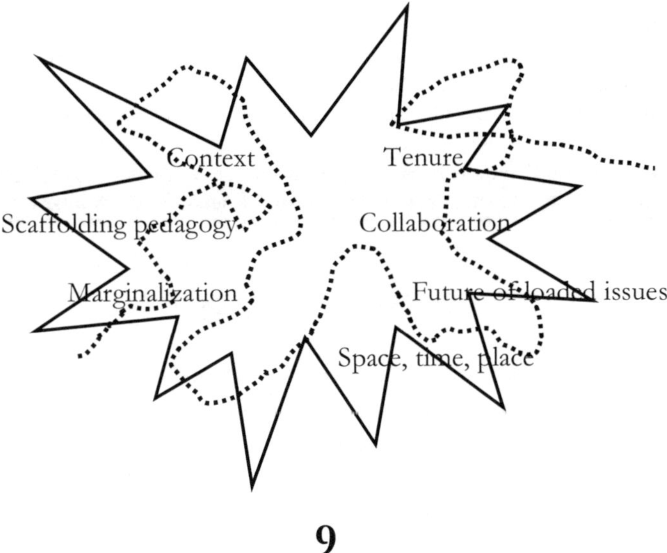

9

Unloading the Loaded Matrix: (Re)charging Our Minds

In this section we (re)charge our thinking and reflect on our text as we consider the future of loaded issues in English education. We believe that new loaded issues will continually emerge and warrant further investigation. Though we cannot predict for the spacetime shifts that emerge overnight, we can prepare ourselves with an understanding that issues will surface that require immediate attention in preservice teacher education. We can be lighthouses for potentially loaded issues and be better equipped to work with them when they do emerge. As we draw to a close in this section, we (re)call topics previously addressed and offer important considerations for English teacher educators and preservice teachers. We also think forward about how preservice teachers and English educators can continue to collaborate on loaded topics that are on the horizon in this new century. As we were considering our closing chapter, several guiding questions surfaced for us. We were concerned about empowering preservice teachers but also protecting them when they did decide to make a stand on loaded issues.

Focus questions for chapter 9:

1. **Are preservice teachers developmentally ready to address loaded issues prior to becoming an inservice teacher?**
2. **What could be the possible redress for tackling loaded issues prior to becoming an inservice teacher?**
3. **How can English educators support preservice teachers in applying university-based learning that tends to be loaded in the secondary schools?**

Scaffolding Pedagogy

Just as a child should be developmentally ready to learn and be taught certain skills in life, a preservice teacher, we suggest, also needs to be prepared in order to assimilate specific learning while developing a meta-perspective of the field. Britzman (1991) confirms this by reminding us that a preservice teacher is marginally situated in two worlds: that of the inchoate educator who is making meaning of what a teacher is and does, and that of still being educated. Reflecting on who a preservice teacher is can help guide us toward making decisions about how to best scaffold pedagogy.

Preservice Teacher Marginalization

Preservice teachers are people who are becoming teachers, and with that comes a multitude of complex factors. Unlike most professions where people have had less exposure prior to their entrance into that profession, preservice student teachers have already experienced over thirteen thousand hours of observation of what a teacher does and who a teacher is based on their own compulsory schooling (Britzman, 1991). To a large degree, their role as a preservice teacher is predetermined because of institutional and social expectations. Consequently, preservice student teachers are confronted with how past knowledge/experience, the construction of the self by his/her teacher preparatory program, bump up against that of new and traditional teaching pedagogy and teaching practices. The struggle herein is how to make sense of the two, when new and old traditions collide and are each veritable.

Bakhtin (1981) refers to this type of struggle as the power struggle of a dialogical relationship and the tension between an authoritative discourse, the voice of authority, and an internally persuasive discourse, or one's own voice. An authoritative discourse is a discourse that:

> Operates within a variety of social contexts and partly determines our "symbolic practices," or the normative categories that organize and disorganize our perceptions. It

> is "received" and static knowledge, dispensed in a style that eludes the knower, but dictates, in some ways, the knower's frames of references and the discursive practices that sustain them. Bakhtin termed such discourse the "word of the father, adult, teacher, etc." in that these positions already have the power to authorize subjects. (Britzman, 1991, pp. 20–21)

On the other hand, an internally persuasive discourse is similar to an authoritative discourse except that it is "denied all privilege" (Bakhtin, 1981, p. 342). An internally persuasive discourse,

> Pulls one away from norms and admits a variety of contradictory social discourses. As renegade knowledge, internally persuasive discourse has no institutional privilege, because its practices are in opposition to socially sanctioned views and normative meanings. It is the discourse of subversion. Internally persuasive discourse is, as Bakhtin argues, "half ours," and as we struggle to make it our own and as it clashes with other internally persuasive discourses, "this discourse is able to reveal ever newer ways to mean."(Britzman, 1991, p. 21)

An internally persuasive discourse is tentative because it is still becoming and negotiating schooled meanings and identities. Preservice teachers are vulnerable to being misshaped by authoritative discourses that may be biased, prejudiced, or which may poorly reflect the true lives of students. Once preservice teachers become comfortable with themselves as teachers, they may feel the tension between what others expect with that of what feels internally right. When preservice teachers are invalidated by an authoritative discourse, it can demean a student and may even position her/him to change teaching pedagogy and practice or, in some cases, leave the profession altogether. By addressing loaded issues, our hope is that preservice teachers will gain confidence with their teaching identities so that their internal and authoritative discourses meld, and can help them assert themselves when issues are loaded.

However, what happens when preservice teachers reject cultural norms or institutional norms which are attempting to co-construct them? What happens when there is tension between authoritative discourse and a preservice teacher's internally persuasive discourse? What happens when preservice teachers flat out reject authoritative discourse? Can preservice teachers still become teachers? Should they move toward teaching in an alternative school or a school that best reflects their values? What does this mean for preservice teachers?

When preservice teachers stand outside of specific expectations of a teacher and outside of dominant culture, their preservice teachers' identities may destabilize. Schools that insist on using one dominant language are inconsiderate about how spaces are created in the school (and perpetuate marginalization), or that hang artifacts in the hallways (and force teachers to post messages only in their classrooms for the status quo), send painful messages that "otherness" (Minh-Ha, 1989) is not acceptable and may position some of these preservice teachers as "outsiders," sadly destabilizing their teacher identities.

Preservice teachers' use of discourse can also position the self as an outsider when they speak out against the majority who teach or even when they speak to reinforce status quo ideologies (in a school that is liberal). When teachers who are part of the majority community in a school reinforce a preservice teacher's stance as an "outsider," the preservice teacher who is outside of the majority may feel even further marginalized and the preservice teacher identity can destabilize. However, as a survival tool, teachers who resist being subsumed by traditional dominant teaching pedagogy, practice, theory and/or ideology can create social spaces to survive their own marginalized preservice teaching experiences.

When preservice teachers are marginalized in their own schools, they may create micro-cultures of support (heterotopias) with other teachers, their peers, family, friends, or former teachers who think similarly or share in similar social, political, or pedagogical concepts. Freire (1970) refers to this as conscientization, a critical consciousness that "permits one to respond to the socio-cultural realities that shapes one's circumstances by developing, in concert with others, interventions that interrupt forms of oppression and thus make available creative practices" (as in Britzman, 1991, p. 25). This process may catalyze preservice teacher restabilization and lead to eventual teacher identity stabilization. When preservice teachers fail to have any support, though, they are likely to leave the profession altogether.

We believe that instilling a sense of how to identify, unpack, and address loaded issues will reinforce a sense of confidence in preservice teachers and may buffer them from experiencing psychasthenia is probable that when they do speak out about controversial issues, others who embody and activate social justice in the schools will align themselves with them, forming a heterotopia. We hope that the support they receive will affirm their pedagogies and establish a network of like-minded individuals that they can turn to for materials, camaraderie, and advice.

Timing

Many factors affect the development of pedagogy: beliefs (Fisher, Fox, & Paille, 1996; Fox, 1993; Holt-Reynolds, 1992; Knowles, 1992; Knowles & Holt-Reynolds, 1991; Moss, 1992); background values (Carter & Doyle, 1995; Dill & Associates, 1990; Farr, 1997; Fox, 1994; Grossman, 1990; Grossman, Wilson, & Shulman, 1989; Lortie, 1975; Nespor, 1987; Parsons, 2003; Smagorinsky, Cook, & Johnson, 2003; Vygotsky, 1987); concepts and preconceptions about teaching; beginning teacher knowledge (Apple, 2002; Clandinin & Connelly, 1995; Elbaz, 1983; Fisher, Fox, & Paille, 1996; Shulman 1987; Travers, 2000; Zeus, 2004); age; life experience; and culture. We therefore pose a concern: is it just to introduce loaded issues to preservice teachers when they are just learning about themselves as teachers and trying to make meaning of different theories of practice? We agree that some loaded issues should be introduced slowly and over time so as not to overwhelm them because it is difficult enough to be an inchoate teacher who is trying to assess learning and understand how race, class, and gender factor into learning, let alone take on some of the more subversive issues that can undermine learning in the classroom. We recommend that it is best to gather information informally and formally about methods students and, from there, determine the pace at which one thinks them capable of assimilating loaded issues into their forming pedagogies.

Students' personal histories can help the methods instructor determine the readiness of preservice teachers to assimilate information about loaded issues. Life experience is probably the single most important factor in determining readiness, which makes it difficult to assess whole group readiness (see collaboration). Having whole group discussions as well as assigning dialogical journaling are good places to begin to decode student readiness. In determining readiness, the methods instructor might ask preservice teachers to reflect on some of these questions: tell me about yourself and where did you grow up? Describe in detail the communities you grew up in—school, neighborhood, cultures, home; describe if there were any things about you that got you into trouble; describe any community issues you knew about; name and describe any social issues that you knew about while growing up; and describe your complicity in any of these issues or ways in which you challenged them. Once the instructor takes the pulse of the class, s/he will be better able to determine where to begin and the order in which to address the issues.

In order to adequately support students in developing their pedagogies, the instructor should rank the order to address the issues as determined through students' responses (appendix A). The instructor may want to introduce loaded issues within the context of the matrix as a way to help preservice teachers visualize the simultaneity of the issues. Next, fostering a discussion around safety can help establish a foundation in which the issues can be unloaded and discussed. Lastly, it is also important for the instructor to consider scaffolding the loaded issues along with classroom efficacy, potential redress that they may face, and the law's stance. Preservice teachers should come to understand that they should bring up loaded issues over time and contextually in their classes and with great forethought, as simply to impose an idea can prove disastrous. As instructors unpack loaded issues, it would benefit preservice teachers to understand the importance of space, time, and place as it relates to context.

Space, Time, and Place

Many of us have heard the saying, "there is a time and place for that." This saying is worthy of our attention when we work with preservice teachers as they should understand that loaded topics cannot be unloaded and unpacked without pre-planning and collaboration with cooperating teachers. Though it is not inappropriate to discuss loaded issues, as a fledgling educator, it is best to have a rationale and justification for teaching certain topics that may be perceived as controversial. In other words, loaded topics should be brought up in the context of about *what, where, and when* it is being taught or through curricular expectations. The rationale should be linked to appropriate standards and clearly articulate the nature of loaded issues that would require any parental or administrative pre-approval (appendix B—sample letter). Preservice teachers should be reminded that if they are ever in doubt about the loaded nature of material, then it is better to be safe than sorry, and sending home a note can ensure them against potential redress. For instance, when teaching a unit on *Song of Solomon* it would behoove the preservice teacher to articulate the "who, what, when, why and how" (rationale, goals/objectives, standards, procedures, modifications—-ESL and learning "otherly-abled," materials/resources, assessments, and/or anchors) of the text along with the assessments. Additionally, the thematic topics related to the text must be clearly contextualized. Related to *Song of Solomon*, topics might include bigotry and prejudice, sexual and emotional abuse, and several of the "ISMs." Milner and Milner state that "even careful plans cannot always protect you" (2003, p. 229). They refer to other strategies new teachers can try besides sending a note home for an individual text, such as sending a syllabus of the key texts or films that are planned to be taught for that year and inviting parents to examine them first, then contact the teacher for different assignments if there are any qualms about those selected (p. 229). Most importantly, they emphasize that an "openness and willingness to communicate about students' learning can't prevent all fights, but it makes them less likely and equips you better to face them if they come" (p. 229).

(Re)visiting Loaded Issues

We return to the loaded issues that were discussed throughout the text and consider what is on the horizon of spacetime change as it pertains to them. There are figurative meteors and asteroids that are always moving throughout the universe and which have the potential to collide with the matrix. However, we can keep ourselves continuously appraised about the rulings on loaded issues and about the different climates that can generate collisions. Contrary to popular belief, the more we do locally, the more potential we have to impact thinking globally. Change does begin with the self.

There are several areas that we can keep ourselves posted about that are likely to impact policy and laws that are active during any spacetime. The warning signs that pose the greatest potential that can impact change include: changes in national and international political leaders, reforms to current teaching acts, a large shift in political parties holding positions of power, war, a downturn in the deficit, hostility with other countries, amendments that write prejudice into the Constitution, and the proximity and the inevitability of global warming/climate change. When we see such threats to change amassing on the horizon, we need to keep ourselves alert and informed by whatever means we gather information without losing sight of our students who are the citizens that we are helping to co-construct.

As we complete this book, it has been five years since September 11, 2001. Several texts including films and documentaries have chronicled that day, a life-changing event in American history impacting people around the world. Oliver Stone's *World Trade Center* (2006) is one such recollection involving a New York City Port Authority police officer and his home and workplace families. John McLoughlin's leadership during the events of 9/11 is an analogy for the delicate relationship between university educators and preservice teachers. In this film we learn that McLoughlin (played by Nicholas Cage) is a well-respected and knowledgeable law enforcement officer who has had considerable experience in terrorist operations and saving lives. His fellow officers have good reason to trust his strong, steady, and calm leadership because he witnessed firsthand the earlier bombing of the Trade Center in 1993 and was there to assist with the investigation and clean-up. Because he knows the blueprints of the World Trade Center buildings, he begins to establish plans for getting people down from the higher floors of the tower, and appears to have the situation under control on that fateful day; his team follows him into Tower One, sticks close to him, and does everything he asks of them. As experienced as he is, however, McLoughlin cannot foresee the enormity of the tragedy that is about to literally fall on top of them all, even though he appears to be one of the most knowledgeable and experienced personnel at the scene. Our point paralleling teacher education is this: no matter how many years we teach and mentor, no matter how much we read and study old and new pedagogies, no matter how many school sites we visit, observations we make, school personnel we collaborate with or students we serve, there will always be something that we cannot totally prepare for; there is always something new for us to learn. There will always be something that we cannot control; and when we think we have seen everything we could possibly see in teacher training, there is always something we did not know before, there is always another way or a better way. We cannot predict the Columbines, the book banning, the favoritism, the funding cutbacks, or the natural or conspired disasters that may produce lasting effects on a university or school community. We can, however, make new teachers aware of what has been, what is, and what could be based upon our experiences and the shaping of our identities, and we can only pledge to prepare them as best we can to make decisions to become the best educators they can be, knowing that there is always the unknown.

Lore about Tenure

As individuals move from preservice to inservice, there are other loaded issues that are invisible and that warrant further attention. One of these issues is tenure. A concern that surfaced for us with regard to tenure was how does one behave as a citizen in the teaching and school community relating to the loaded issues that we've unpacked throughout the chapters?

Tenure is a cornerstone of academic freedom in the United States and a "semi-permanent" contract between the individual and the institution that assures due process and that an individual will not be dismissed without just cause. Due process means that the individual "has a formal hearing before an unbiased person or panel, where the school administration has the burden to prove the charges. The teacher has the right to testify and to call and cross-examine witnesses and to have the assistance of a lawyer" (NEA, 2006). At the university level with an appointment of full-time instructor or a higher rank, tenure is granted after a probationary period and a lengthy application process generally between the fifth and no later than the seventh year. A professor who has achieved tenure can be fired for incompetence or gross misconduct if the administration has determined that there is a strong enough case. Generally, if a professor with tenure is fired by the university, he/she can typically sue with great effort.

In most states there are tenure laws that prevent public school teachers from being fired without just cause and due process. Normally after three years (tenure for teachers can range from two to five years), teachers who satisfactorily meet job expectations earn tenure. While it does not absolutely guarantee a job, it does provide some security. When a teacher has not yet earned tenure, there is minimal job protection. Nineteen states have agreed to provide teachers reasons for the nonrenewal decision if a teacher is terminated prior to earning tenure. Results from an NEA survey reveal that several states have job protections for beginning teachers "that minimize the risk that they will suffer arbitrary nonrenewals. These states include: Alaska, Arkansas, Delaware, Indiana, Kentucky, Nebraska, New Jersey, Ohio, Oklahoma, Oregon, Pennsylvania, Vermont, and West Virginia" (NEA, 2006). There are also "several states where nontenured teachers enjoy few or no rights in connection with nonrenewal decisions. These include: Alabama, California, Colorado, Florida, Illinois, Maine, Maryland, Massachusetts, Missouri, North Carolina, South Dakota, Utah, and Wyoming" (NEA, 2006). Beginning and veteran teachers have no state tenure laws in Georgia, Mississippi, and Texas.

When we are informed about our rights, it can make a difference about how we behave in our school communities. An informed individual is one empowered to either act in accordance with status quo ideals or to challenge the system in hopes of its betterment. It is risky to take chances in a school that is dissonant from the individual's beliefs, and it may have consequences for job renewal. We therefore pose, how can we best prepare preservice teachers then to consider outcomes and quality of life before they risk job loss, their careers, and even their happiness? This list can serve as a helpful reminder and a possibility for assignments in methods. We recommend asking preservice teachers to do some of this groundwork while in methods and *prior* to applying for a full-time teaching position.

1. Research the Hatch Act laws in their states.
2. Inform themselves about state tenure laws.
3. Inform themselves about "nondiscrimination laws" especially as they pertain to GLBT teachers.
4. Consider how one's lifestyle may be affirmed or challenged in a particular school district.
5. Consider the type of physical (mountains, hills, flats, farmland) and cultural environment in which one wants to both live and teach: urban, rural, or suburban.
6. Consider one's values (religion, the environment, politics, culture) and which kinds of schools and districts may challenge, affirm, or disaffirm them.
7. Consider how important income is and which states have better pay in comparison to cost of living.
8. Consider the assessment culture in the state—such as with standardized testing and the types of assessment required.
9. Consider professional development opportunities—does the individual want to have opportunities to continue to grow as a teacher or is that not significant? Is there funding available?
10. Consider collegiality, support systems, and access to socializing.

Our ultimate hope is that we help preservice teachers embrace who they are in all their multiple identities so that they can share the diverse sides of themselves with their classroom students. When we honor and embrace all of who we are in an authentic way, we are more likely to enjoy our lives and our professions. Honesty begets honesty and what we put forth is likely to inspire the same in our students. Students with an affirmed and authentic sense of self are likely to be citizens who can and will act on and transform the worlds in which they each live.

Future of Loaded Issues

In order to effectively prepare ourselves for the changes that occur and so that we aren't defenseless in their presence, we have compiled a list of some strategies to use with our preservice teachers that they can also use in their secondary classrooms.

➡Teaching Points

∞Methods Courses

Assignments for Preservice Teachers—Furthering Inquiry for Social Action

•Consider what would or could possibly impact policy changes at school. How might they best prepare themselves for such shifts?

•Create a new loaded matrix that includes other issues that are important to discuss in methods.

•Consider a proleptic loaded matrix. What would be in it? What might impact how it will change in spacetime?

•Design a lesson that takes into consideration spacetime and the loaded matrix. How might they teach about the future in such a way that it helps their own students consider ways to imagine future change?

•Identify issues that are loaded and need to be addressed during this spacetime. Research the topic and then design a lesson plan that addresses its impact on schooling.

•Ask students to create scenarios for the class to role-play about loaded issues. Include responses from parents, teachers, administrators, students, university instructors, preservice teachers, and school board members. What is the issue? What would they each say? What was the outcome?

•Ask students to identify a loaded issue that they would like to learn more about. Consider ways to support them in conducting empirical research on the issue through site visits, interviews, phone calls, rallies, and so on. Then consider how they would teach about the issue to secondary students. Report findings to class.

•Write a teaching philosophy that includes a pedagogy. It should be student centered and English language arts focused. In order to do this write-up, students should ask themselves, "*What are my belief systems?*" and "*how do those belief systems create my pedagogy?*" Be sure to draw upon prior readings, discussions and field experiences. When describing the pedagogy, be succinct and explicit with concrete examples. Support answers with references.

•Create a top-ten list of behaviors and/or statements to commit to never do in the classroom.

➡*Teaching Points*

∞Secondary Classrooms

•Ask students to identify loaded issues in their schools and in their local and national communities. Work with them to consider ways to unload them proactively.

•Ask students to identify a loaded issue that they would like to learn more about. Consider ways to support them in conducting empirical research on the issue through site visits, interviews, phone calls, rallies, and so on. Then consider how they would teach others in their school about their findings. Report the findings to class.

•Ask students to create scenarios for the class to role-play about loaded issues. Include what they think responses would be from parents, teachers, administrators, students, university instructors, preservice teachers, and school board members. What is the issue? What would they each say? What might the outcome be?

•Create a top-ten list of behaviors and/or statements to commit to never do in the classroom and in the local community.

•Ask students to identify what may emerge as a loaded issue in the future. Ask them how they can prepare themselves for what might befall. How can they educate others about the possibility of its presence?

Collaboration

In reflecting on the loaded matrix and all of the participants impacted by it, there are a number of voices concomitantly contributing to the outcomes about the issues presented. While multiple perspectives have a hand in helping individuals come to an understanding about how loaded issues unload and play out in schools, the complexity of opinions and problem solving as a collective merits attention. Collaboration can offer key support to preservice teachers who are at early stages in their teaching career, can help them consider solutions as a collective whole, and can greatly benefit them.

Though by no means is our list of collaborative ideas exhaustive nor is it prescriptive rather, it suggests that a series of ideas when put into practice have the potential to benefit individuals. In teaching social justice, a cornerstone of such work is to enlist all of the voices that have a stake in the outcome, and for those who may not have access to attend a collaborative event, it is all the more important that particular pillars are in place so that the voices of the voiceless are also heard and accounted for.

Collaboration is an activity that requires either the presence of a person, or one who can speak in the absence of more than one person, who together seek to achieve an outcome. It requires that the individuals present listen and discuss topics and try to reach a mutually satisfying outcome. Not without tension, collaborative work often demands that individuals be willing to show up physically, emotionally, and mentally, work with rather than against the flow toward a mutual outcome, foster a sense of interdependency not dependency, are accountable for one's actions, and retain an open mind about feedback and revision. These ideas can be applied to both university and secondary classrooms.

Ground Rules

There are some basic ground rules that can help move collaborative activity along. First, in deciding on the outcome of the collaborative activity, it is important that all people's voices are spoken or accounted for. This means that in the absence of someone, that someone either has a written statement or email with their input. When deciding on the outcome, it is also important that everyone has time to speak and be heard about the outcome. In the case of a stalemate, a silent vote can be taken until the group decides on the outcome. Next, tasks should be divided up so that no one person takes on more or less work than others. Third, group members should have at least two peer collaborators they can go to for feedback or help with their tasks. Fourth, collaborators should choose a task for which they have an interest or investment. Fifth, timelines and deadlines should be honored in order to maintain group harmony. Lastly, although problems are often inevitable in a group setting, it is important that issues be addressed when they surface and collectively problem-solved.

Spacetime of Collaboration

There are spaces and times that can contribute to a positive experience of collaboration. It is often difficult to find a space and a time that contribute to everyone's satisfaction, so there should be some give and take about spaces and times that work for everyone. Finding a place that is central to the proximity of travel can help, and selecting a time that does not impact jobs, childcare, or other responsibilities can also contribute to group accord. It is often helpful if the group agrees to have food present especially if the time of the meeting coincides with mealtime.

Collaborative Ideas

There are infinite ways to collaborate on projects. We present a number of collaborative ideas that we have found helpful over the years as they relate to loaded issues. Since there are many voices in the matrix, it is all the more imperative that the kinds of collaboration that are used contribute to a unified outcome; otherwise we defeat our own purposes.

•Host town hall meetings or public forums.
•Research projects that are empirically based and designed to integrate multiple voices and perspectives.
•Debate and conduct well-developed seminars.
•Design, develop, and activate a social action project.
•Write a how-to manual for peers.
•Write and perform a play.
•Write and perform a song or compose music.
•Design a cooking show and cook/discuss solutions.
•Invent a solution to a loaded issue and activate it.
•Host a rehearsed and scripted faux dinner party and have people take on different perspectives.
•Do a TV talk show with rehearsed parts and have people take on different perspectives.
•Script a comedy routine and perform it.
•Select a cause, volunteer, and then support it.

Benefits of Collaboration

When we collaborate, we have the potential to grow and expand our understanding about loaded issues. Ways in which we can benefit from collaboration include understanding group dynamics, more opportunities to problem solve, potential for increase in self-understanding, developing interdependence skills, gaining multiple points of view, seeing life through others' eyes, expanding one's worldview, and rethinking previously held beliefs. Each of these potential areas for growth has great implications for efficacy in the classroom with students and assignment development. A hope of collaboration is that what may be difficult for someone to understand or work through, another may be able to support the individual to work through the tensions. As a result, both people benefit from the experience.

(Re)charging Our Thinking

Ethan, Beth, and Acazia have helped us consider and (re)consider approaches to supporting them, understand, and apply university-based learning to their secondary classrooms. They have helped us pay closer attention to the issues facing each of them during this spacetime and inspired us to do our homework. Our preservice teachers are the voices that we must listen to as they have firstspace exposure to the classrooms. While English educators may be removed to some degree from the day-to-day teaching required of preservice teachers in secondary schools, as we stay open to their experiences, we have opportunities to help our field grow and shift with the changing times.

We have come to understand something about ourselves as collaborators on this book. Despite our twenty-year age difference, we realize that each of our backgrounds and the times in which our teaching identities were co-constructed by the spacetime of each of our own matrices has taught us much about the change in English teacher education. As such, we noted that each matrix is an archive of history and can be studied as a marker of time. When we began this project we cajoled each other that Linda was "old school" and sj was "new school," but what we now appreciate is that we are each an amalgam of old and new and that one impacts the other in a co-mentoring fashion and pushes us each into new directions as we trailblaze into the future.

Launching the Loaded Matrix into Spacetime

We end where this book project began by unpacking the loaded teacher matrix and now launch it into the future. We hope that by discussing the loaded matrix, we have provided an additional set of tools for preservice educators and their students to apply and activate in the context of the matrix of their own lives. The matrix can be manipulated, played with, (re)shaped, and lifted to fit a multitude of contexts, and as such, we entrust that it has earned its place as part of the discourse within teacher education.

We can continue to play with the matrix as a "methodological frame to study the environment for educators and as a space wherein participants are contextually situated" (Miller, 2007). Although imaginary and real, the matrix provides a way to illuminate loaded issues given a spacetime and how such intricate relationships are networked. The components embodied by the matrix during any spacetime should continue to be viewed not atomistically but relationally because a holistic approach can guard individuals from a body/mind split. The matrix's place within methodology can be utilized as a tool for analysis about the issues facing individuals within any spacetime. By looking at the matrix during different times and by examining the relationships within it and within different spaces, the matrix can have efficacy in other research contexts and spacetimes. As social justice educators who strive to live and activate social justice within each of our own matrices, unpacking the loaded matrix typifies social justice during any given spacetime.

We want preservice teachers to have the confidence about how to think through and make decisions about loaded issues when they surface. We hope that their internally persuasive discourse becomes their authoritative discourse and that inchoate and veteran teachers alike, and cross-generationally, will mentor one another about the spacetime of issues. Inchoate teachers who are fresh out of a university program are likely to have the most current readings on issues in English education while veteran teachers have the experience and expertise of both the application of pedagogy and firstspace experience of teaching; sharing experiences can work to the benefit of everyone.

In looking back over all of the loaded issues that we have unpacked throughout the text—

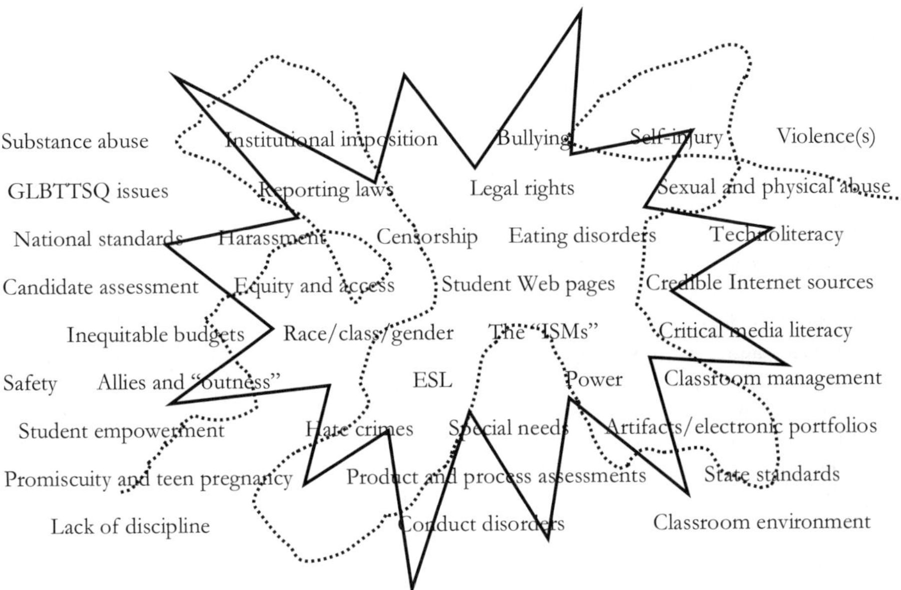

we assert that the loaded issues facing preservice teachers during this spacetime will differ from the loaded issues during a different spacetime. As we stay open and conscientious to the issues facing preservice teachers and their students, we honor them when we affirm what they name as crucial and urgent topics for discussion. Together, we all have great potential to become empowered by learning from one another as we move from preservice to inservice, unpacking the loaded teacher matrix, and negotiating space and time between university and secondary English language arts classrooms.

Appendix A: Loaded Issues

Rank according to where you want to begin. 1 marks the place to begin.

___Allies and "outness"
___Artifacts
___Bullying
___Candidate assessment
___Censorship
___Classroom environment
___Classroom management
___Conduct disorders
___Credible Internet sources
___Critical media literacy
___Eating disorders
___Electronic portfolios
___Equity and access
___ESL
___GLBTTSQ issues
___Harassment
___*Hate crimes*
___Inequitable budgets
___Institutional imposition
___INTASC
___Lack of discipline
___Legal rights
___*National standards*
___Power
___Product and process assessments
___Promiscuity and teen pregnancy
___Race/class/gender
___Reporting laws
___Safety
___Self-injury
___Sexual and physical abuse
___Special needs
___Standards (student, candidate assessment, teacher education)
___Student empowerment
___Student web pages
___Substance abuse
___Technoliteracy
___The "ISMs
___Violence(s)

Appendix B: Sample Letter to Parents

Dear Parents or Guardians of Dr. Miller's Senior AP English Classes,

As part of the unit I am teaching on oppression, the students will be reading Toni Morrison's *Song of Solomon*. The book addresses some touchy topics that I want you to be appraised of prior to our reading. We will look at how prejudice manifests and some of its root causes, and sexual and emotional abuse. Each of these topics will be carefully addressed with detailed units and expert guest speakers from the local rape crisis center will be invited in to help us work through concerns that may arise.

Please sign below if you grant your son or daughter consent to participate in the reading. Should you so choose not to allow your child to read the text, I will replace it with a suitable text and no retribution shall come to your child based on your decision. Feel free to contact me if you have any concerns regarding the text or if you would like to sit in on classes.

Thank you,

sj Miller, PhD
Assistant Professor English Education, IUP

Please tear off the bottom and return the following school day.

For parents or guardians:

_________________________ (sign and date)
I permit my son/daughter____________ (name) to read *Song of Solomon* in Dr. Miller's class.

_________________________ (sign and date)
I DO NOT permit by son/daughter to read *Song of Solomon* in Dr. Miller's class.

If you opt to not allow your child to participate, please provide an explanation and/or call me.

EXPLAIN BELOW

For Administrator:
I__________________ (sign and date) support Dr. Miller in teaching Morrison's *Song of Solomon*. Dr. Miller has provided lesson plans, which clearly detail, support, and meet curricular expectations and state standards.

References

Apple, M. (2002). *Official knowledge.* New York: Routledge.

Bakhtin, M. M. (1981). *The dialogical imagination: Four essays by M.M. Bakhtin* (M. Holquist & C. Emerson, Trans.). Austin: University of Texas Press.

Britzman, D. (1991). *Practice makes practice.* Albany: State University of New York.

Carter, K., & Doyle, W. (1995). Preconceptions in learning to teach. *The Educational Forum, 59*(Winter), 186–195.

Clandinin, D. J., & Connelly, M. F. (1995). *Teachers' professional knowledge landscapes.* New York: Teachers College Press.

Dill, D., & Associates. (1990). *What teachers need to know.* San Francisco: Jossey-Bass Inc.

Elbaz, F. (1983). *Teacher thinking: A study of practical knowledge.* New York: Nichols.

Farr, J. (1997). Becoming a balanced teacher: Idealist goals, realist expectations. *English Journal, 96*(Oct), 106–109.

Fisher, C. J., Fox, D. L., Paille, E. (1996). Teacher education in the English language arts and reading. In J. Sikula, T.J. Buttery, & E. Guyton (Eds.), *Handbook of research on teacher education* (2nd ed., pp. 410–441). New York: Macmillan.

Fox, D. (1993). The influence of context, community, and culture: Contrasting cases of teacher knowledge development. In D. J. Leu & C. K. Kinzer (Eds.), *Examining central issues in literacy research* (pp. 345–351). Chicago: National Reading Conference.

———. (1994). What is literature? Two preservice teachers' conceptions of literature and of the teaching of literature. In C. K. Kinzer & D. J. Leu (Eds.), *Multidimensional aspects of literacy research, theory and practice.* Chicago: National Reading Conference.

Freire, P. (1970). *Pedagogy of the oppressed.* New York: Continuum Publishing.

Golightly, N., & Lee, D. J. Jr. (Producers). Oliver Stone (Director). (2006). *World Trade Center.* [Motion Picture]. United States: Paramount Pictures.

Grossman, P. (1990). *The making of a teacher.* New York: Teachers College Press.

Grossman, P. L., Wilson, S. M., & Shulman, L. S. (1989). Teachers of substance: Subject matter knowledge for teaching. In M. Reynolds (Ed.), *Knowledge base for the beginning teacher* (pp. 23–36). Elmsford: Pergamon.

Holt-Reynolds, D. (1992). Personal history based beliefs as relevant prior knowledge in course work: Can we practice what we teach? *American Educational Research Journal, 29*(2), 325–349.

Knowles, J. G. (1992). Models for teachers' biographies. In I. Goodson (Ed.), *Studying teachers' lives.* New York: Teachers College Press.

Knowles, G., & Holt-Reynolds, D. (1991). Shaping pedagogies through personal histories in preservice teacher education. *Teachers College Record, 93*(1), 87–113.

Lortie, D. C. (1975). *Schoolteacher: A sociological study.* Chicago: University of Chicago Press.

Miller, s. (forthcoming, 2007). (Re)/Re-envisioning preservice teacher identity: Matrixing methodology. In J. Flood, S. B. Heath, & D. Lapp (Eds.), *Handbook of research on teaching literacy through the visual and communicative arts* (Vol. II). Mahwah: Lawrence Erlbaum Associates.

Milner, J. O., & Milner, L. F. M. (2003). *Bridging English* (3rd ed.). Upper Saddle River: Merrill/Prentice Hall.

Minh-Ha, T. (1989). *Woman native other: Writing postcoloniality and feminism.* Bloomington and Indianapolis: Indiana University Press.

Moss, B. (1992). Preservice teachers' reminiscences of positive and negative reading experiences: A qualitative study. In N. Padak, T. Rasinsky, & J. Logan (Eds.), *Literacy research and practice: Foundations for the year 2000* (pp. 29–35). Pittsburgh: College Reading Association.

NEA. *Rights of non-tenured teachers.* Retrieved June 26, 2006 from http://www.nea.org/neatoday/0105/rights.html.

Nespor, J. (1987). The role and beliefs in the practice of teaching. *Journal of Curriculum Studies, 19,* 317–328.

Parsons, P. (2003). A need for reform to align practice with values. *Journalism & Mass Communication Education, 58*(31), 214–218.

Shulman, L. S. (1987). Knowledge and teaching: Foundations of the new reform. *Harvard Educational Review, 57*(1), 1-22.

Smagorinsky, P., Cook, L. S., & Johnson, T. S. (2003). The twisting path of concept development in learning to teach. *Teachers College Record, 105*(8), 1399–1436.

Travers, K. A. (2000). *Preservice teacher identity made visible: A self-study approach.* Paper presented at the AERA, New Orleans.

Vygotsky, L. S. (1934/1987). Thinking and speech. In L. Shulman (Ed.), *Collected works* (Vol. 1, pp. 39-285) (R. Rieber & A. Carton Eds., N. Minick, Trans). New York: Plenum.

Zeus, L. (2004). Theme issue: Disciplinary knowledge and quality education. *Educational Researcher, 33*(5), 3–5.

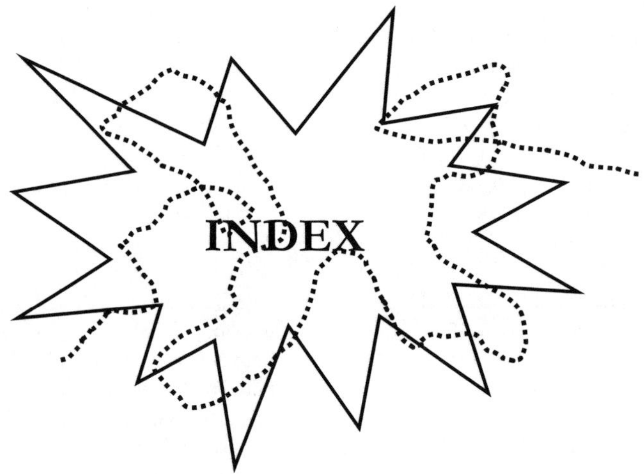

-A-

-B-

-C-

-N-

-O-

-P-

-R-

-S-

sj Miller is Assistant Professor of Secondary English Education at Indiana University of Pennsylvania. S/he has a B.A. in social sciences from the University of California, Berkeley, an M.A. in Jewish studies from the Hebrew Union College, and a Ph.D. in educational thought and sociocultural studies with an emphasis in secondary English education from the University of New Mexico. S/he has published widely in journals and, most notably, won the 2005 Article of the Year Award from the *English Journal.* sj's current research interests are in unpacking English teacher identity in spacetime as preservice teachers experience the larger matrix of the teaching world.

Linda Norris is Associate Professor of English and Director of Undergraduate English education at Indiana University of Pennsylvania. She has a B.A. in English and a B.A. in French from Penn State, and an M.A. in language communications and a Ph.D. in instruction and learning from the University of Pittsburgh, where she won the Doctoral Association of Educators' Outstanding Dissertation Award. She is the co-author of *Making Thinking Visible: Writing, Collaborative Planning, and Classroom Inquiry* (1994).

About the Authors

Studies in the Postmodern Theory of Education

General Editors
Joe L. Kincheloe & Shirley R. Steinberg

Counterpoints publishes the most compelling and imaginative books being written in education today. Grounded on the theoretical advances in criticalism, feminism, and postmodernism in the last two decades of the twentieth century, Counterpoints engages the meaning of these innovations in various forms of educational expression. Committed to the proposition that theoretical literature should be accessible to a variety of audiences, the series insists that its authors avoid esoteric and jargonistic languages that transform educational scholarship into an elite discourse for the initiated. Scholarly work matters only to the degree it affects consciousness and practice at multiple sites. Counterpoints' editorial policy is based on these principles and the ability of scholars to break new ground, to open new conversations, to go where educators have never gone before.

For additional information about this series or for the submission of manuscripts, please contact:

Joe L. Kincheloe & Shirley R. Steinberg
c/o Peter Lang Publishing, Inc.
29 Broadway, 18th floor
New York, New York 10006

To order other books in this series, please contact our Customer Service Department:

(800) 770-LANG (within the U.S.)
(212) 647-7706 (outside the U.S.)
(212) 647-7707 FAX

Or browse online by series:
www.peterlang.com